Canvas of Creation

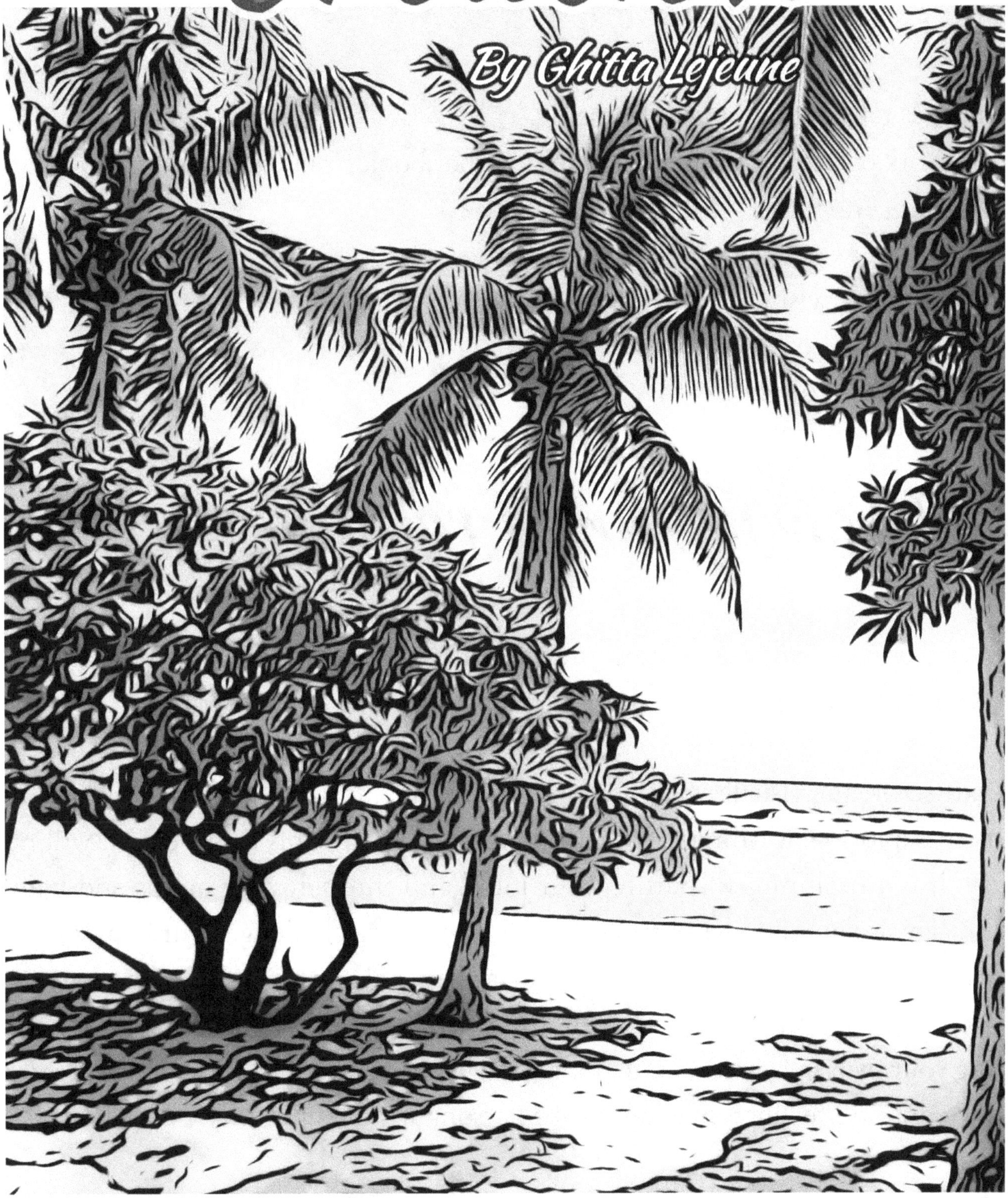

By Ghitta Lejeune

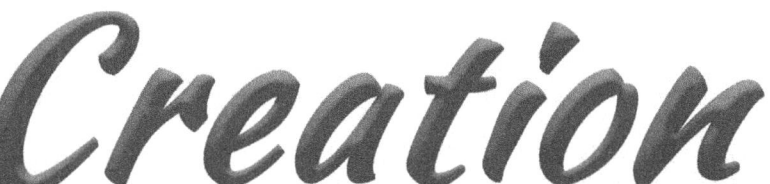

I0462273

Some images taken from pixabay.com
Other artwork created by Ghitta Lejeune from her book *Exhilarating Kingdom of Wonder: Hurricane Gita over Tonga – Mission, Faith, Prayer*

To contact Ghitta, visit.
www.ghittalejeune.com
www.almightysummitestate.com

Art Drawings and Praising

The poetry writing language Ghitta uses is her own interpretation of translating her native German language to English what creates a unique style of writing.

Be the artist, dream, visualize, and put yourself in the midst of the nature display or put colours in exploring, learning, doing something different. This achievement will never go away. It is a beginning of putting your mind and through your minds and hands a mark on canvas paper, is like starting a new adventure to challenge your imagination in a three-dimensional way. The outline of canvas paper gives you the idea and basic tools that you need to finish the picture. It then becomes your own art, one of a kind. Creating your own style with watercolours, acrylic, or pencil, you choose to express your colour moods and feelings, matching your personality and creativity.

Part 1
Canvas of Life

What a wonder that the master of creation gives us a canvas of talents in our mind. It is a beautiful gift of inspiration and fantasy to fill the canvas in us with colourful beauty. I call this inspirational vision what through art we express in all styles, forms, and materials, adding life and love of magical colours to it. A radiant, marvellous and magical transformation then starts in our soul when we love what we do, what then becomes powerful. A passion is then created with a kiss of compassion awakened with determination.

We need to inspire, encourage, and motivate ourselves and one another constantly, because we all have an unbelieve and often hidden talent in us to discover and develop. Did you ever think and were feeling the exhilarating joy, when you mastered a challenge and completed it like you never did before?

When your inner vision, desires, and dreams, becomes a visual achievement and reality; that is the beginning of an unlimited master of exploring of new adventures. We gain new gifts, talents, and skills, what moves our minds and souls. I see it as a blessing that God gives me the choice to make each day a new canvas to paint my own masterpiece. My whole life is a canvas of a thousands of pieces, details of finished or in the process of fragments that I'm working, nurturing, praying, and acting on. My life canvas reflects and molds my moods, circumstances, and emotions. A scalar of billions of strokes of shades what I create with my paintbrushes, a pallet of choices, decisions, opportunities, and colours I am the creator of. My priority is to stay focused on brilliants colours of joy, happiness, motives, reasons, and values, what uplifts and blesses my eyes and soul. Even if we have to paint and go through dark valleys and uncertainties, mist of worries, foggy vision, and scared to see or keep.

Our canvas of life and creation is a picture we explore, trust, and believe, what effects our inner being and how we feel and work out daily. Then we become a master in life. Even sometimes we destroy our life picture and it looks like it may be out of control. In this time I remind myself, that each canvas is a page of my life that with God's help can be replaced, renewed, transformed, redesigned, patched up, corrected or healed. Whatever we like or think, by mistakes and learning, we become a master of our own life canvas to work on 'till perfection, unless we give up and never finish.

My prayer for you and myself, is that God guides us through our steps, thoughts, hands, minds, words, and soul, so our canvas of life will be a blessing and extraordinary as a tool. Creating or filling empty spots in colour in an outline picture, is a playful, enjoying, and satisfying to the end; the result what is a realistic attraction.

Visually, each day we see in our picture, a canvas of our soul spending time with it, rejoicing in completing our picture what no one can do for us. We are accountable, responsible to work under God's umbrella where He is our teacher and creative master. Let no one or nothing stop you. The evolution of creativity will spark and enlighten your inner core. Let your spirit fill your heart with boasting happiness and revolutionary thoughts of your abilities, and let all hesitations go. Believe in God's words and creation, and in yourself and your talents.

Your canvas of life is ready. Take, mix, match, and put your heart and colours in action. A new day to start to work and a new beginning to trust and pray.

Canvas of Sand Clock

Tick, tock, tick, tock...
The time clock in our life is going non-stop.
Each second is one sand corn
what is less of the fullness of our life,
like the sand clock, it goes slowly
but steadily we cannot hold it, stop it,
so long as we are alive.

Tick, tock, tick, tock...
Time is merciful, it heals all sorrow,
eventually, after all.
Time puts Band-Aids over broken souls,
time gives you new strength and hope;
shifts you around to expand your goals.

We do not know when our time is over;
to laugh, cry or breathe.
That's why each second counts,
to do what we want to achieve.

Tick, tock, tick, tock...
the sand clock is running,
time will soften our hearts and grieving.
Time is our counselor, comforter,
and our silent, invisible partner in our daily dealings.
Time is changing us from young to old,
makes us weak or strong, fearful or bold.

Tick, tock, tick, tock...
Each night and day
I come closer to my deadline.
So I have to focus on my actions
and dealings right away.
I do not want to loose time,
with boredom, malice, or unfinished tasks.
Precious time is running
out of my sand clock, very fast.

I am not in panic or fast
with my days. Nor am I in a rush or haste. I
am aware that each second I live,
it can be blessing, productive
or painful and a total waste.

That's why I fill my days as much as I can
with values and qualities and not in vain.
I am committed to do my best
for me and you and fellow man.
To be able to stand for what I believe in,
Instead of being a coward and run.

Tick, tock, tick, tock...
my time is moving forward;
struggles and problems are there to conquer,
specially when I am a matured adult.

Time is my wisdom to let go.
I have to the opportunities,
talents, skills and get my dreams realistically through.

Time is like a doctor who gives me the right medication
to execute dedication
and to avoid depression or hallucinations.

Time is knowledge
as I learn bit by bit everyday more to care and explore,
'till I am experienced, trained, and responsible to share.

Tick, tock, tick, tock...
My sand clock is stuck.
Is somebody out there,
who can shake and make me aware
of how fragile I really am each day
and each second as life is a gift, a gem?
That's why I do not understand
that some people give about their life a damn.
Hell and heaven are opposites and far away,
but time will show
what our choices are and where to go.

Tick, tock, tick, tock..
watch what time it is in your life
on your own clock.
There is time to forgive and forget,
to find a purpose, a passion,
and to love or not to hate.
Don't get bitter, lonely,
or pay back what others did to you.
Time will help to get you safely through.

Tick, tock, tick, tock...
my time is over, I have to stop,
it is your turn, I wish you luck.
Your canvas and sand clock
maybe still have lots of time.
Take your vision and dreams,
and with God's blessing
you have the most creative prospering future
as you are in your life's prime.

In the Beginning...

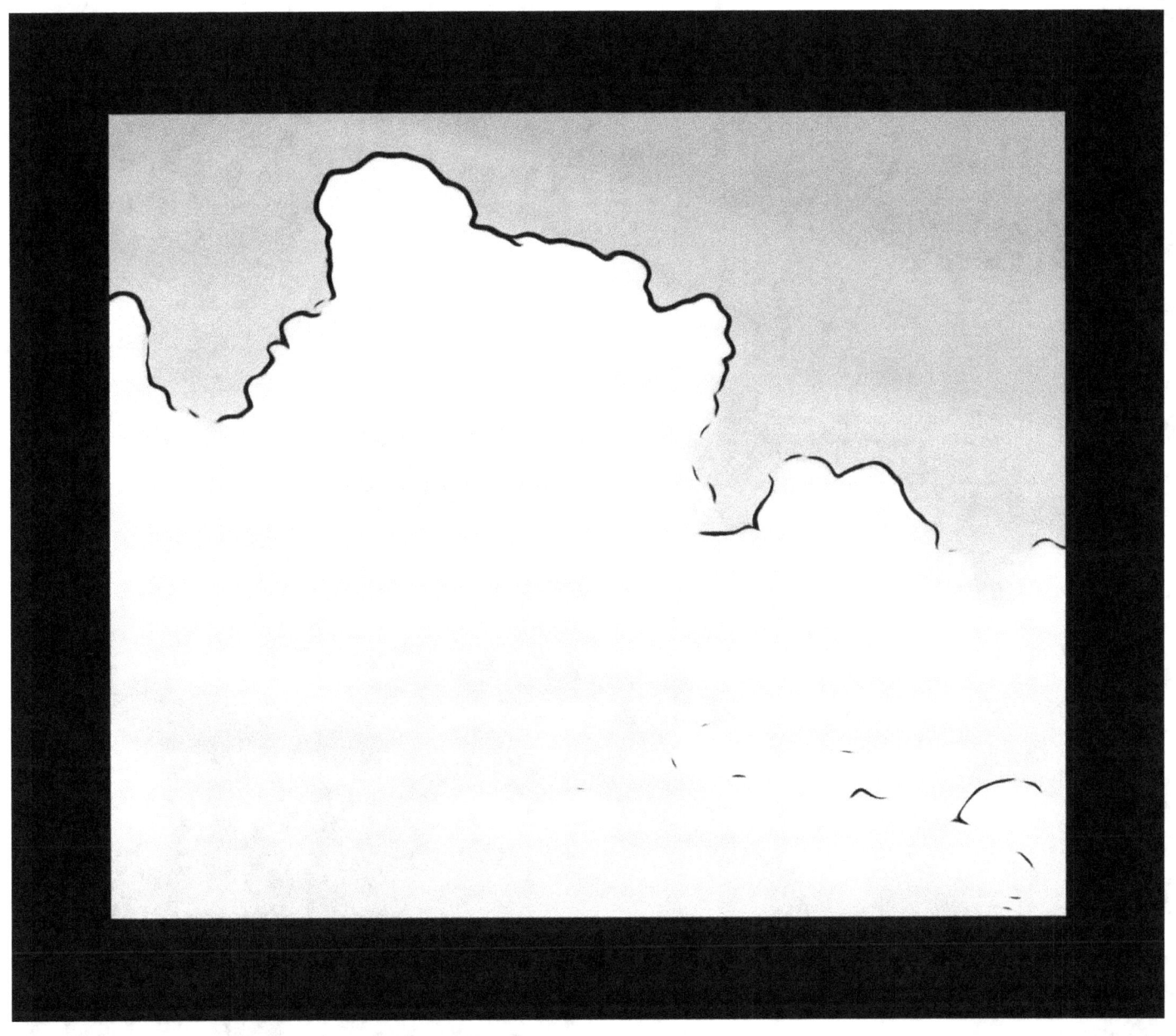

God created the heavens and the earth. Now the earth was formless and empty, darkness was over the surface of the deep, and the Spirit of God was hovering over the waters.

Genesis 1:1-2, NIV

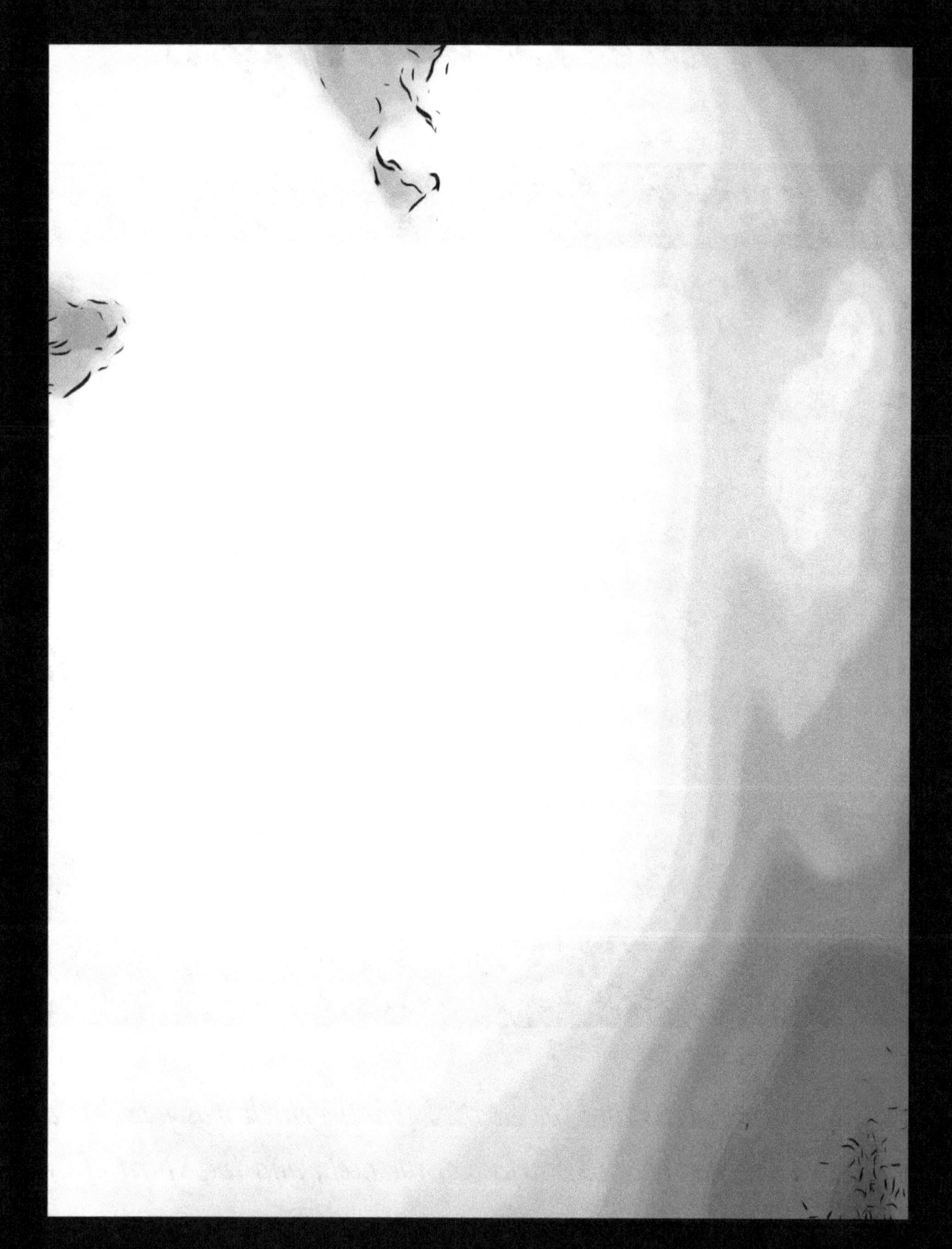

And God said, "Let there be light," and there was light. God saw that the light was good, and he separated the light from the darkness. God called the light "day," and the darkness he called "night." And there was evening, and there was morning—the first day.
Genesis 1:3-5, NIV

And God said, "Let there be a vault between the waters to separate water from water." So God made the vault and separated the water under the vault from the water above it. And it was so. God called the vault "sky." And there was evening, and there was morning—the second day.

Genesis 1:6-8, NIV

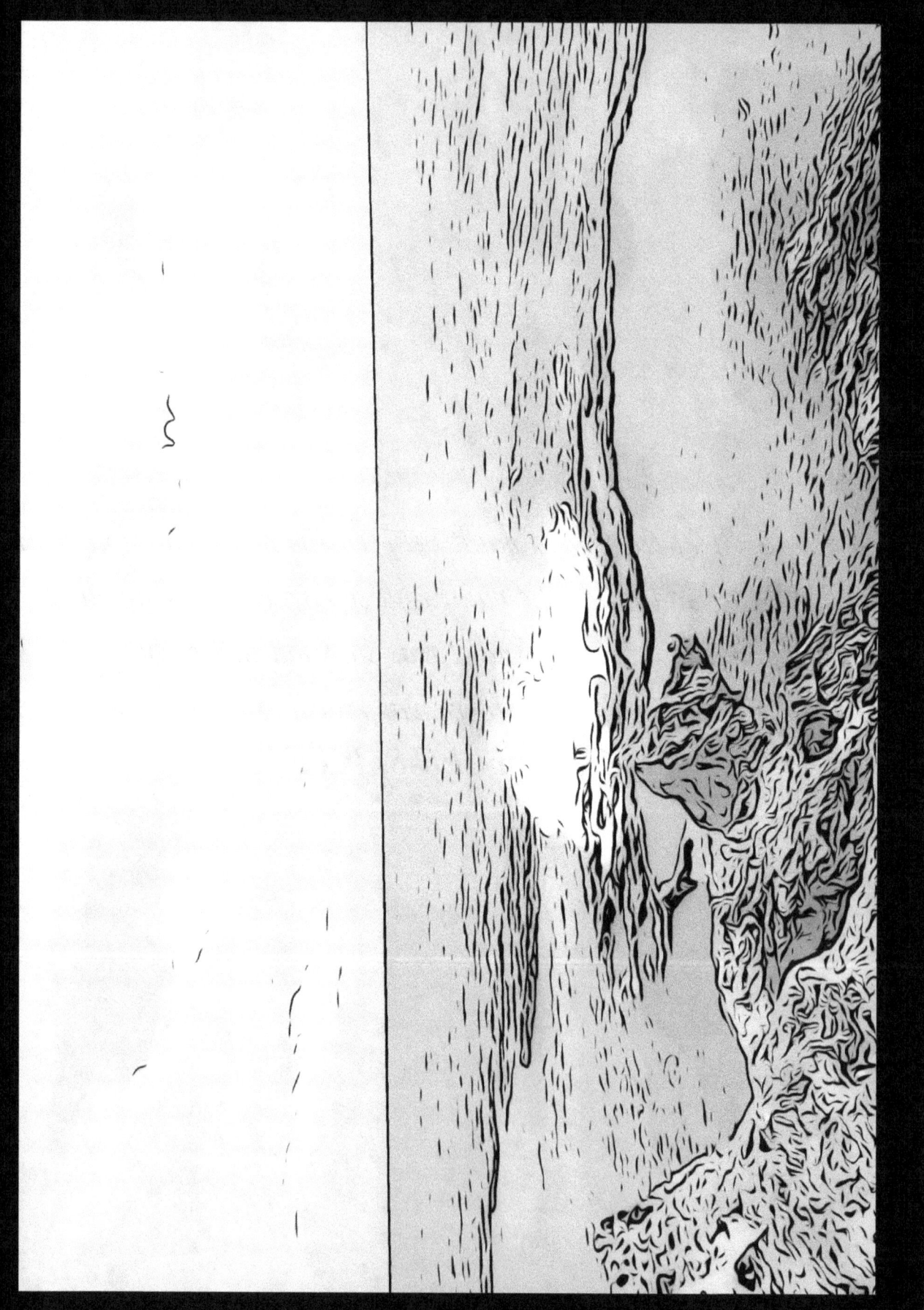

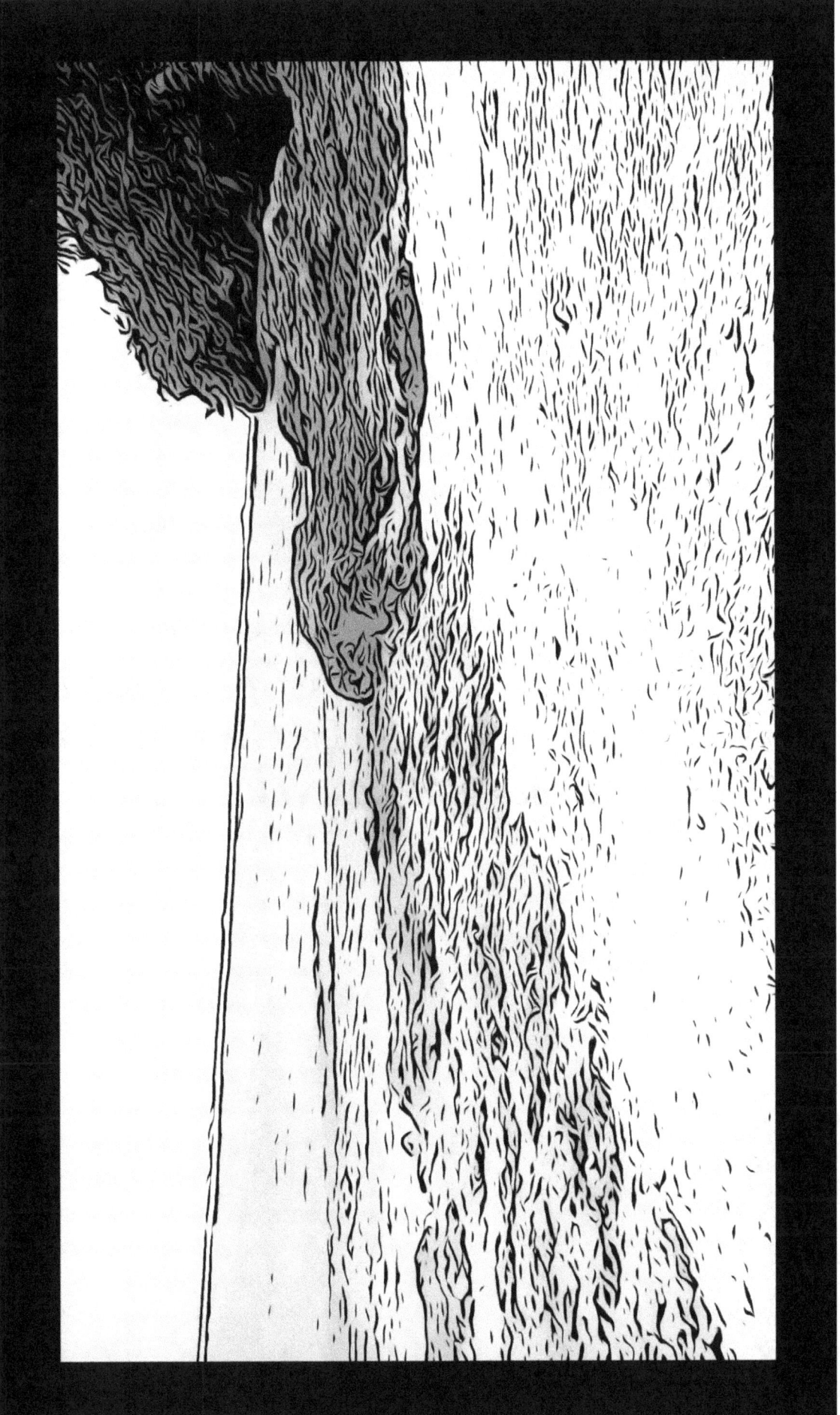

And God said, "Let the water under the sky be gathered to one place, and let dry ground appear." And it was so. God called the dry ground "land," and the gathered waters he called "seas." And God saw that it was good.
Genesis 1:9-10, NIV

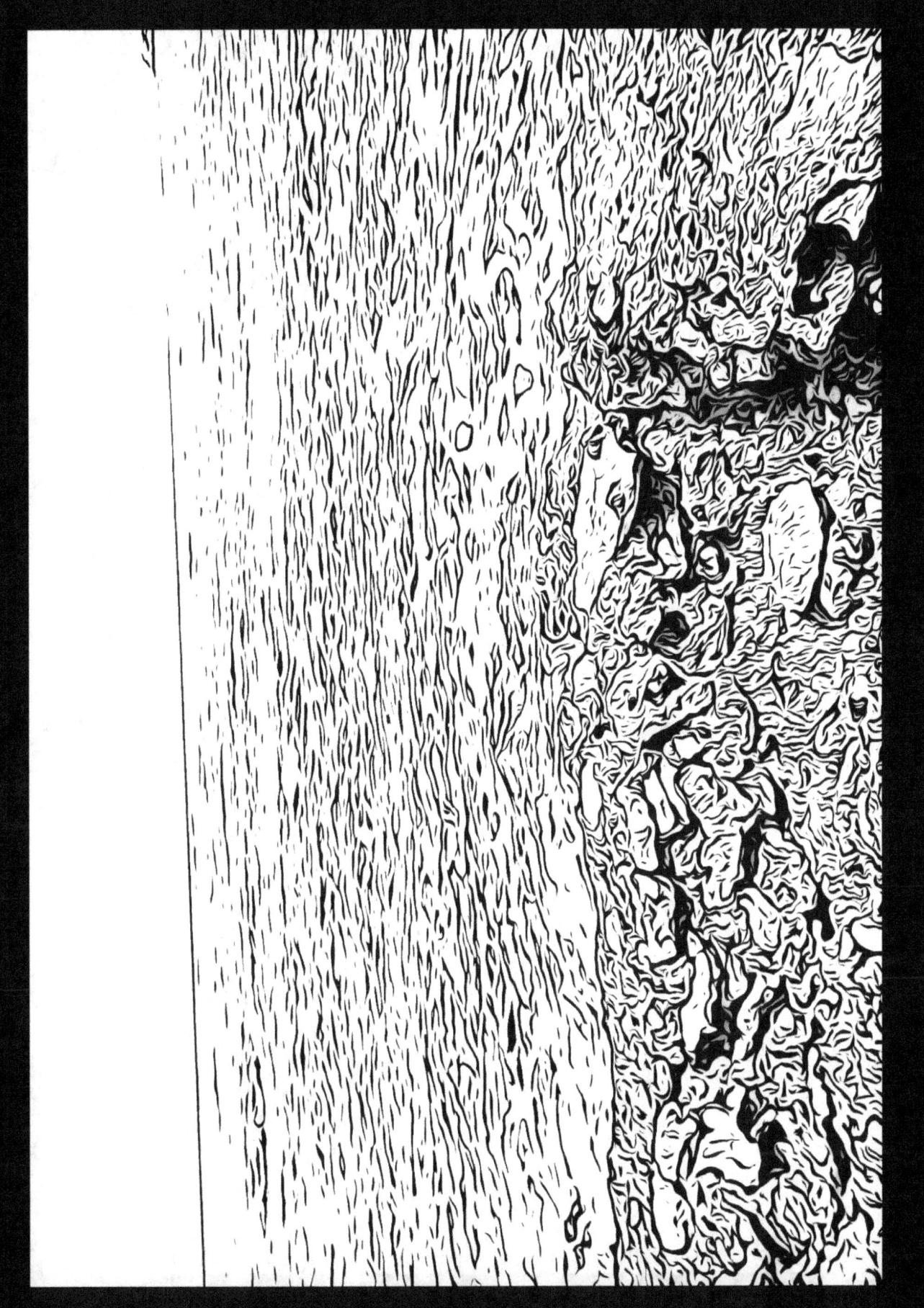

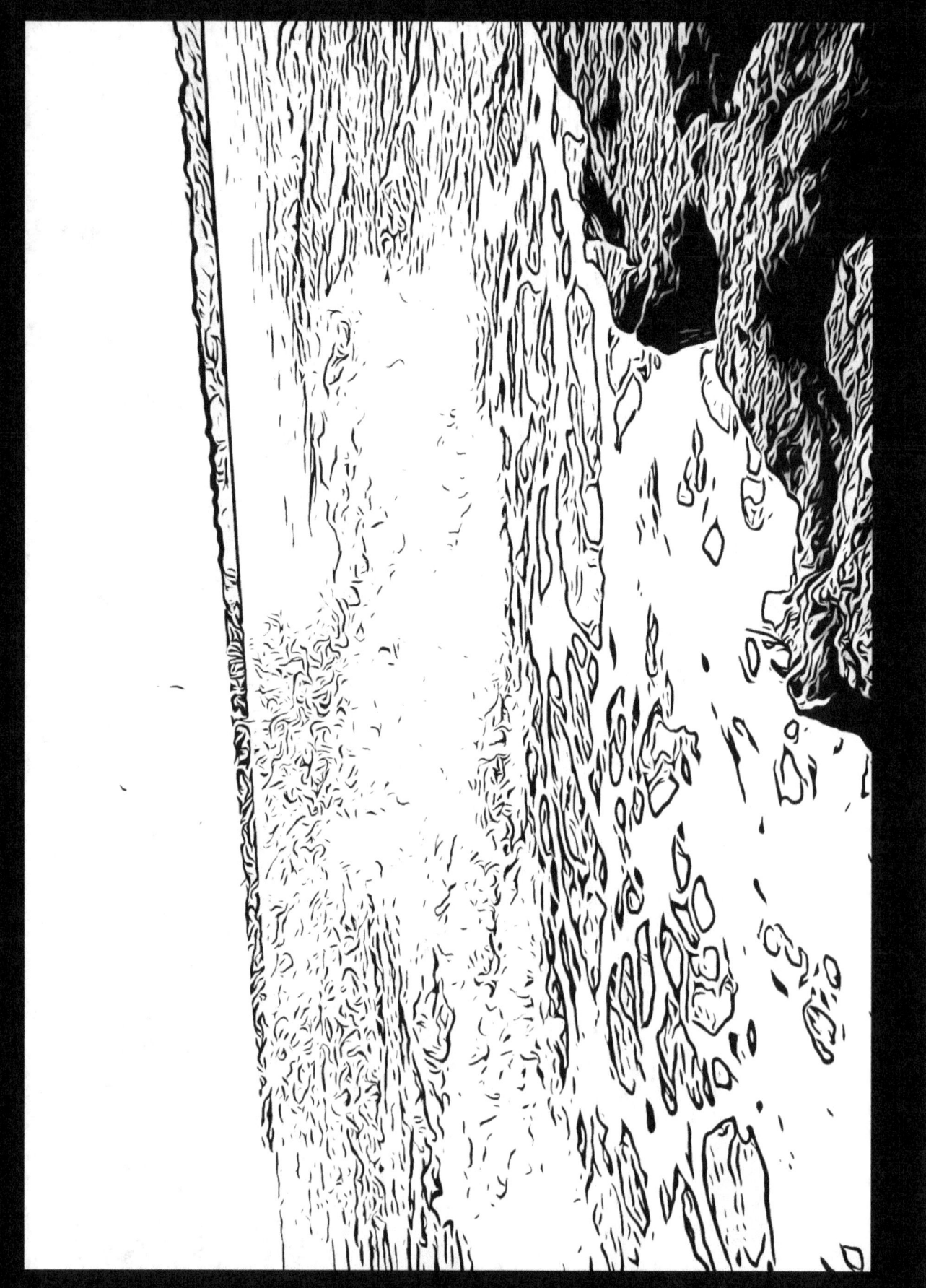

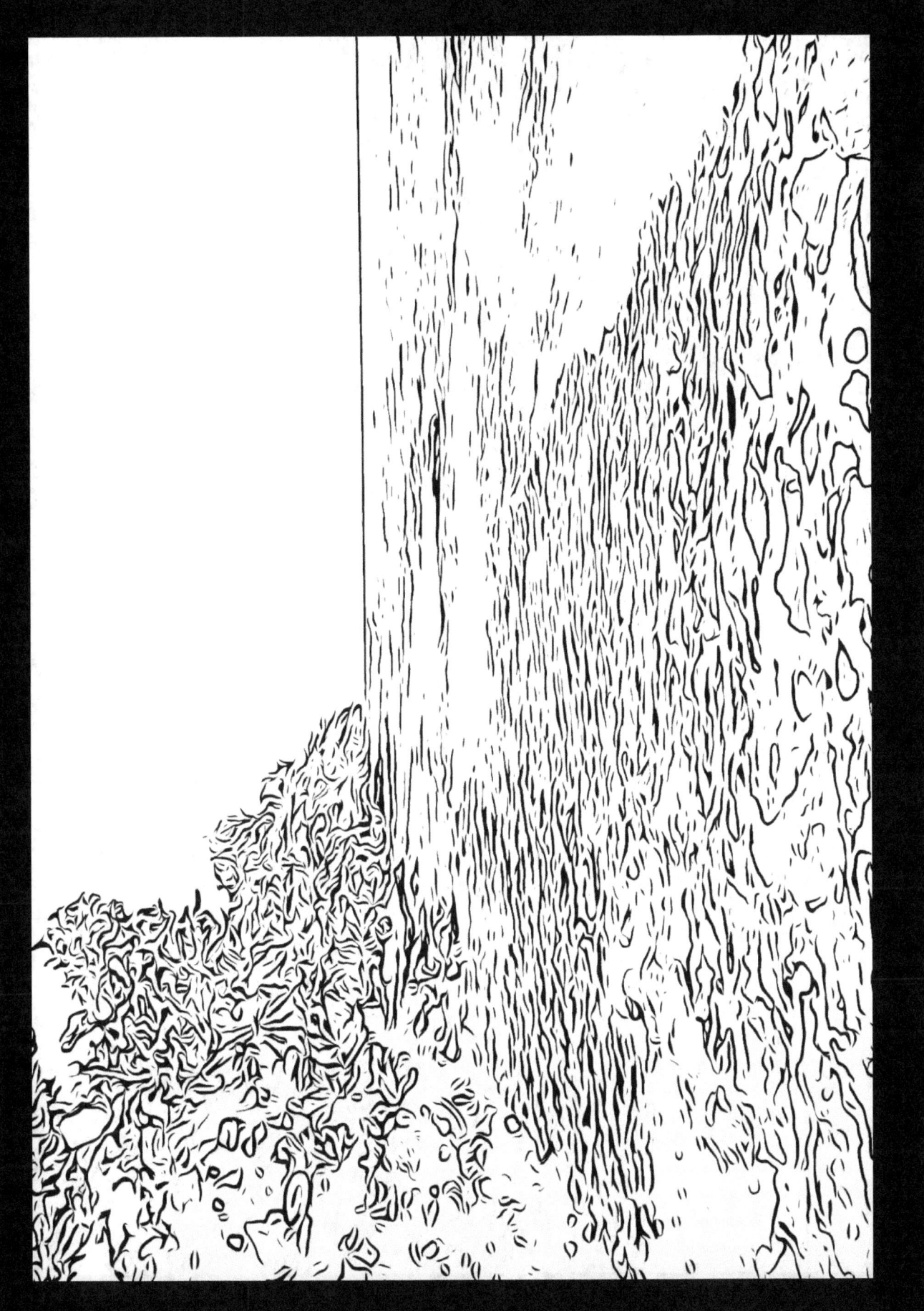

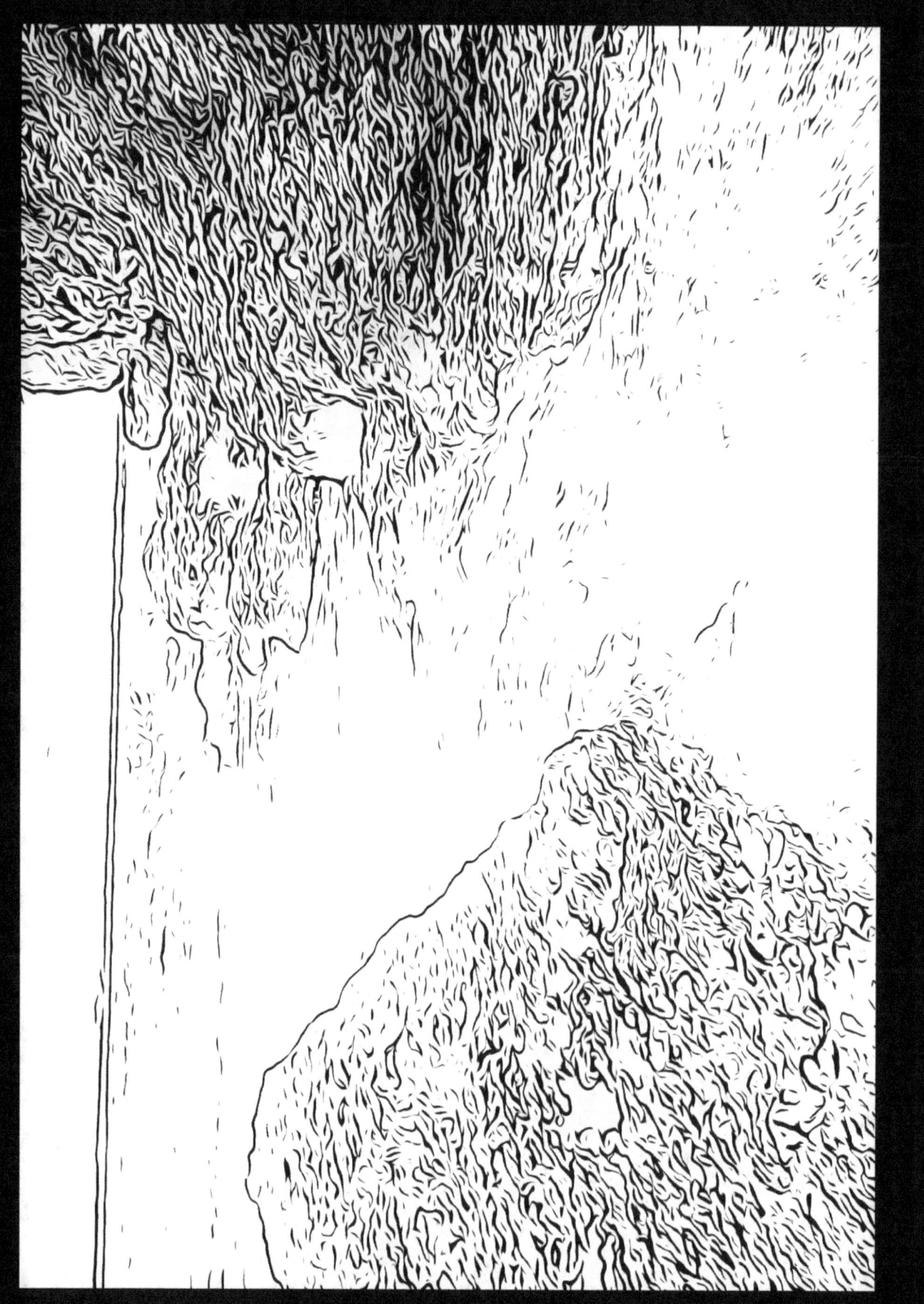

Then God said, "Let the land produce vegetation: seed-bearing plants and trees on the land that bear fruit with seed in it, according to their various kinds." And it was so. The land produced vegetation: plants bearing seed according to their kinds and trees bearing fruit with seed in it according to their kinds. And God saw that it was good. And there was evening, and there was morning—the third day.

Genesis 1:11-13, NIV

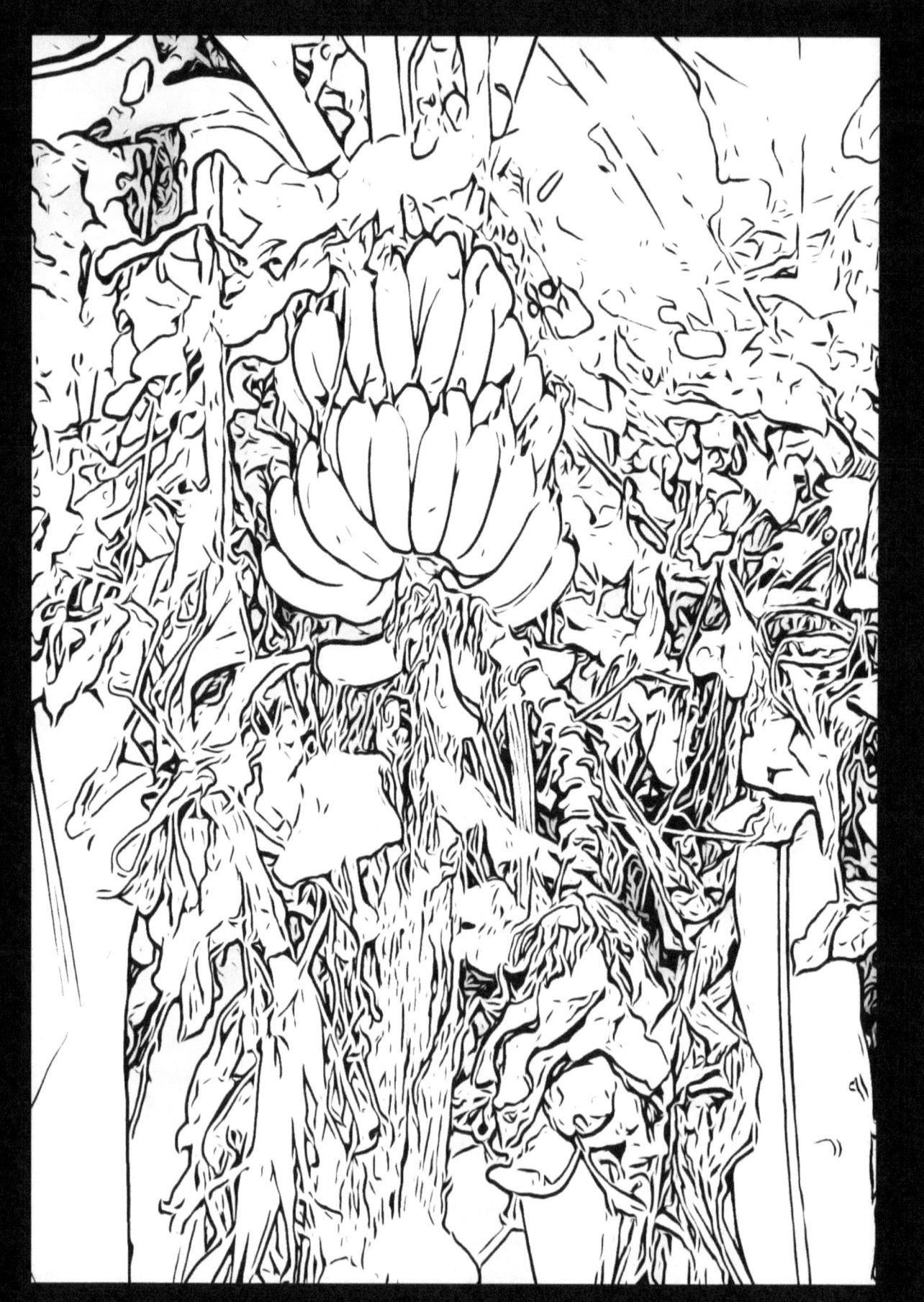

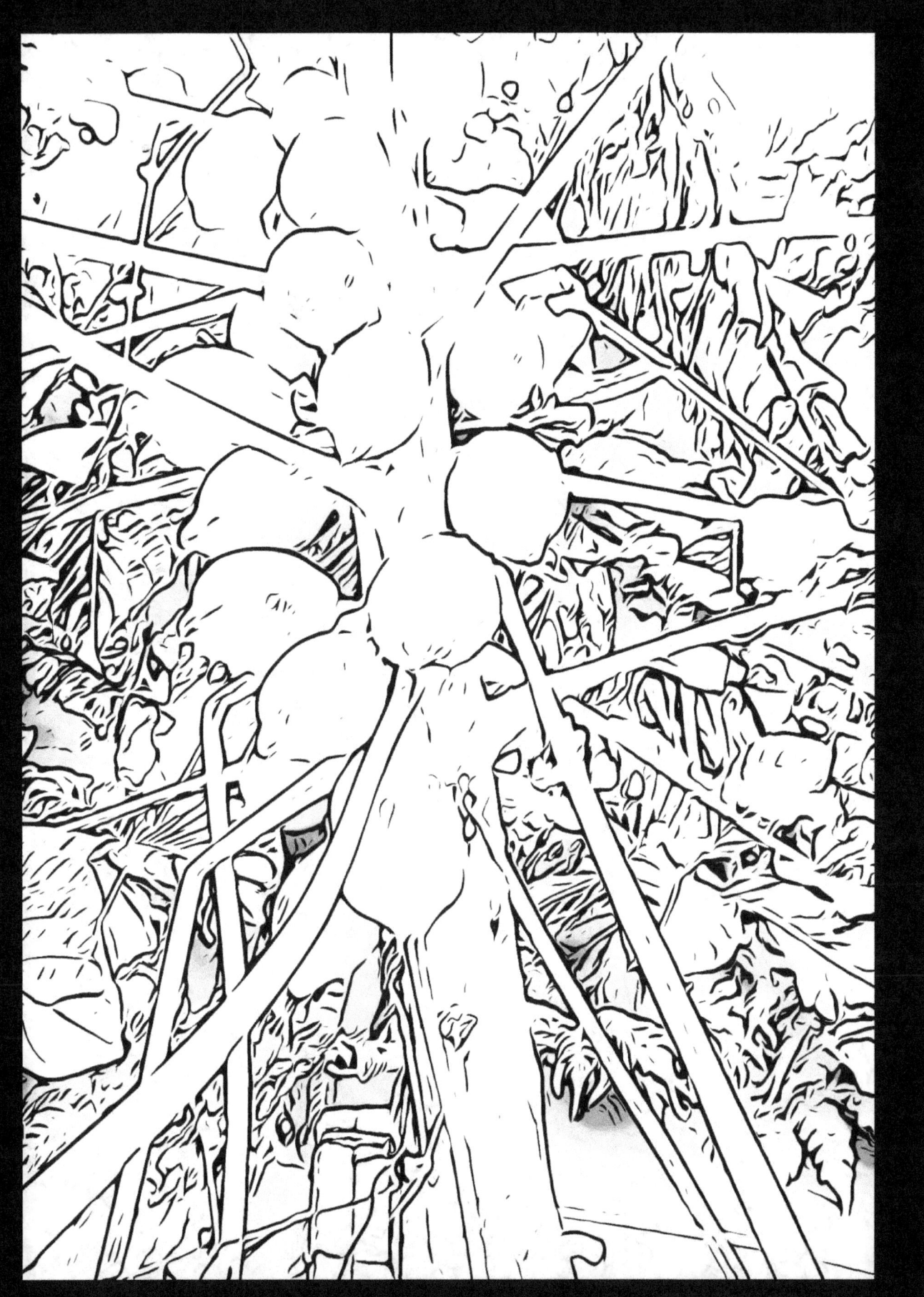

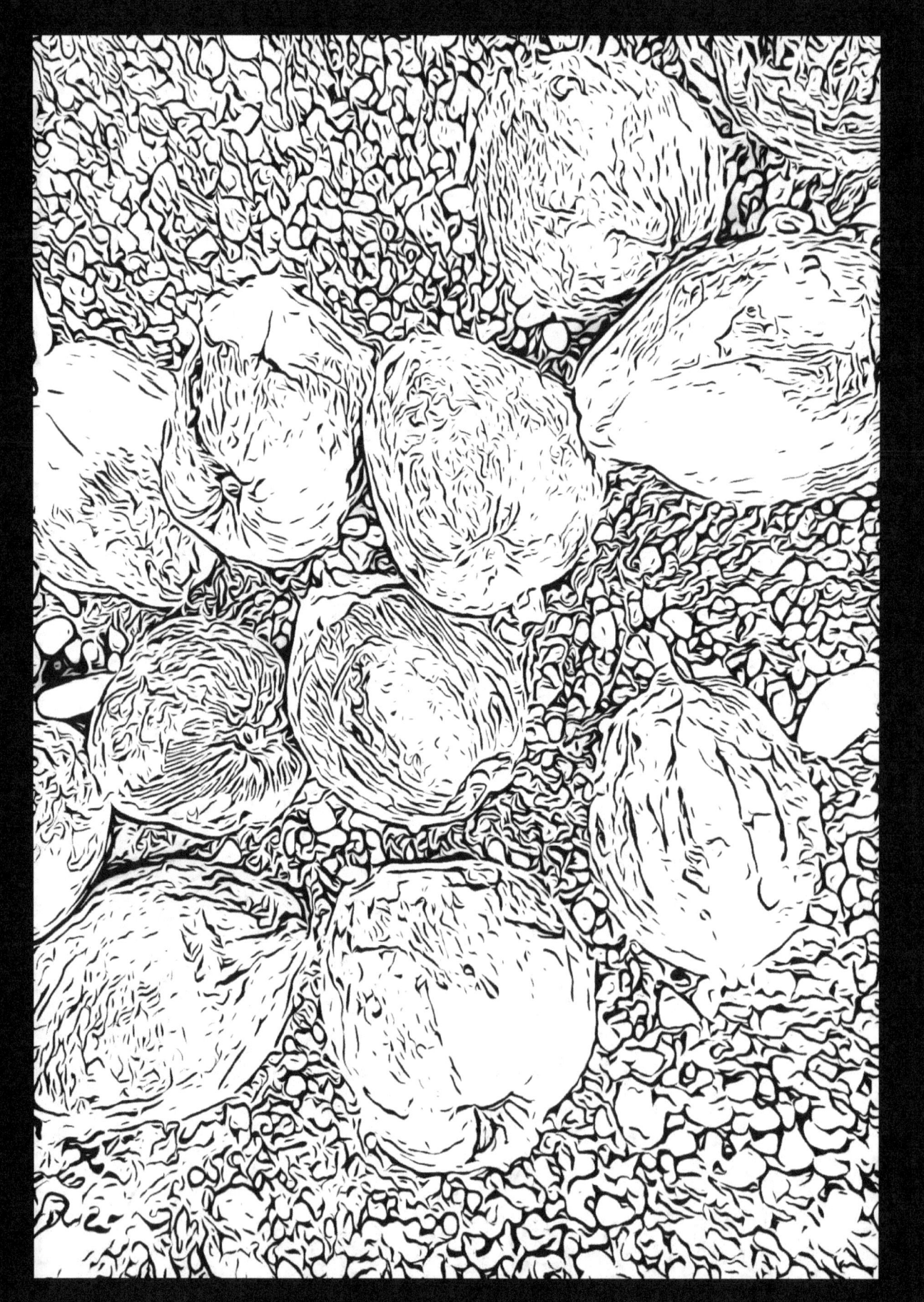

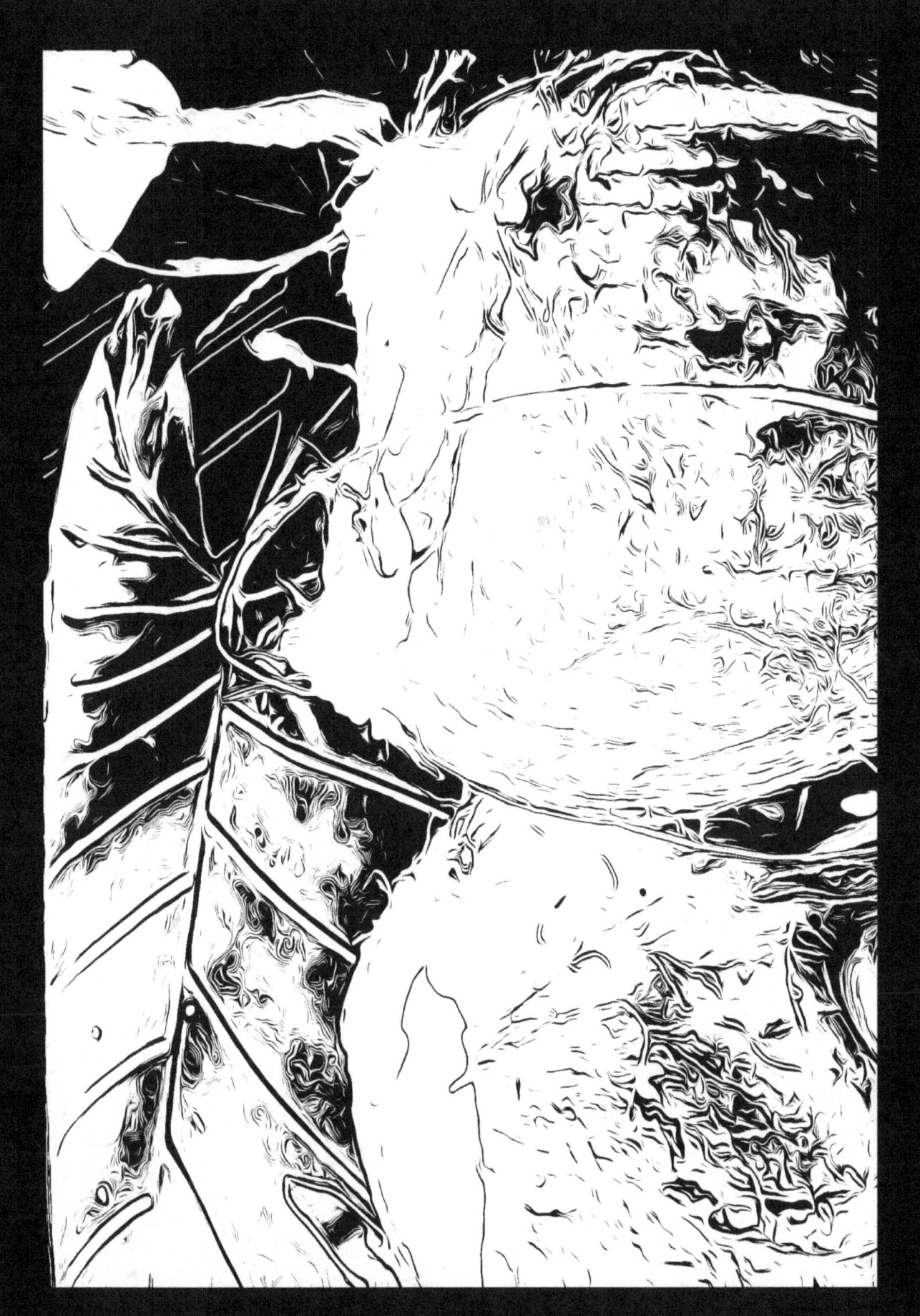

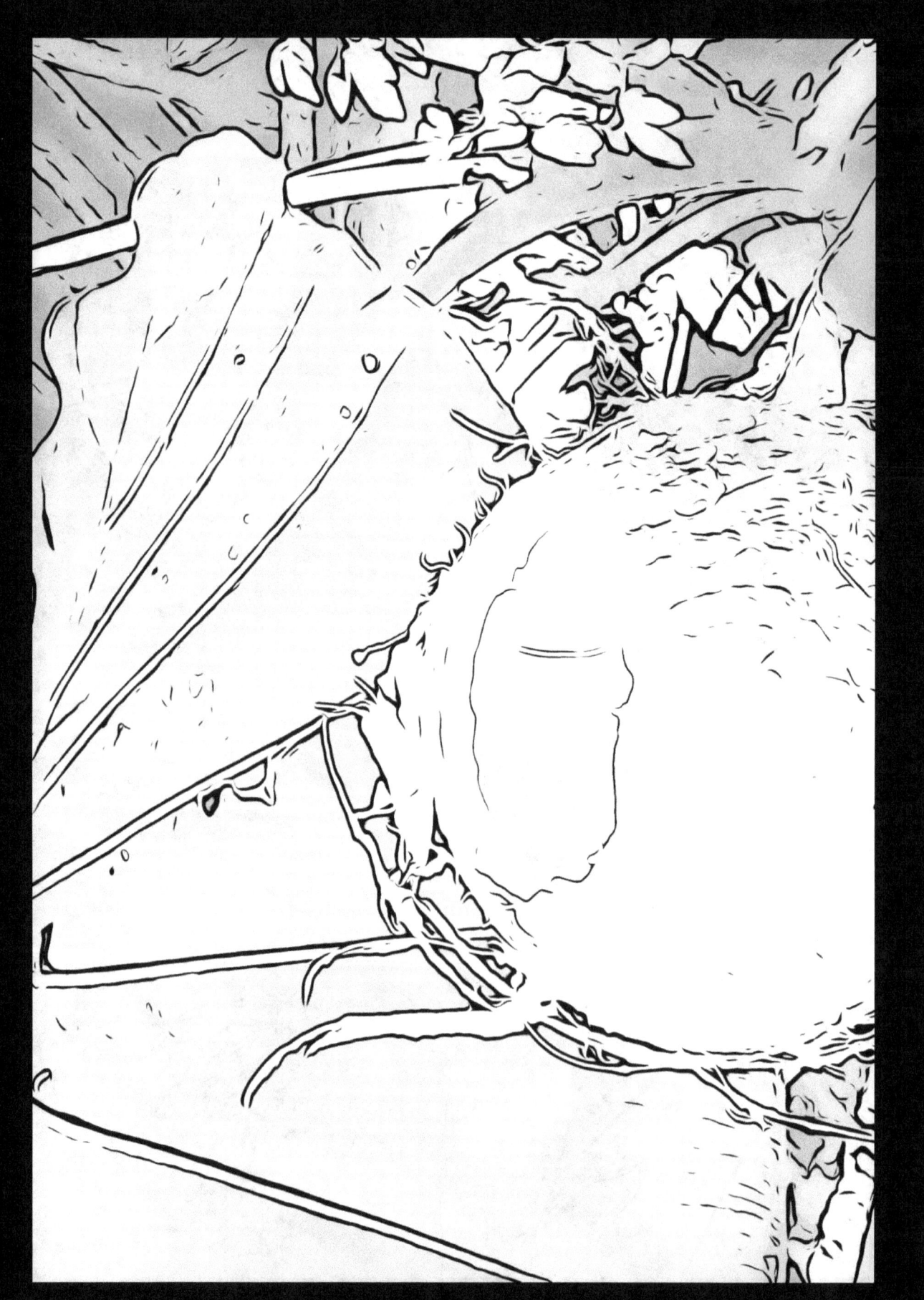

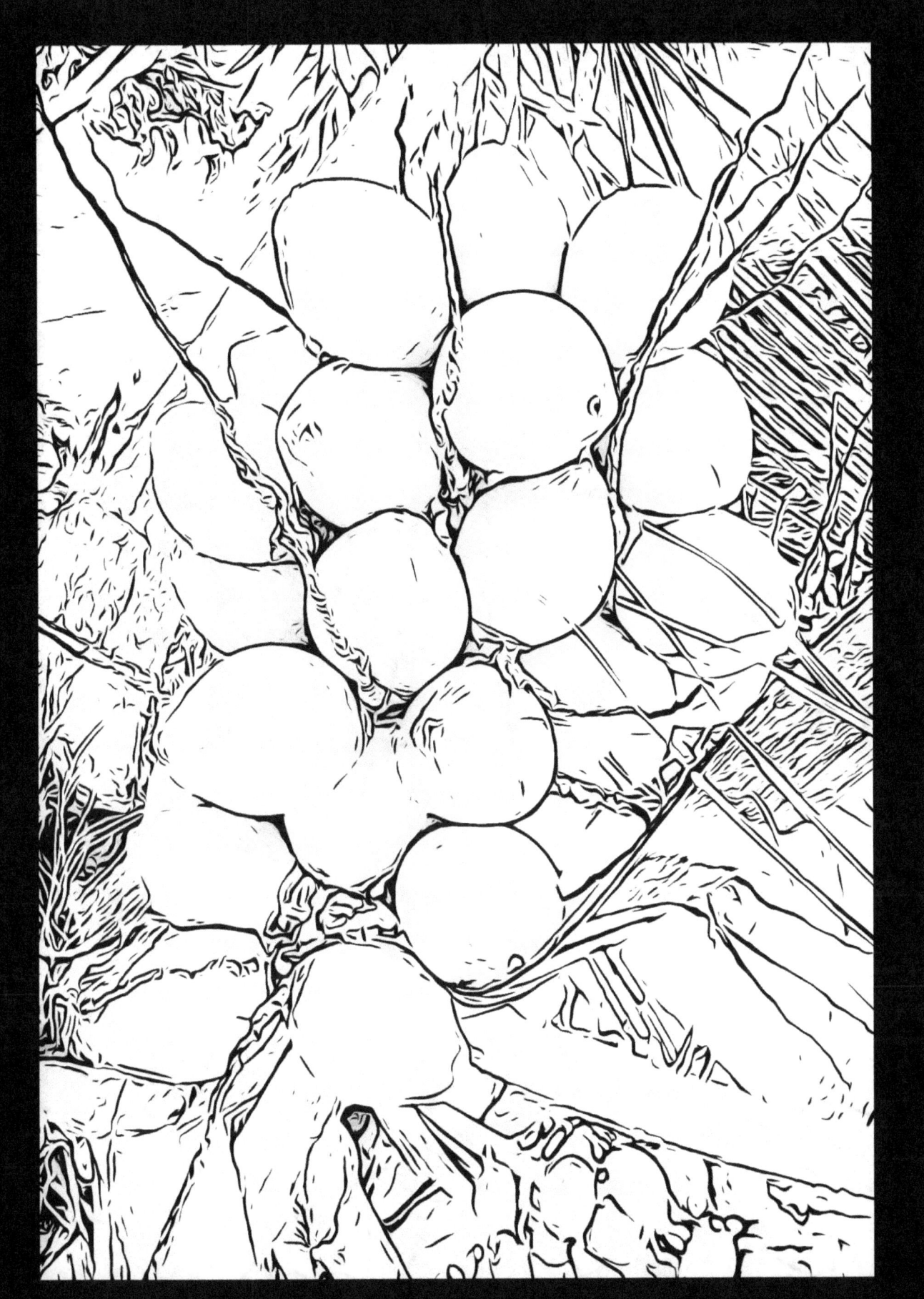

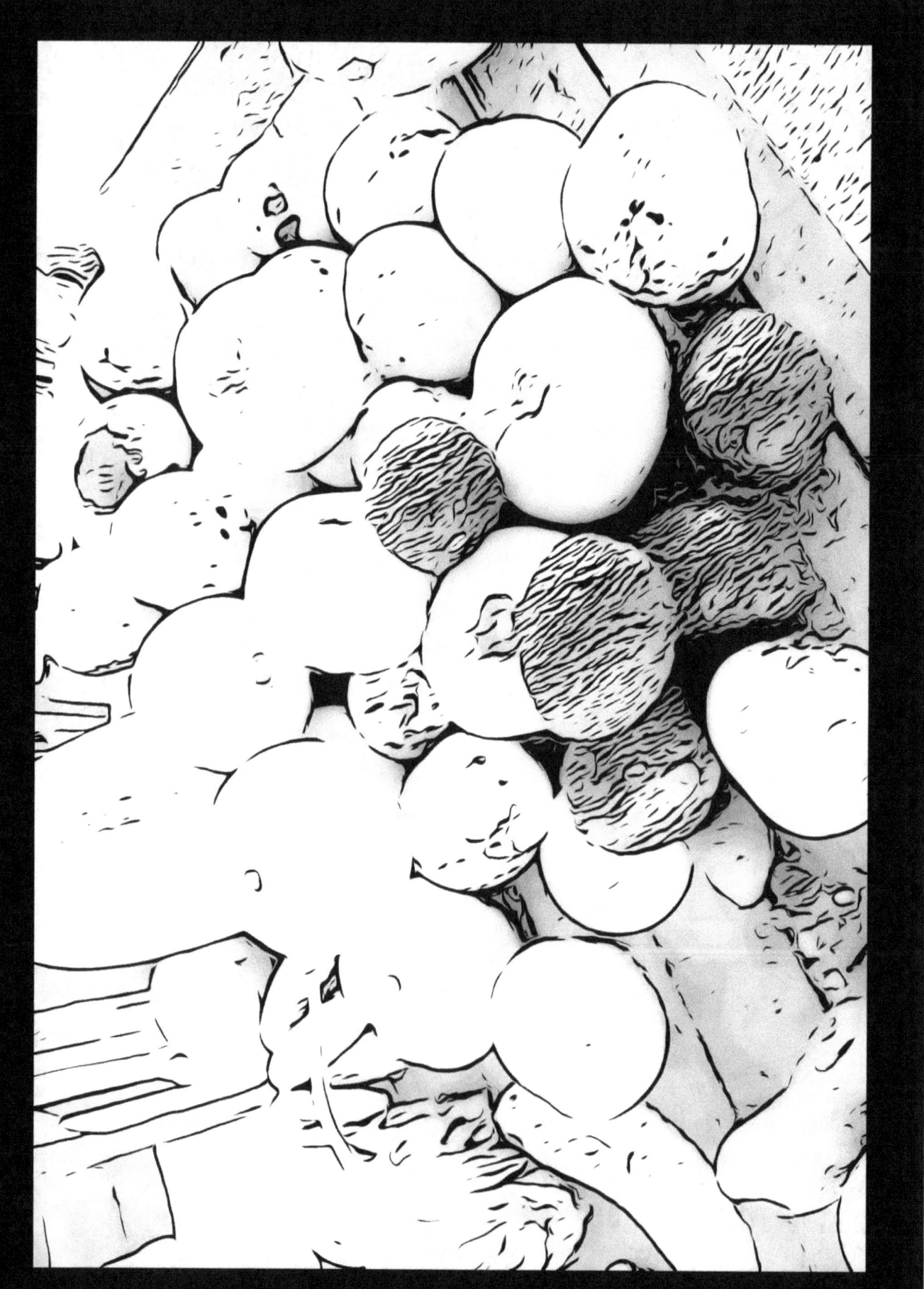

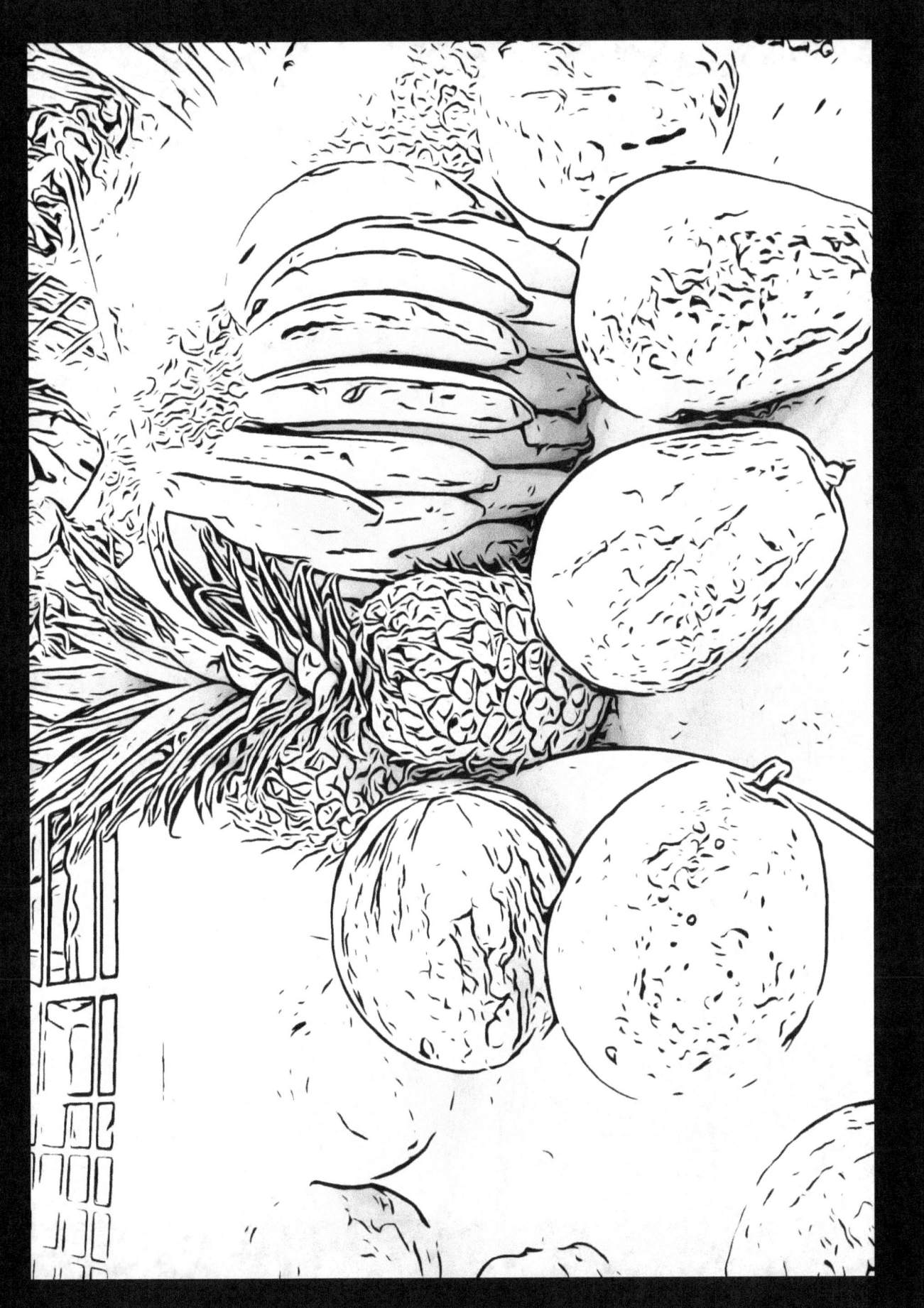

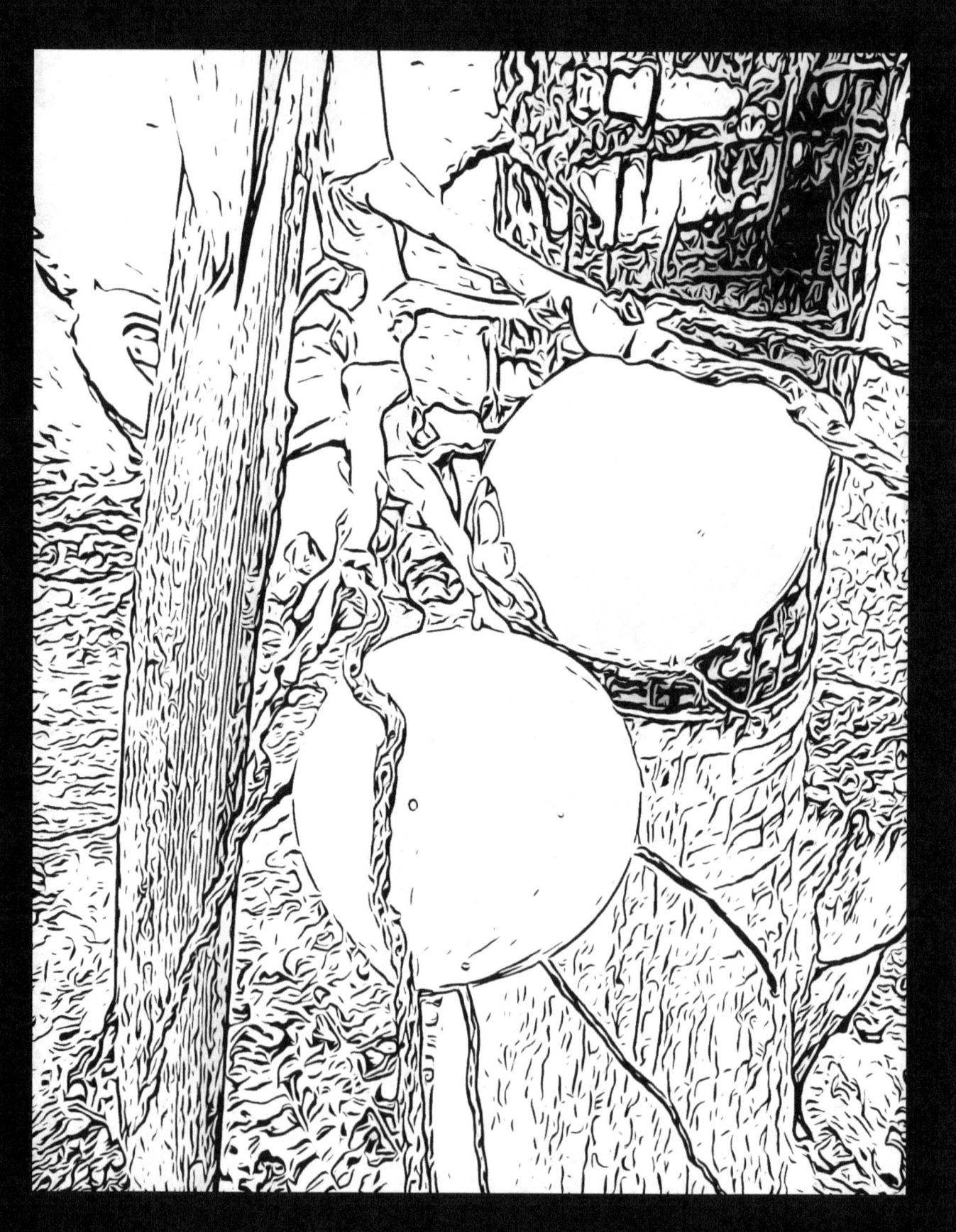

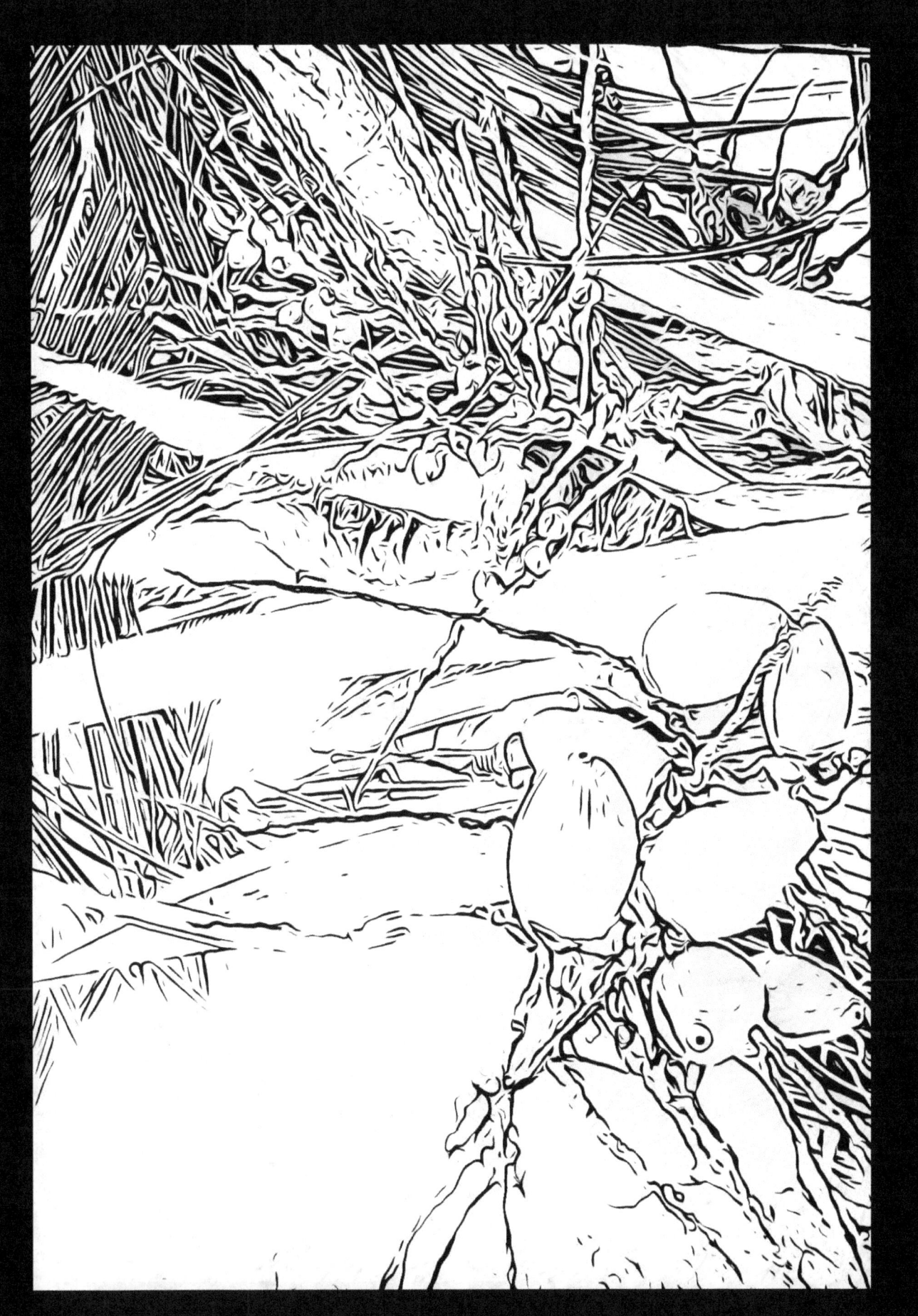

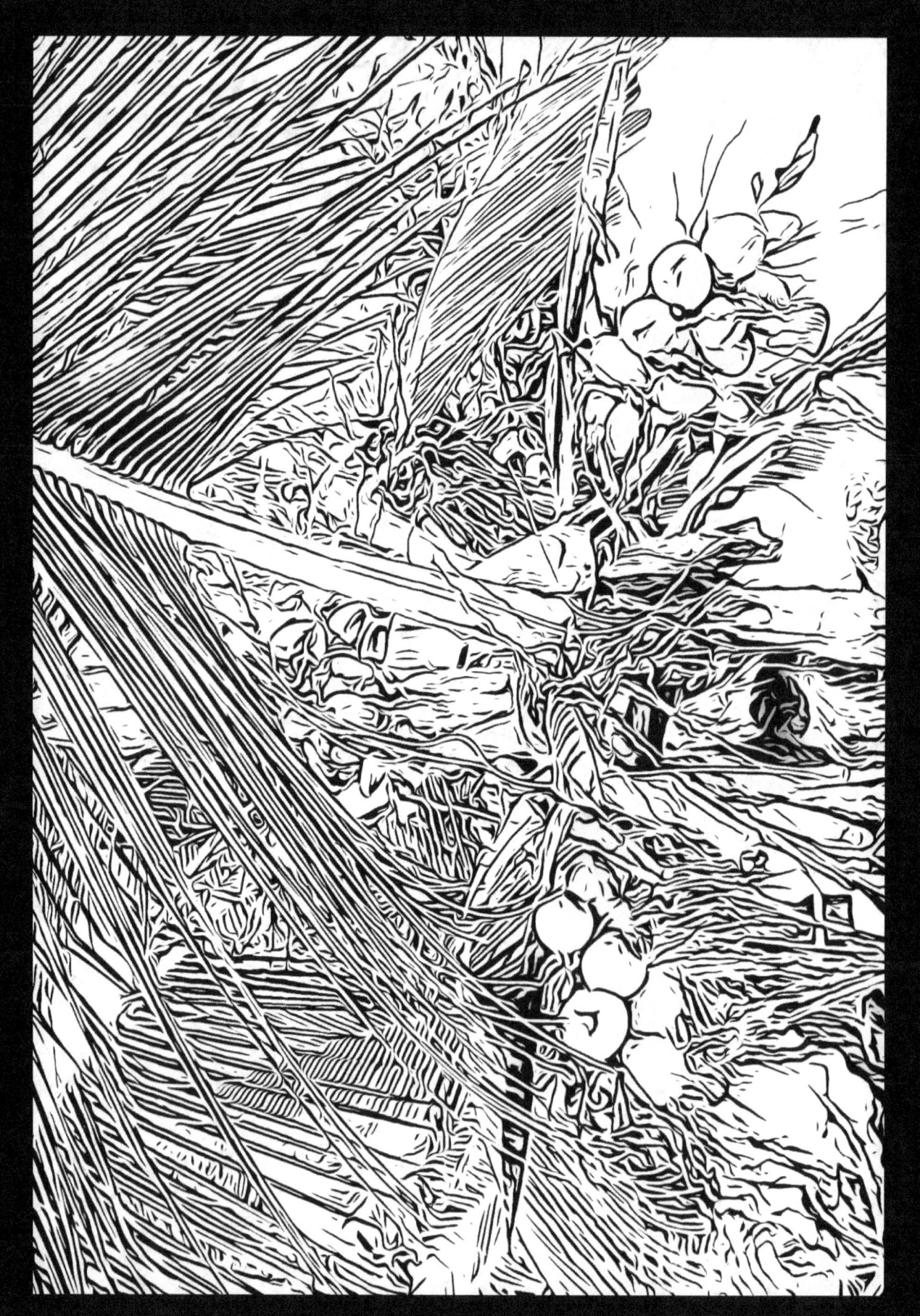

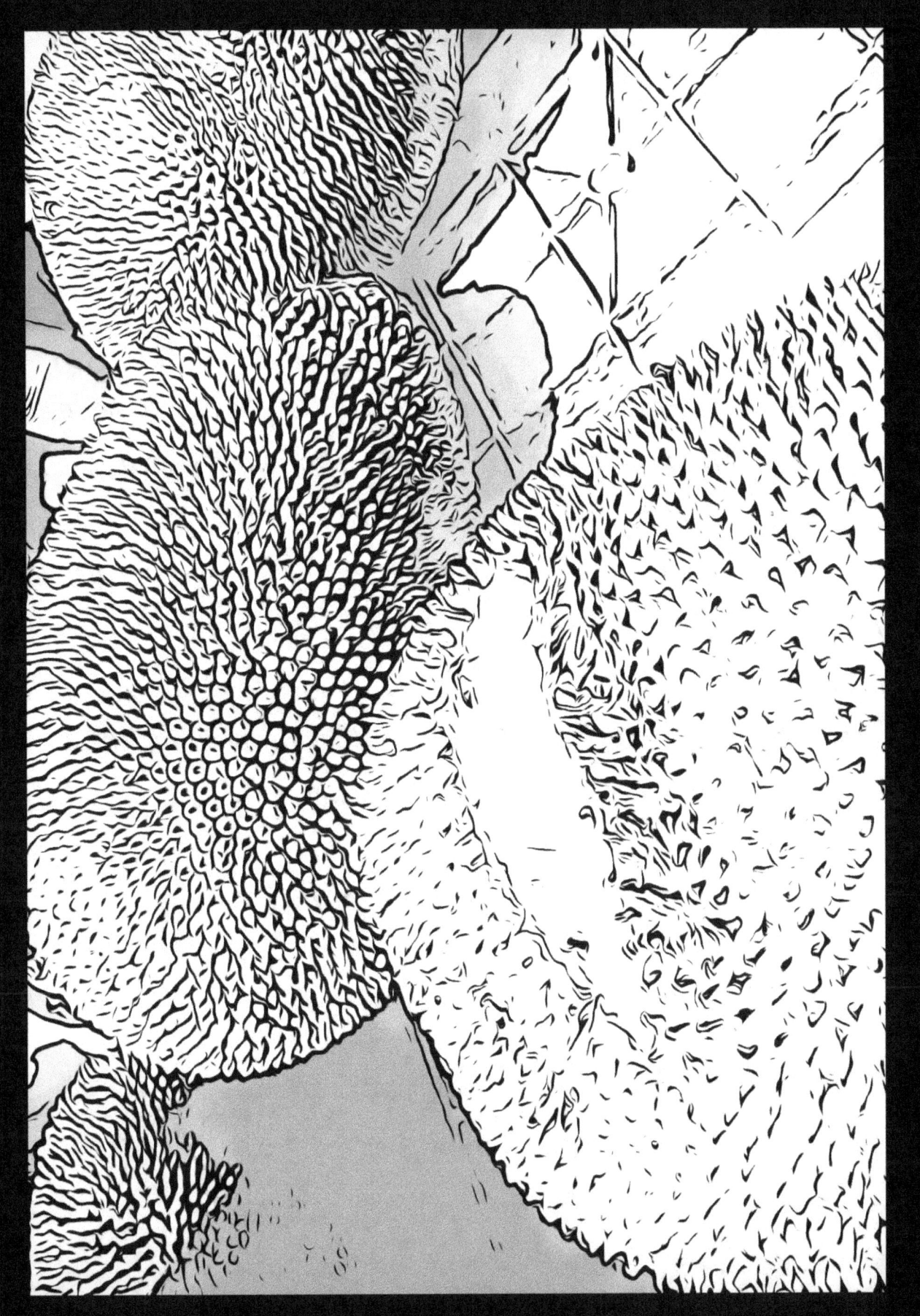

And God said, "Let there be lights in the vault of the sky to separate the day from the night, and let them serve as signs to mark sacred times, and days and years, and let them be lights in the vault of the sky to give light on the earth." And it was so. God made two great lights—the greater light to govern the day and the lesser light to govern the night. He also made the stars. God set them in the vault of the sky to give light on the earth, to govern the day and the night, and to separate light from darkness. And God saw that it was good. And there was evening, and there was morning—the fourth day.

Genesis 1:14-19, NIV

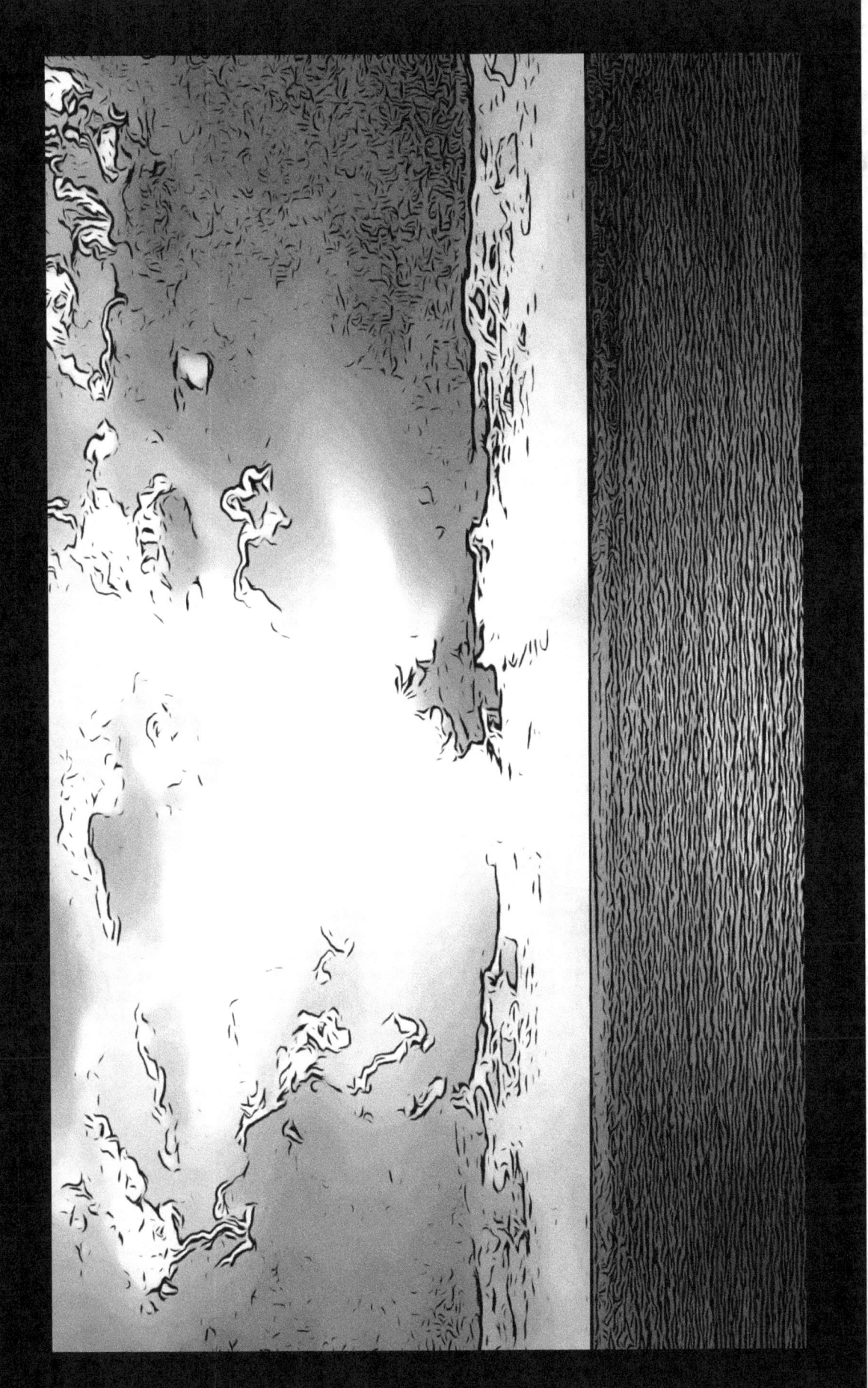

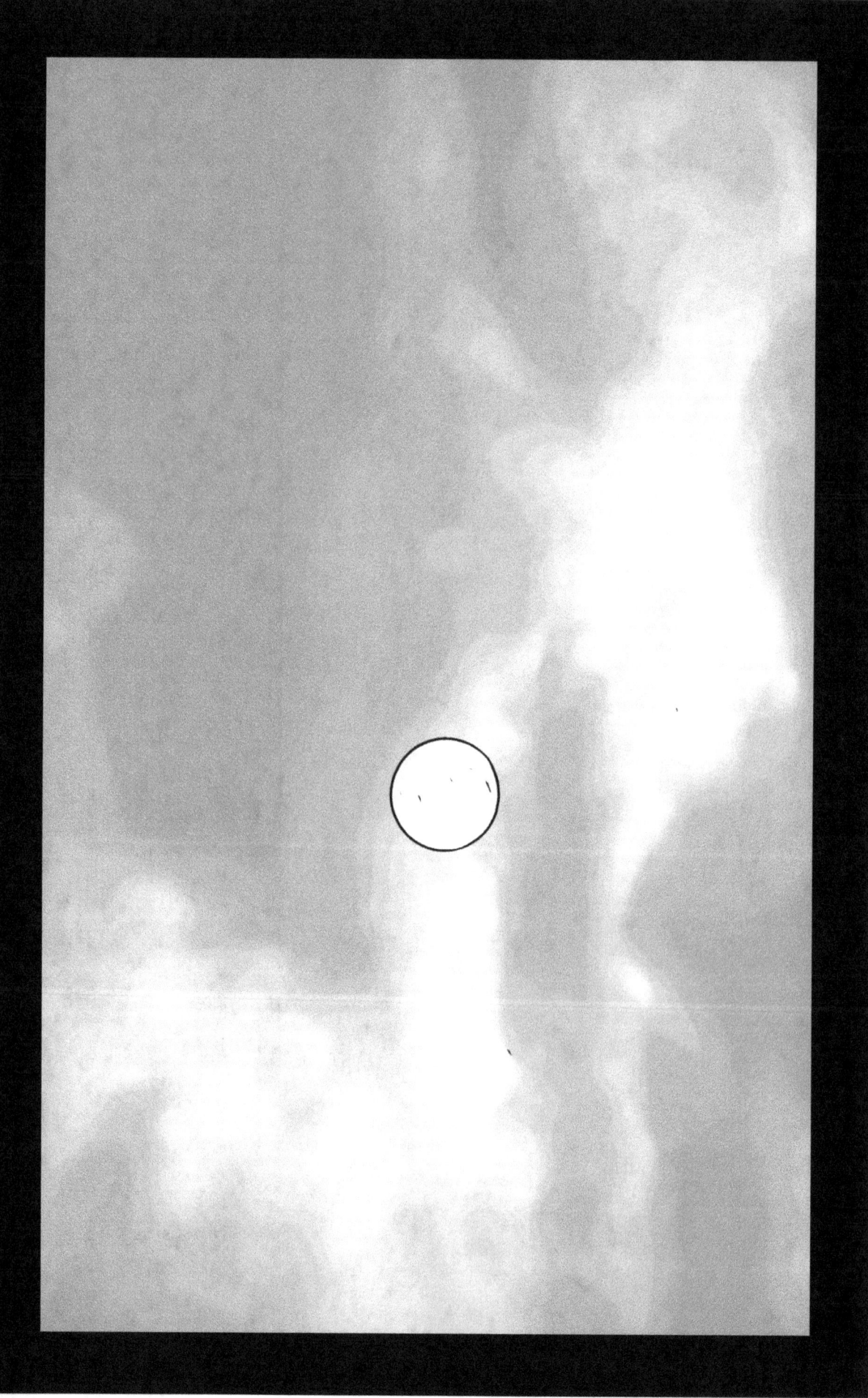

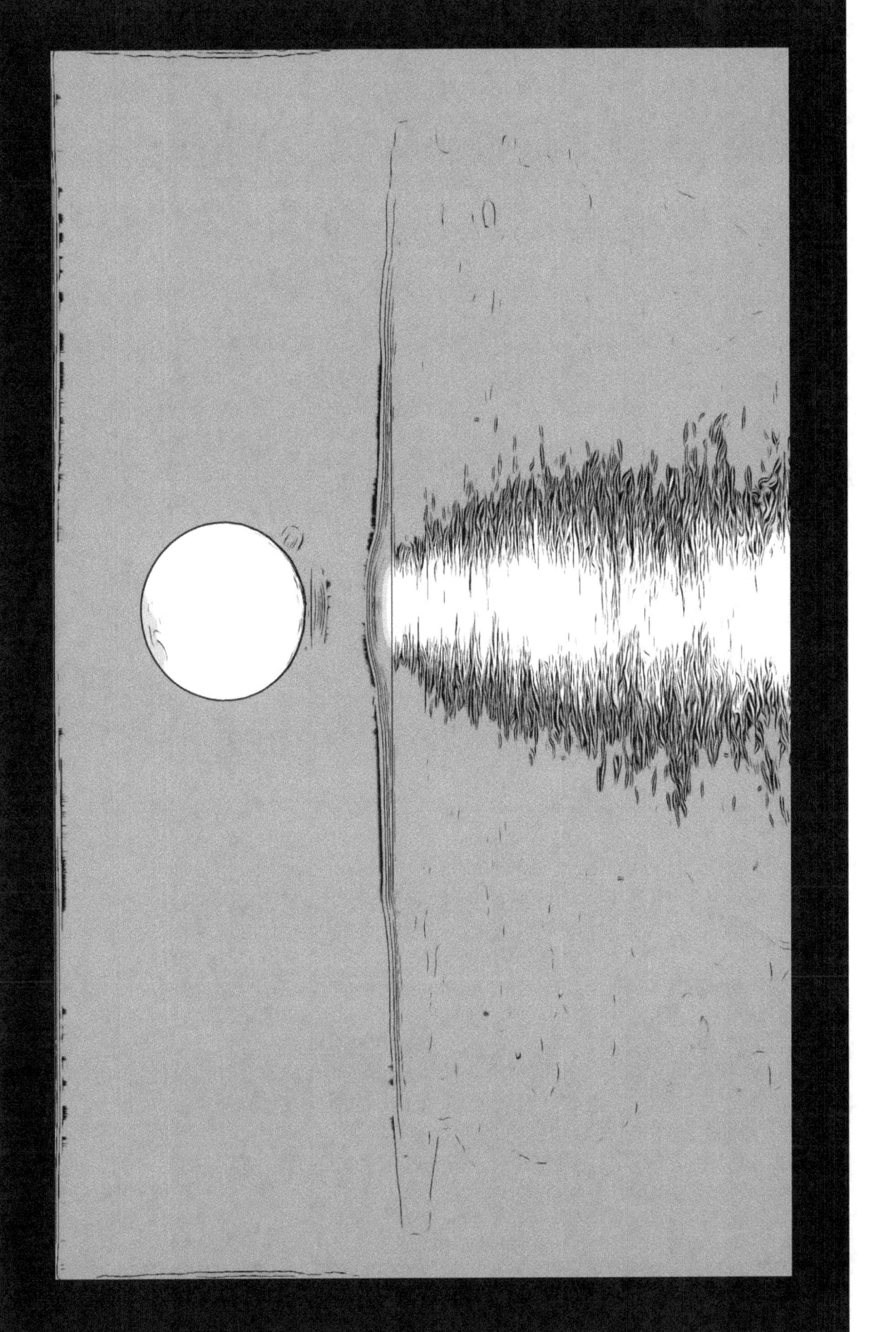

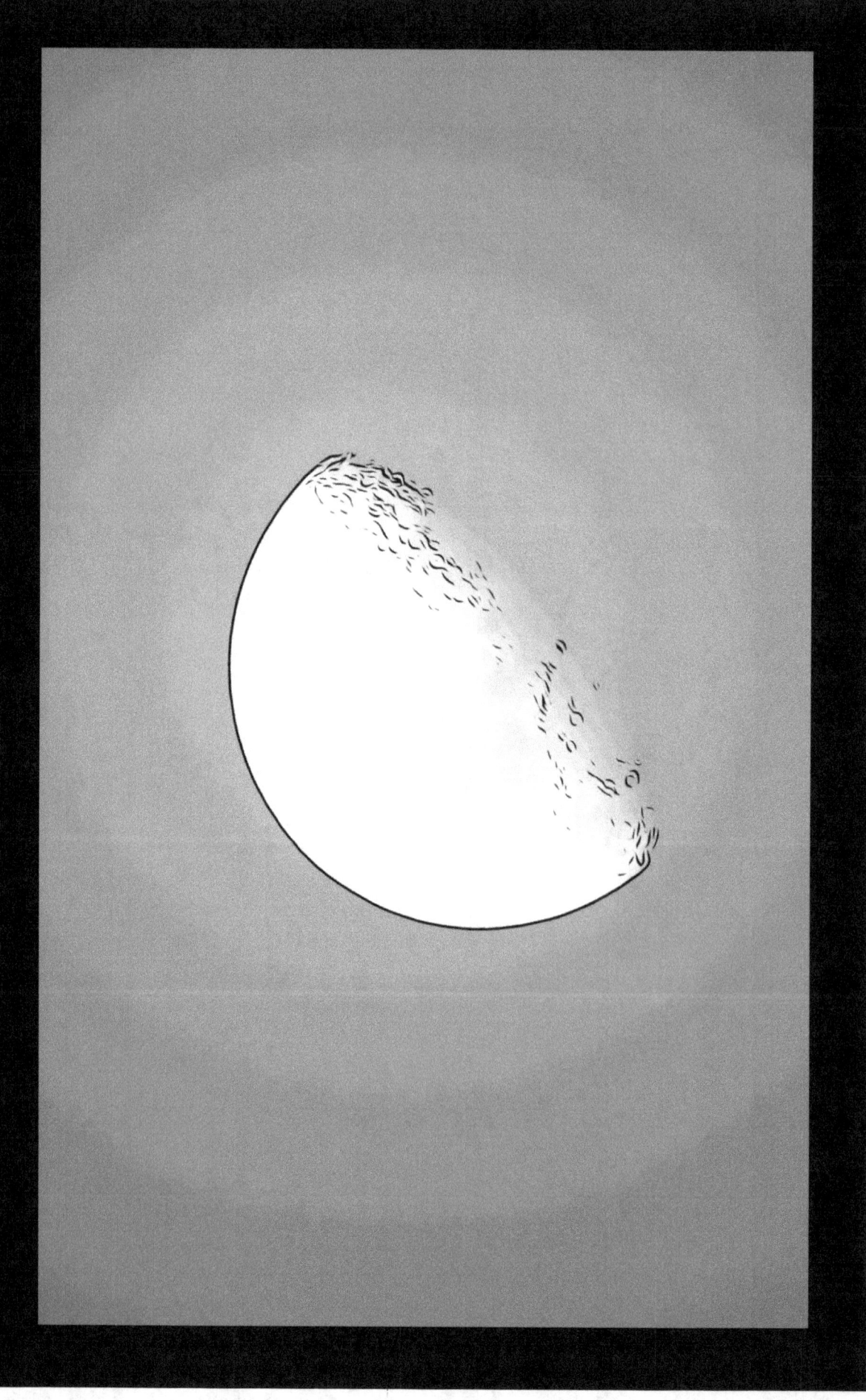

And God said, "Let the water teem with living creatures, and let birds fly above the earth across the vault of the sky." So God created the great creatures of the sea and every living thing with which the water teems and that moves about in it, according to their kinds, and every winged bird according to its kind. And God saw that it was good. God blessed them and said, "Be fruitful and increase in number and fill the water in the seas, and let the birds increase on the earth." And there was evening, and there was morning—the fifth day.

Genesis 1:20-23, NIV

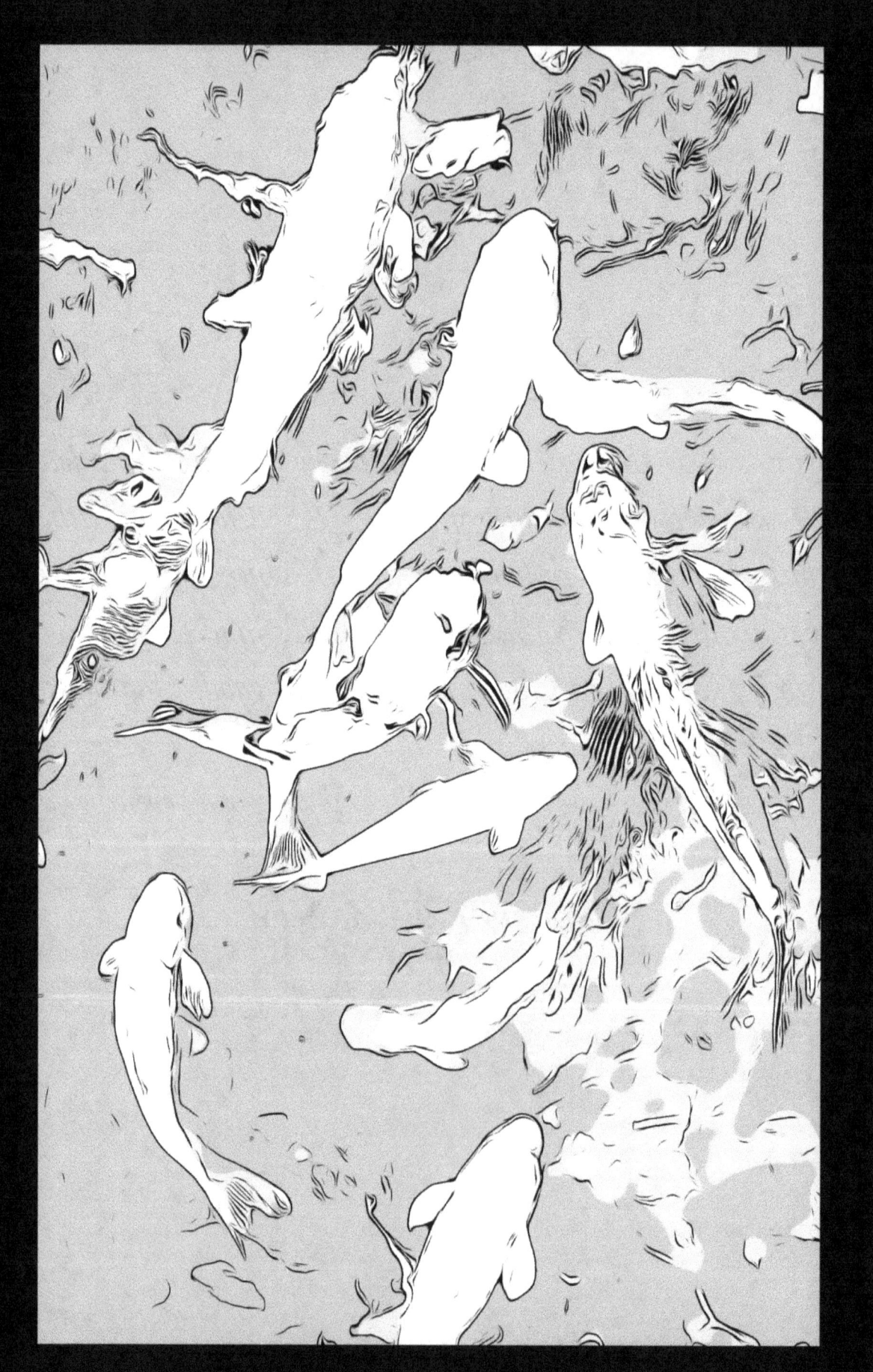

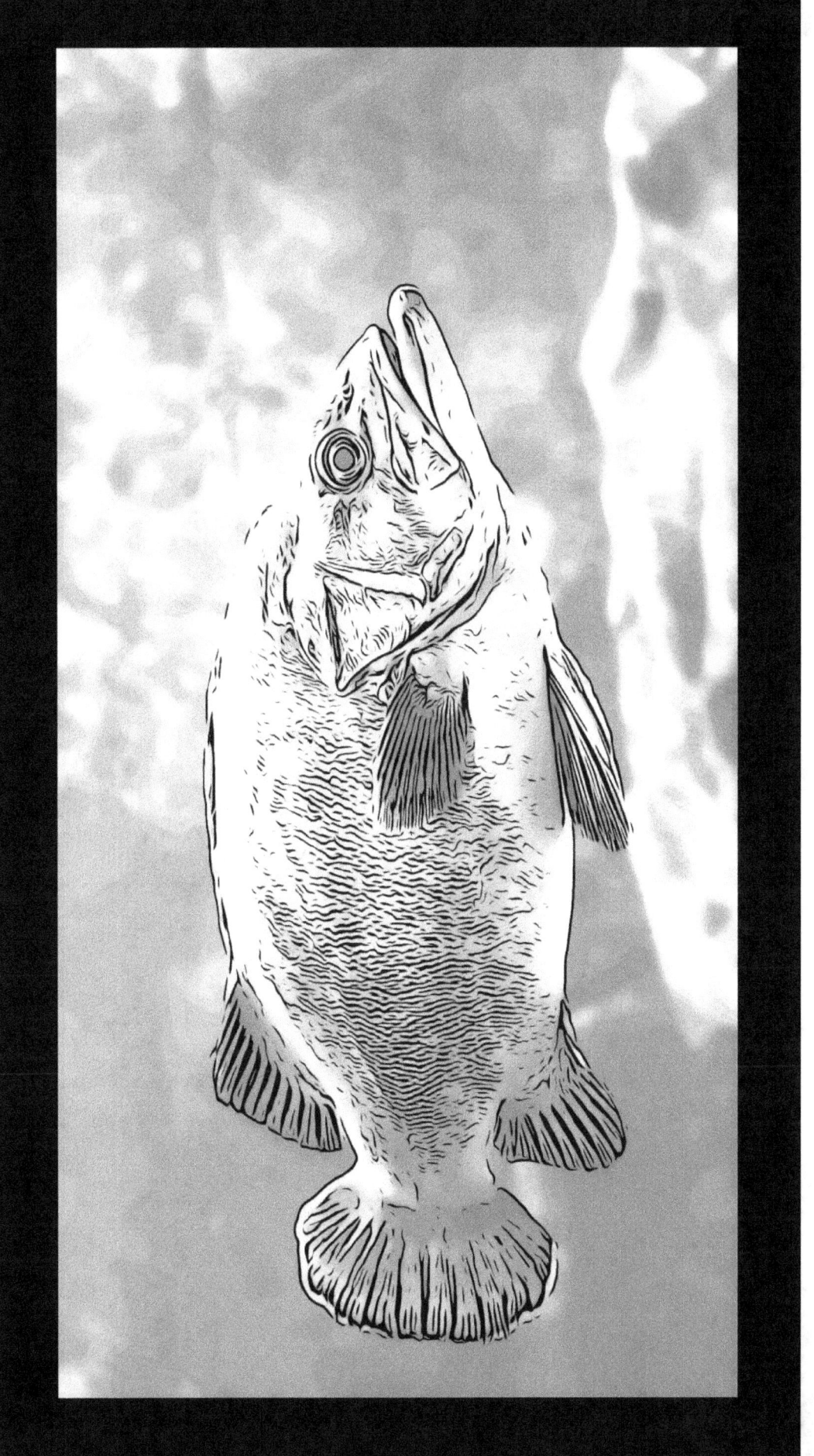

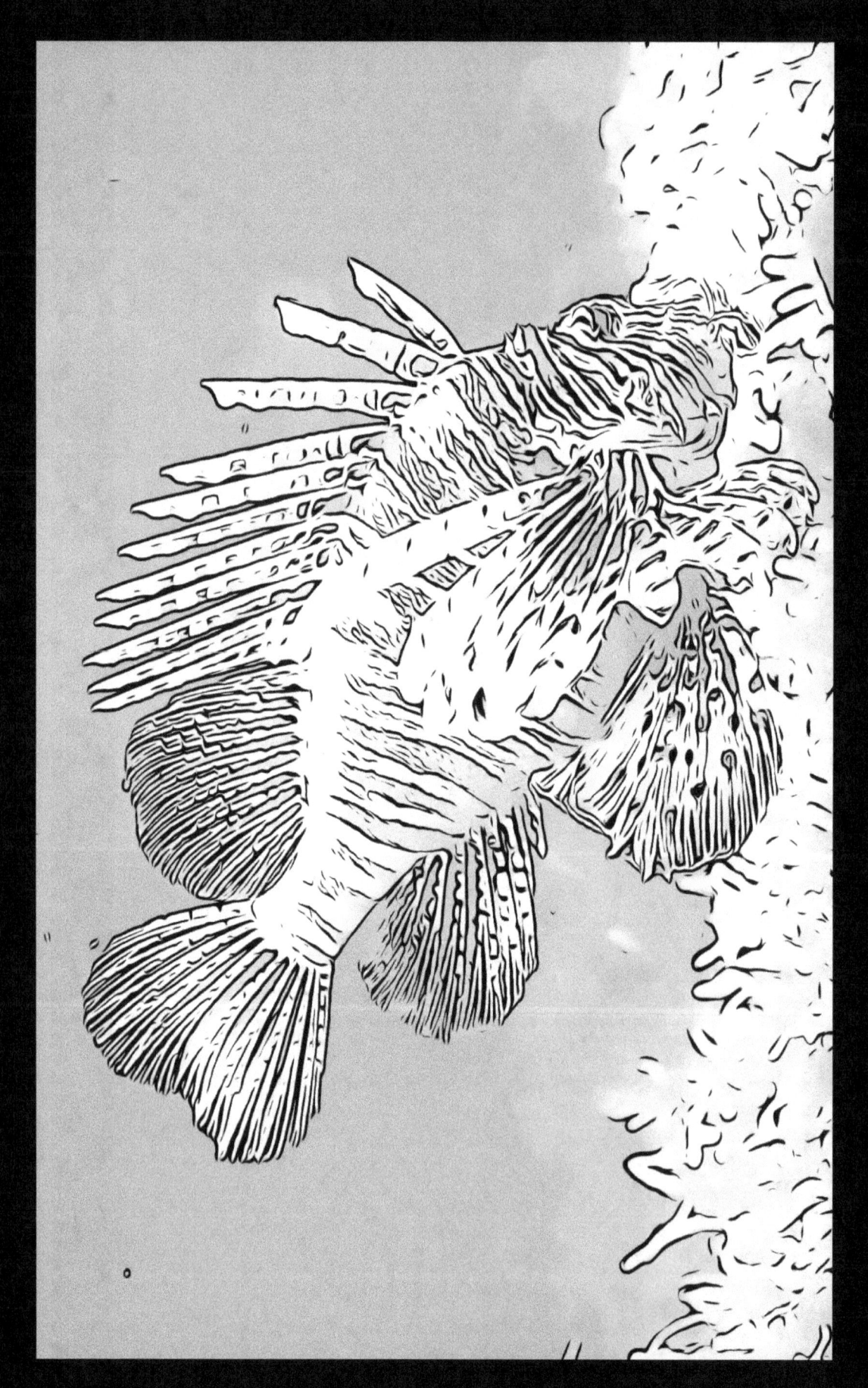

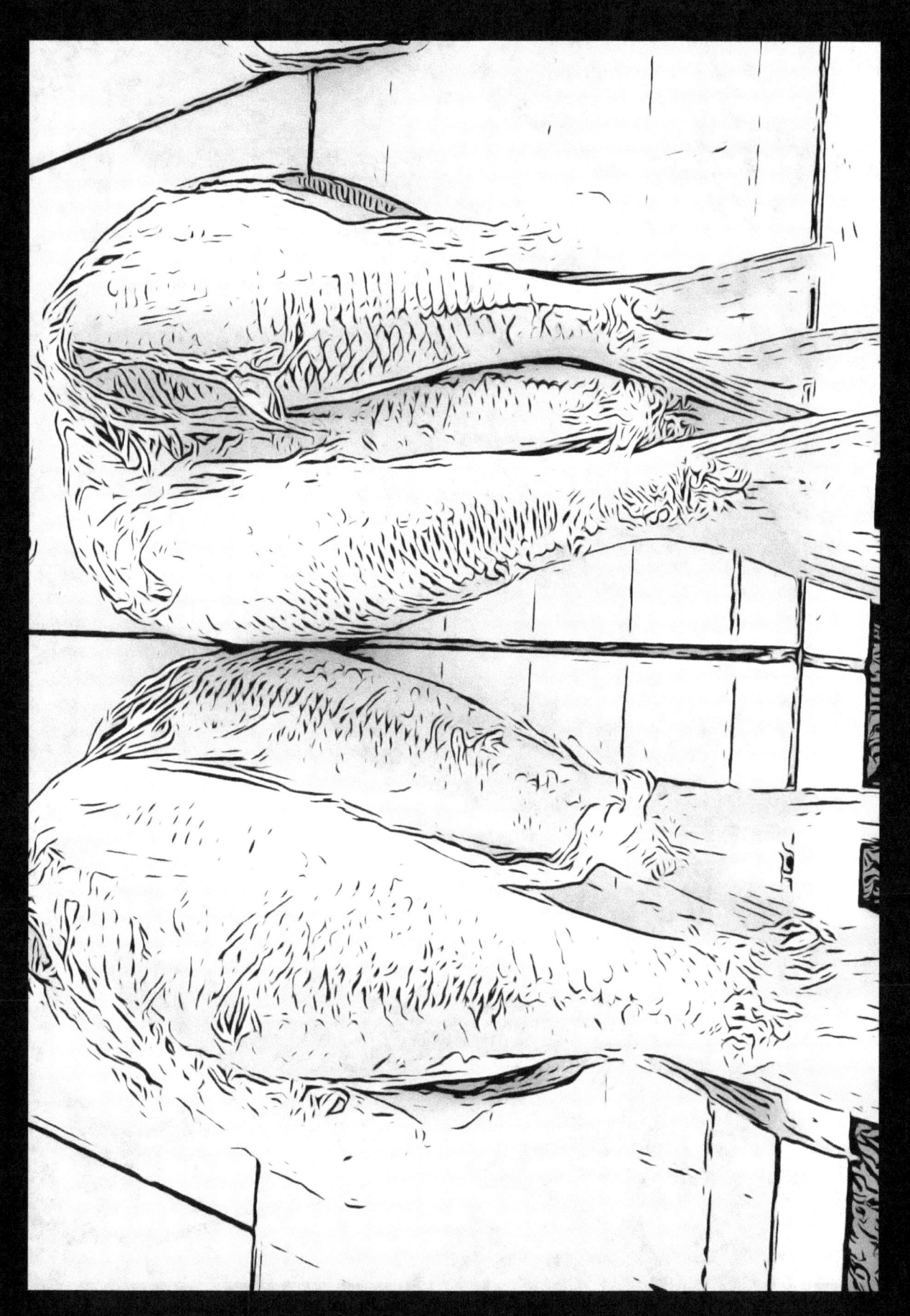

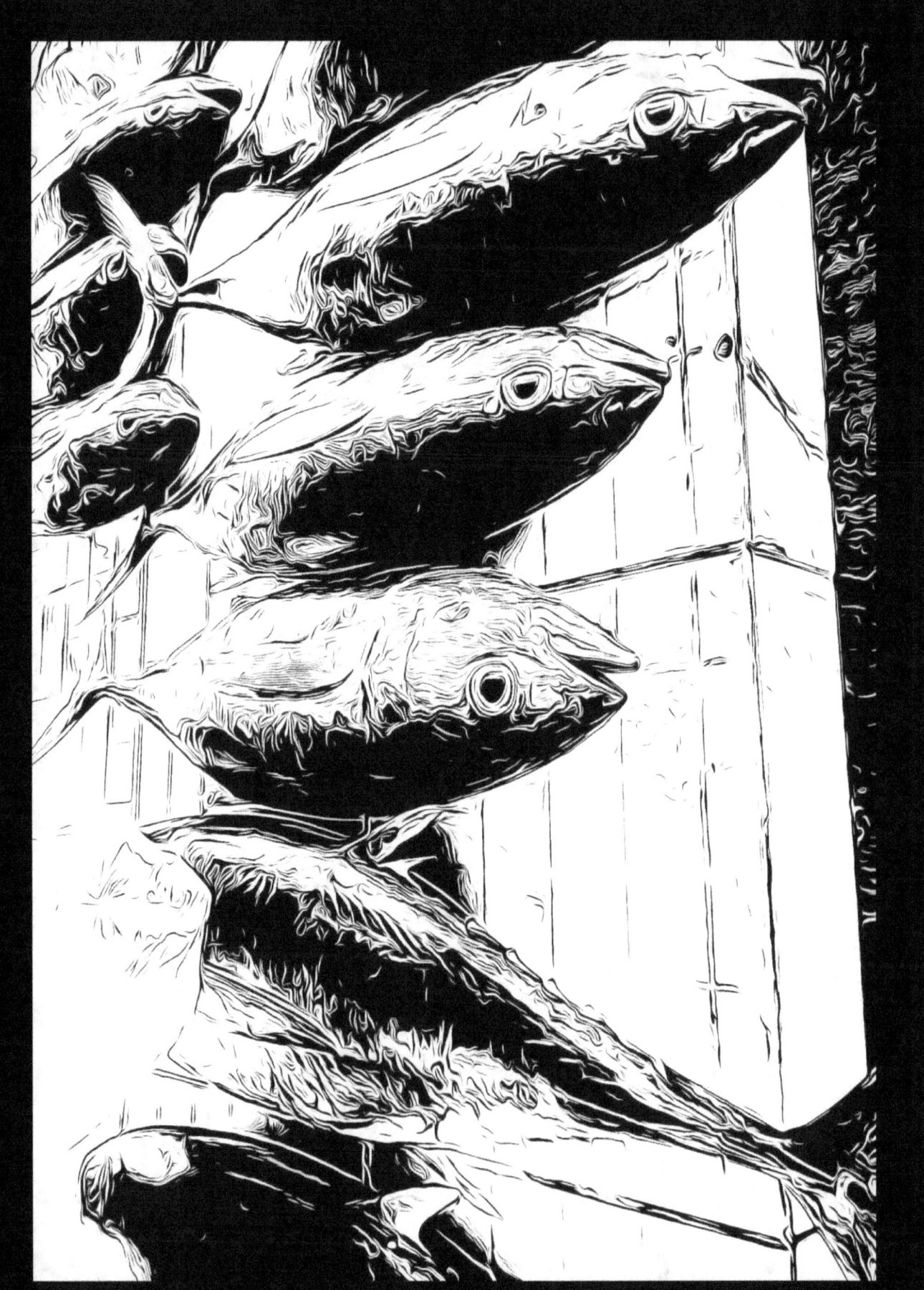

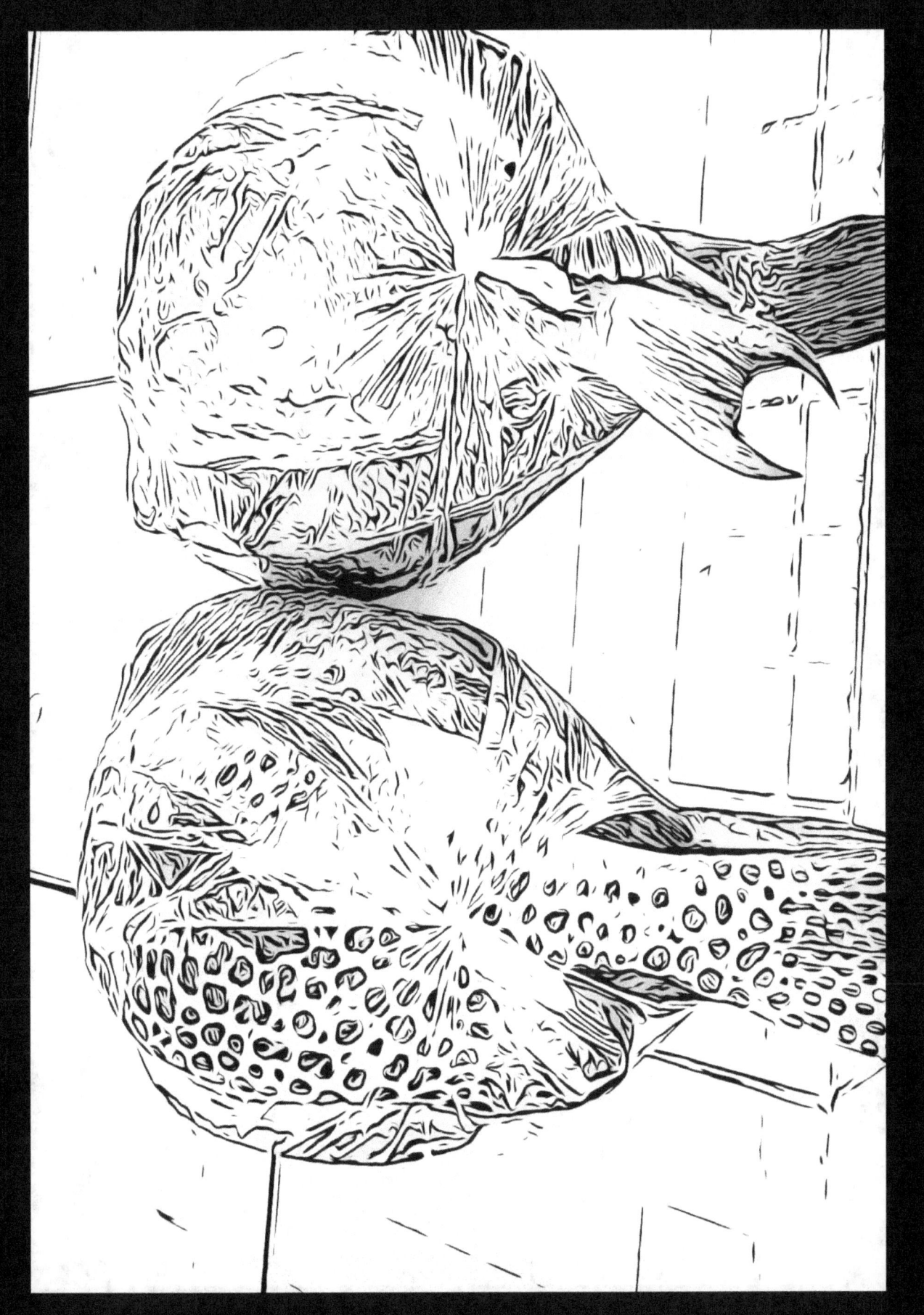

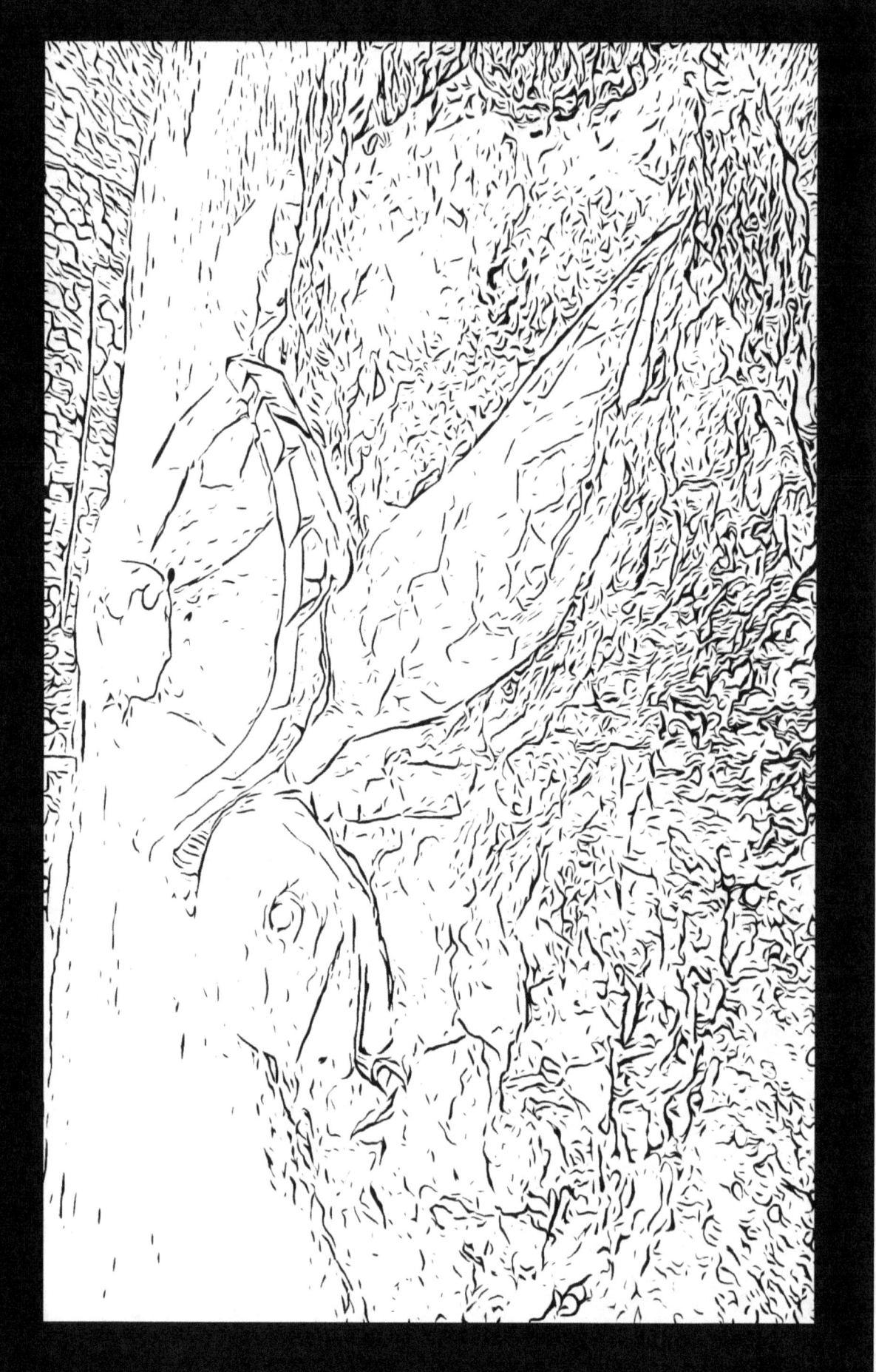

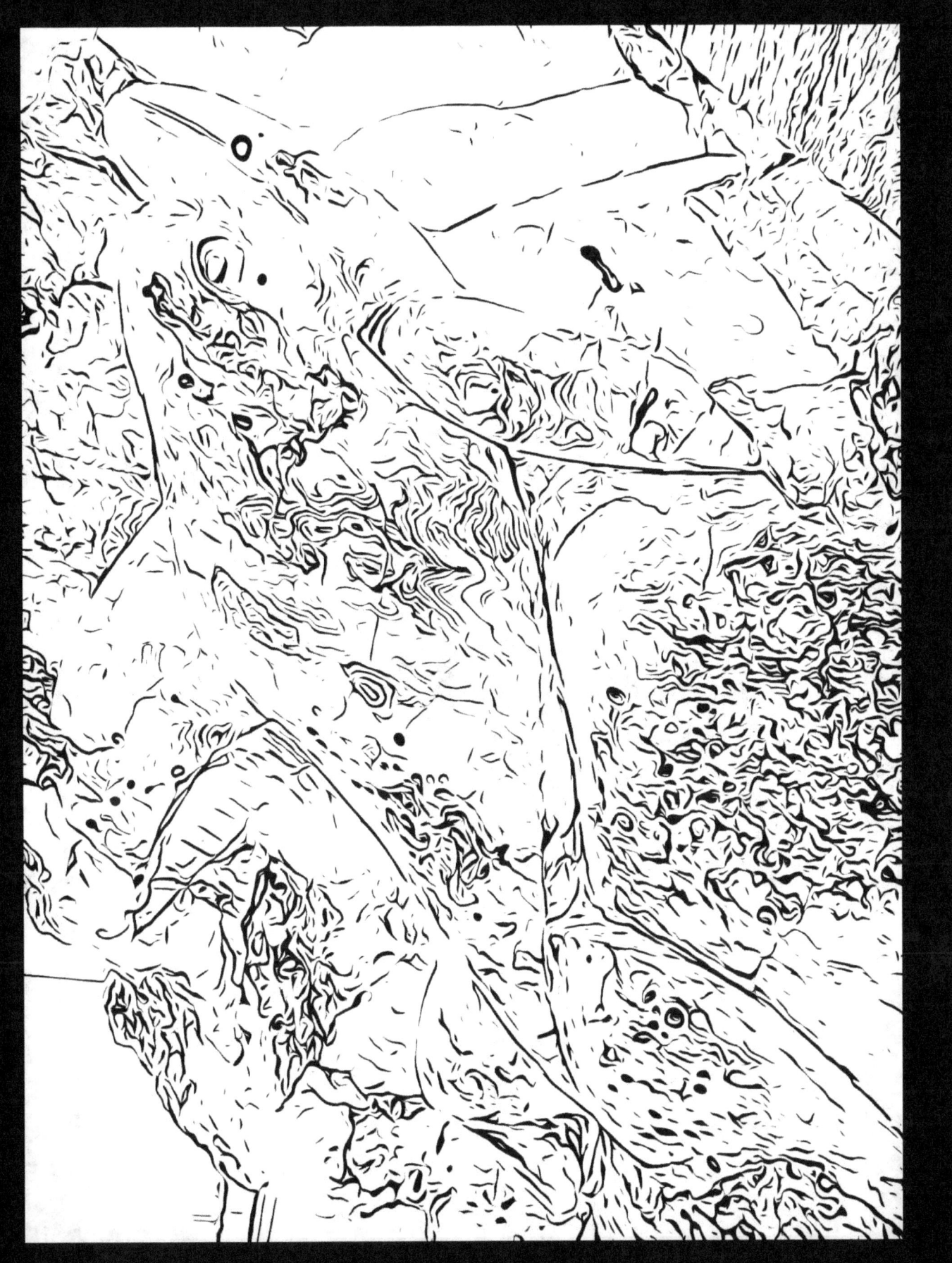

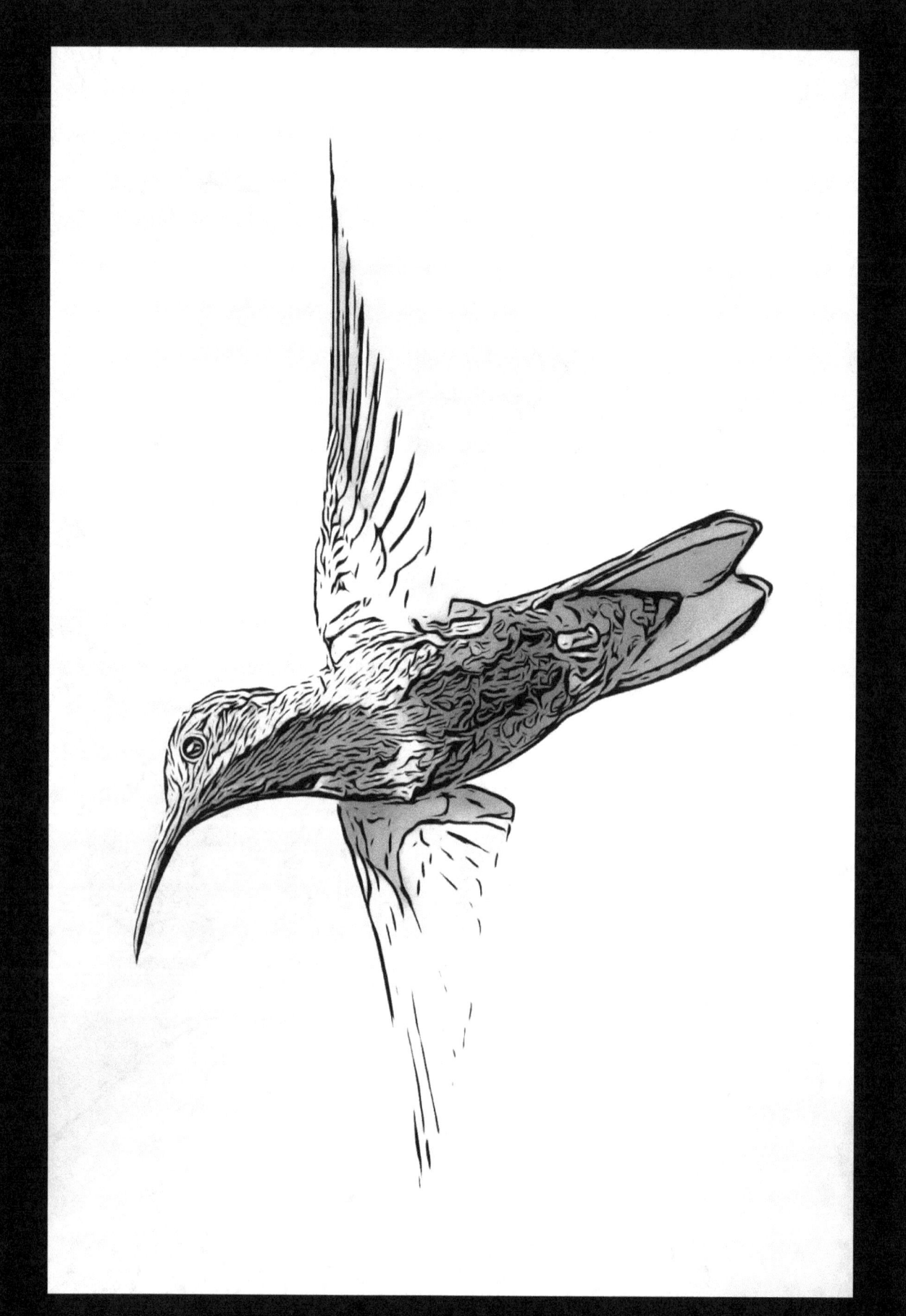

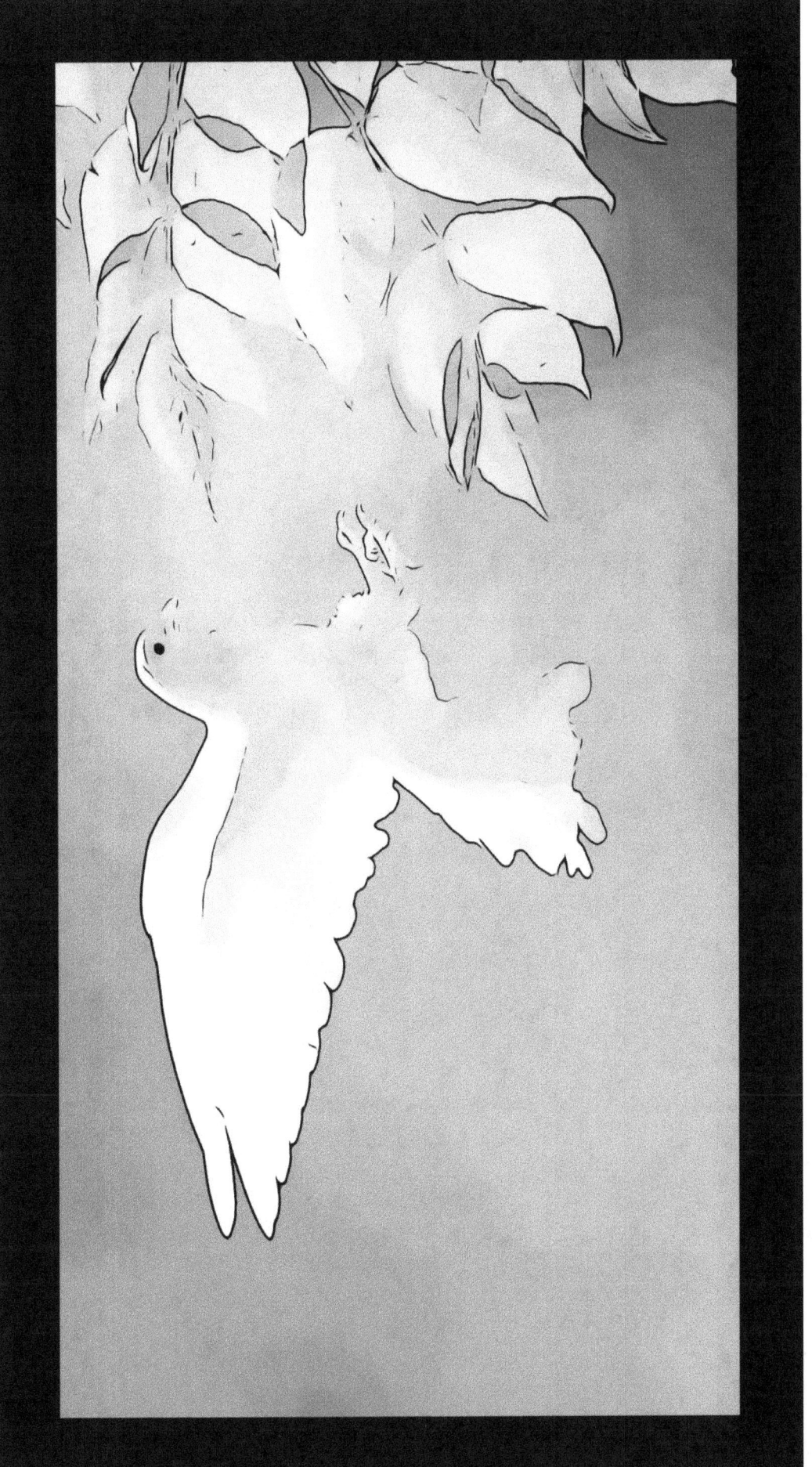

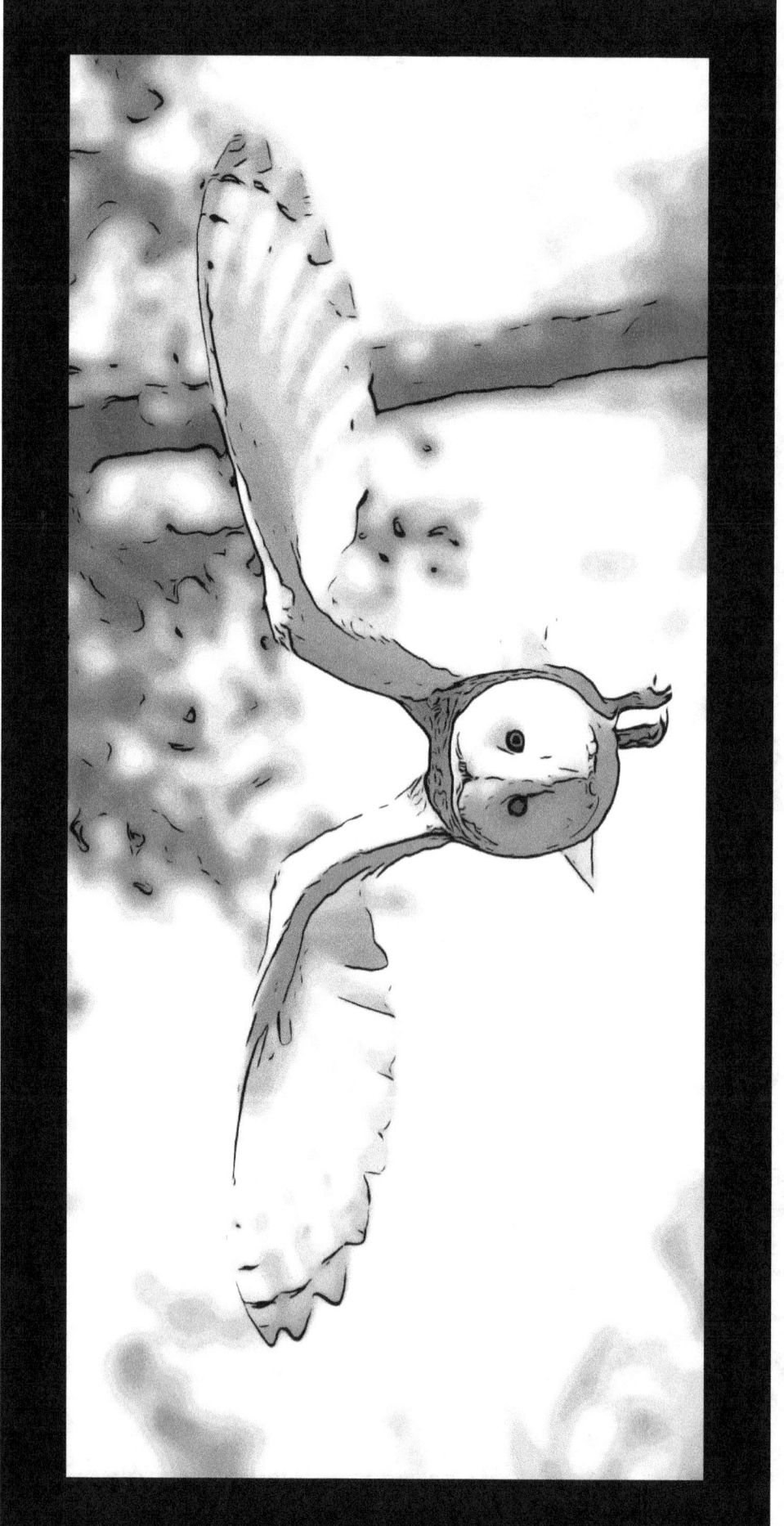

And God said, "Let the land produce living creatures according to their kinds: the livestock, the creatures that move along the ground, and the wild animals, each according to its kind." And it was so. God made the wild animals according to their kinds, the livestock according to their kinds, and all the creatures that move along the ground according to their kinds. And God saw that it was good. Then God said, "Let us make mankind in our image, in our likeness, so that they may rule over the fish in the sea and the birds in the sky, over the livestock and all the wild animals, and over all the creatures that move along the ground."

Genesis 1:24-26, NIV

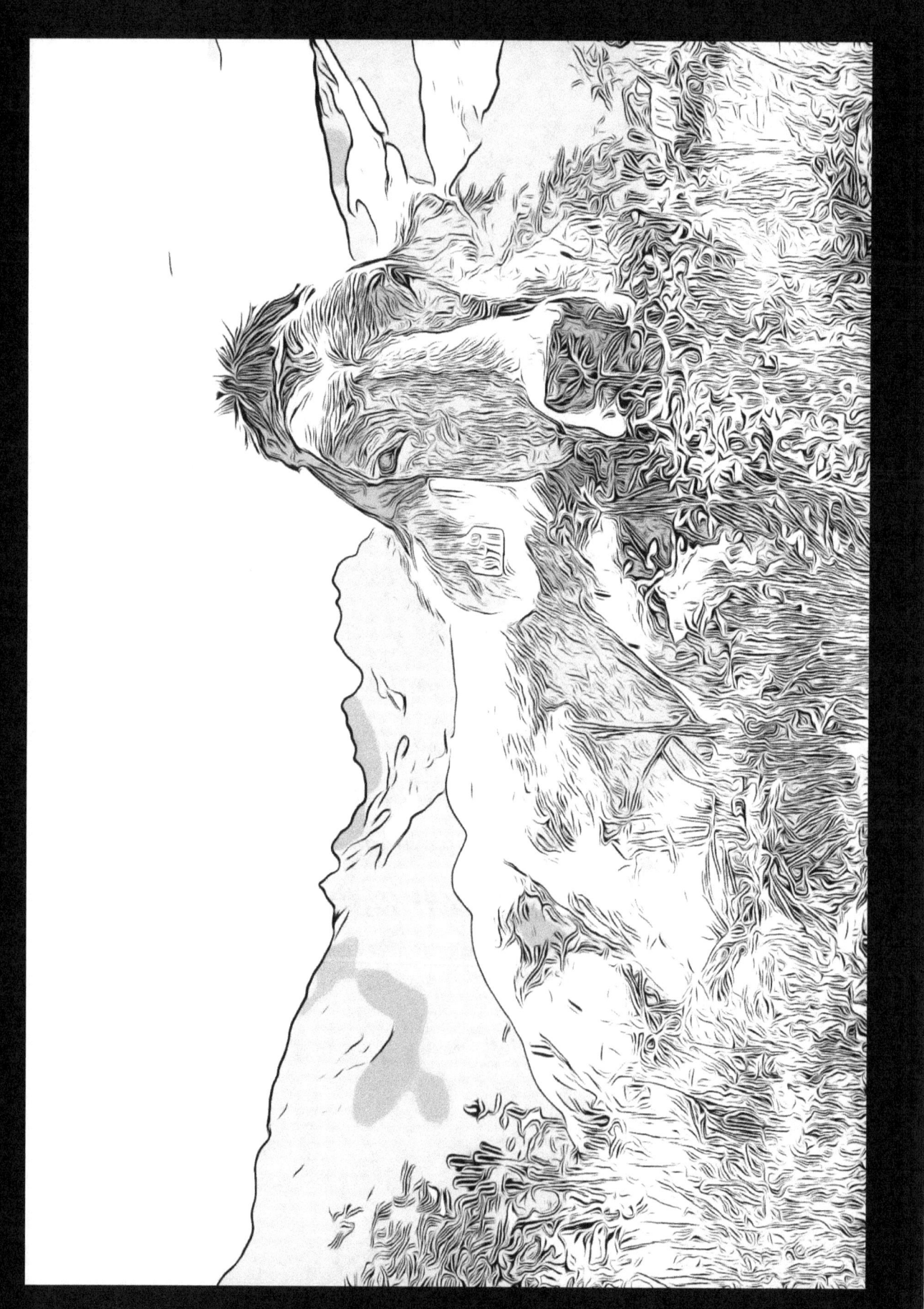

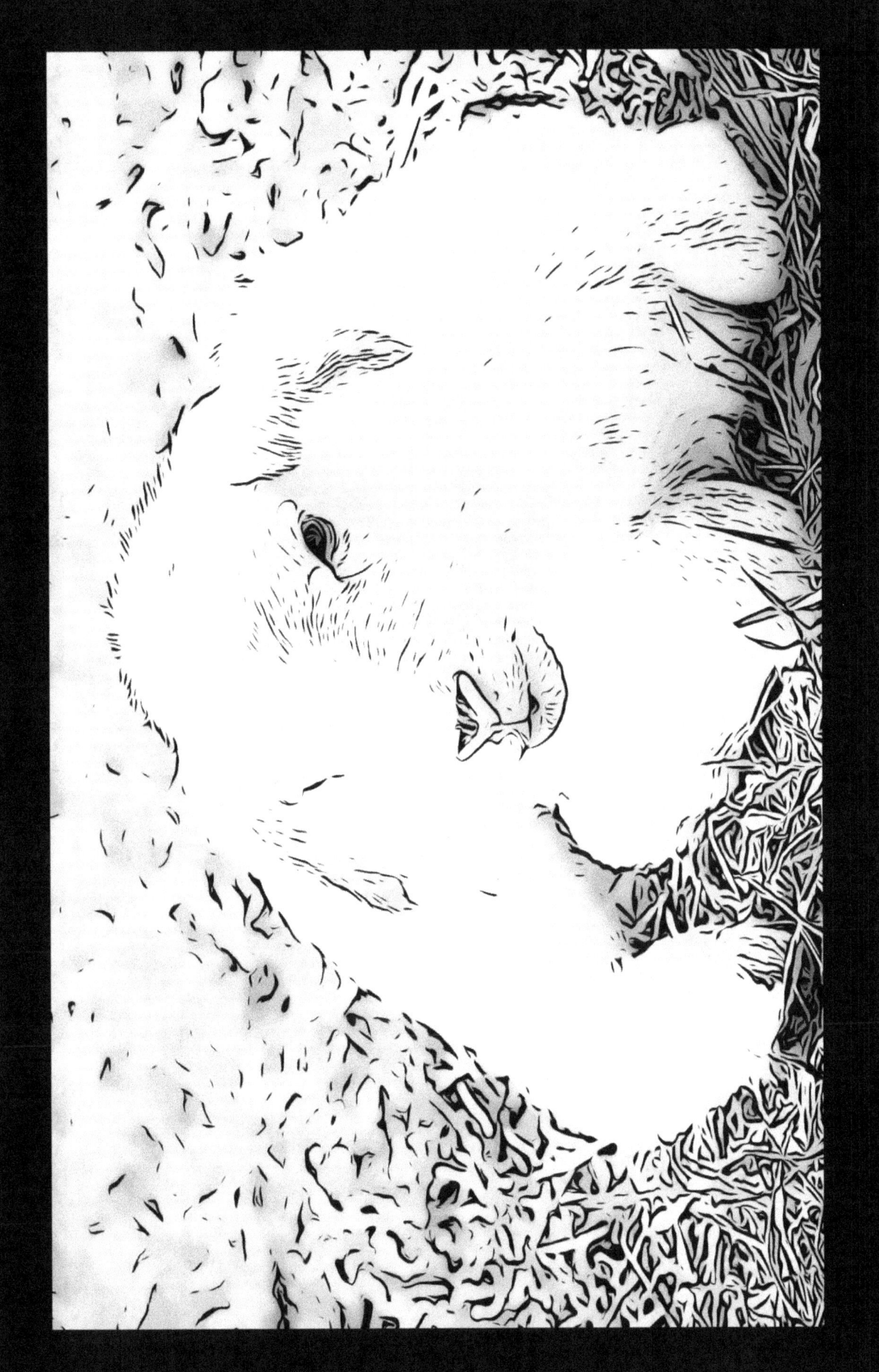

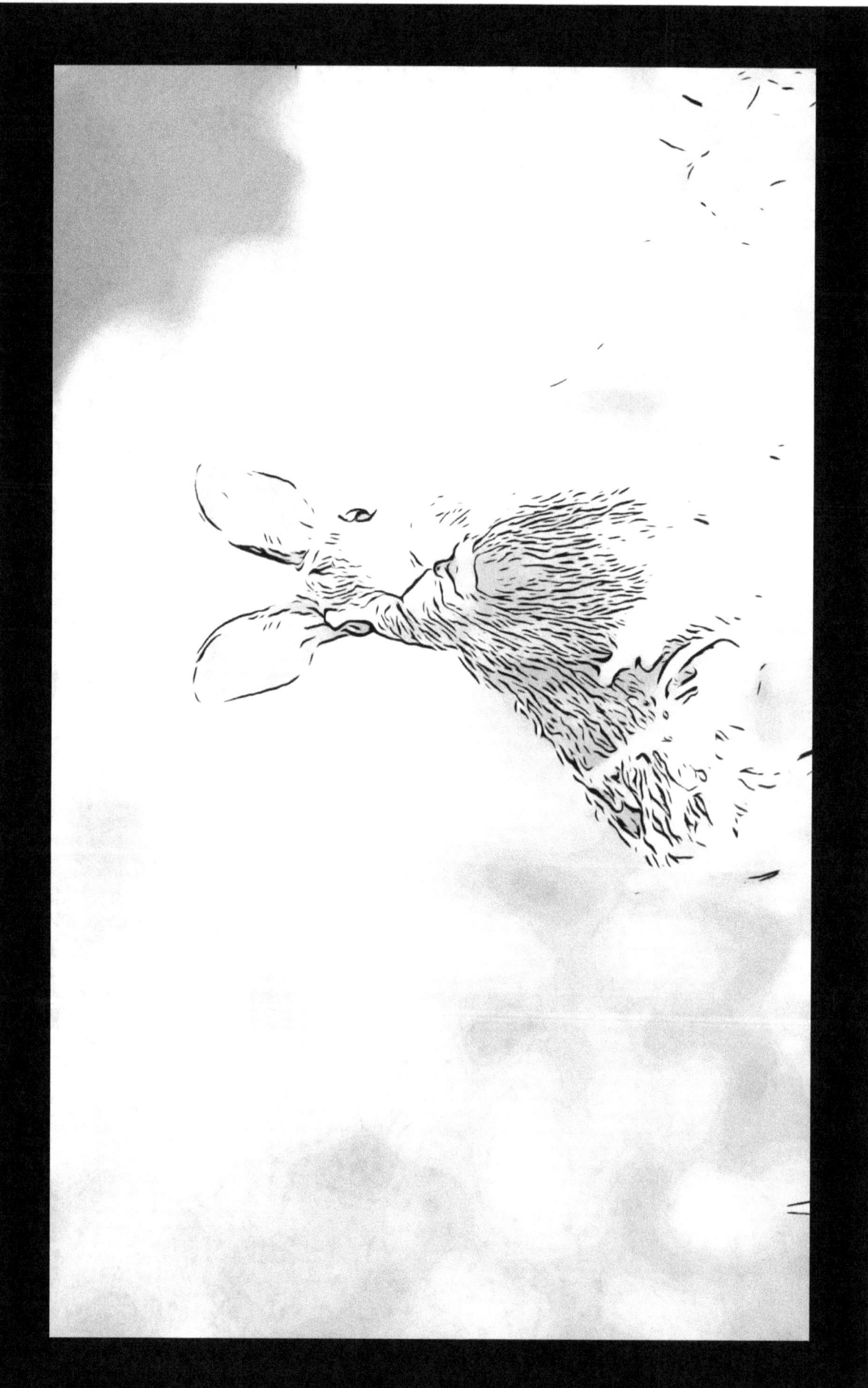

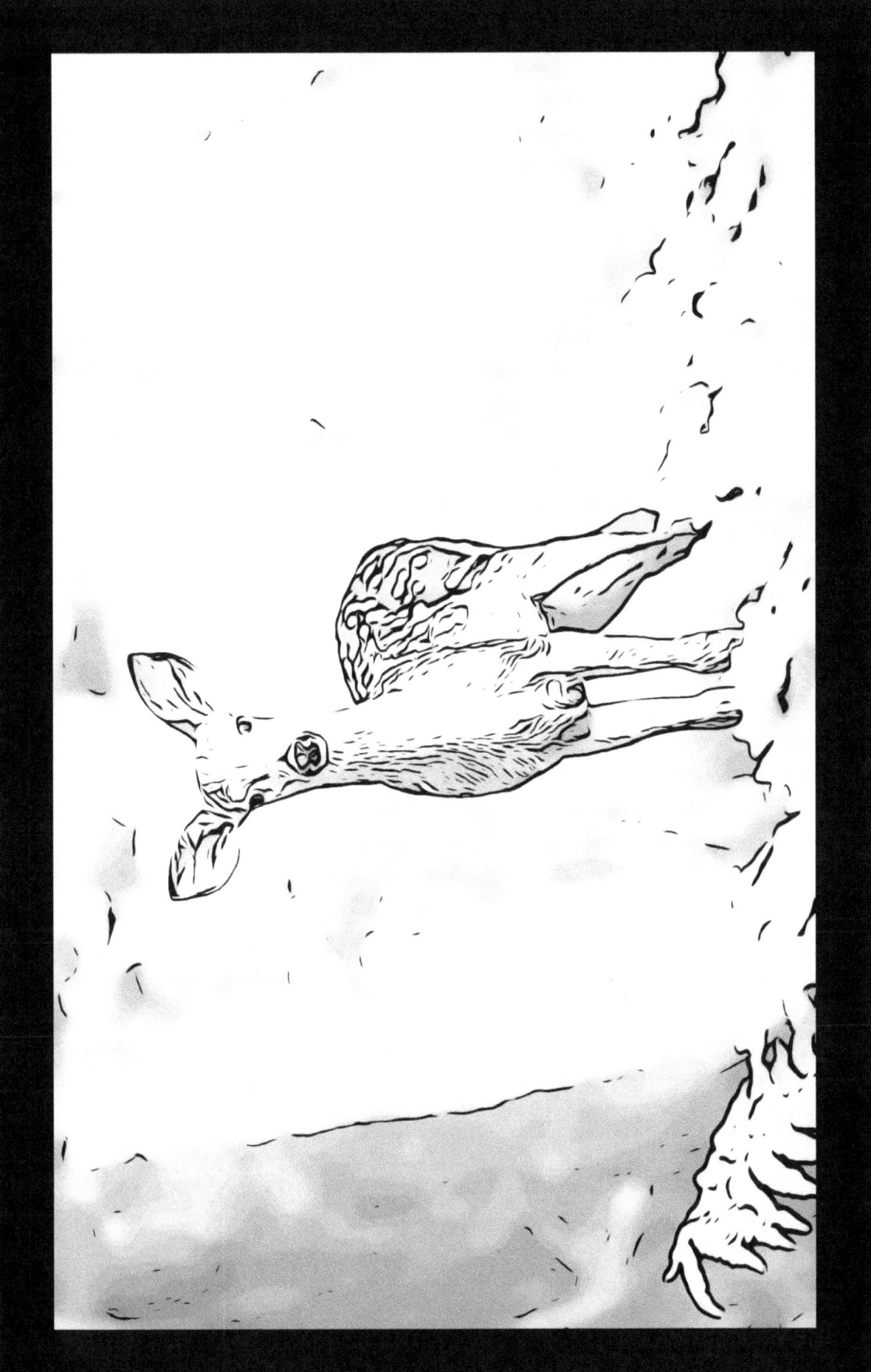

So God created mankind in his own image,
in the image of God he created them;
male and female he created them.
Genesis 1:27, NIV

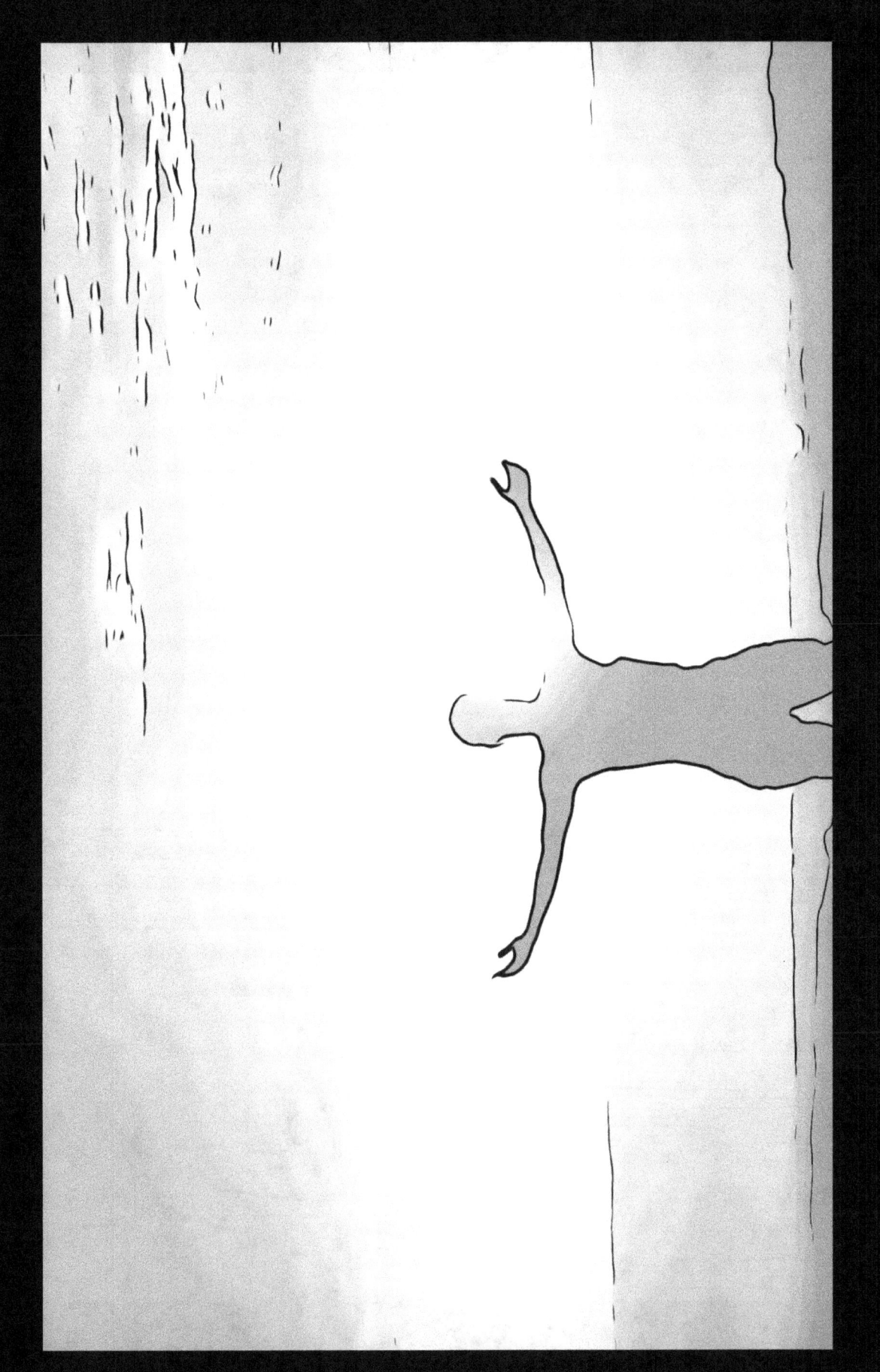

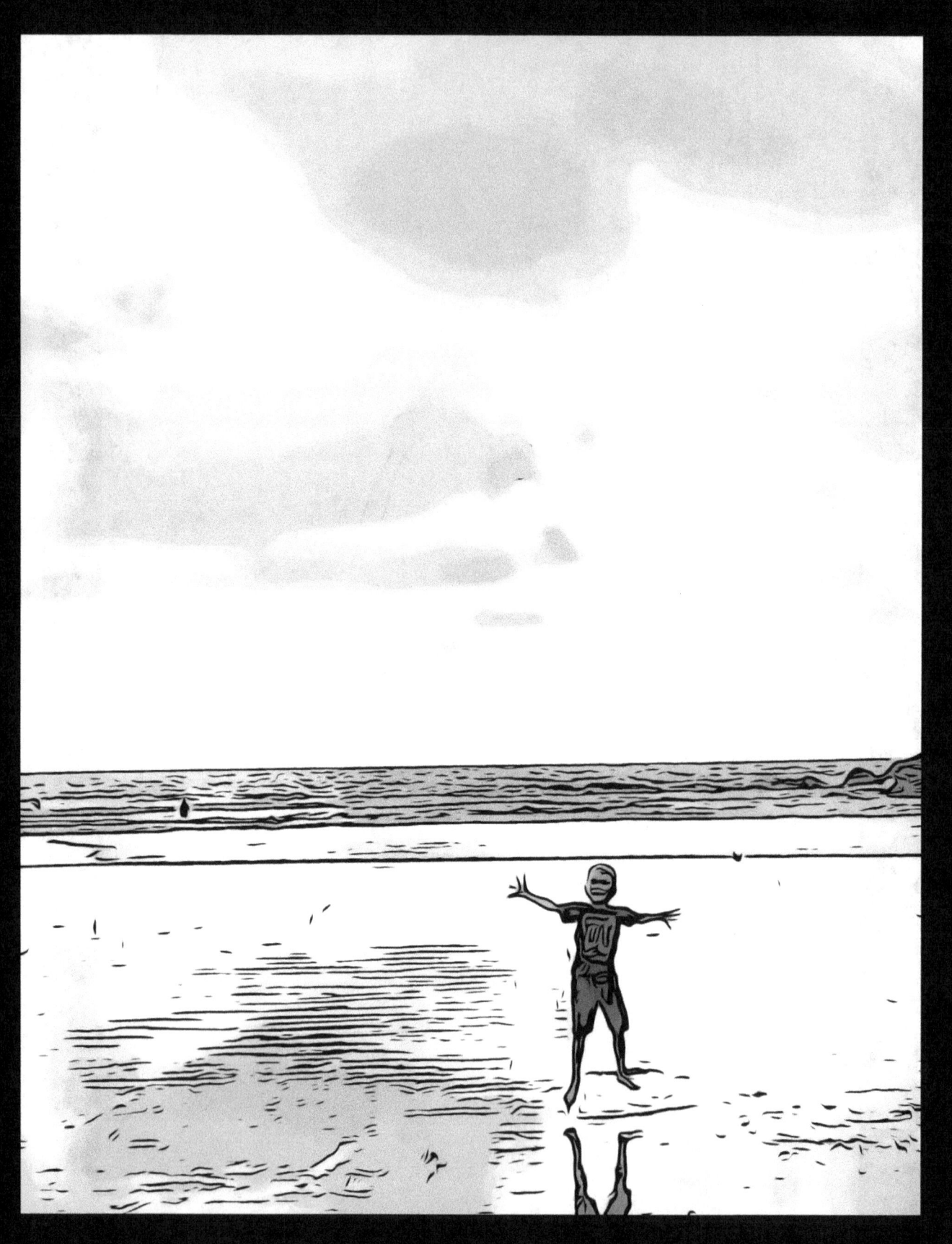

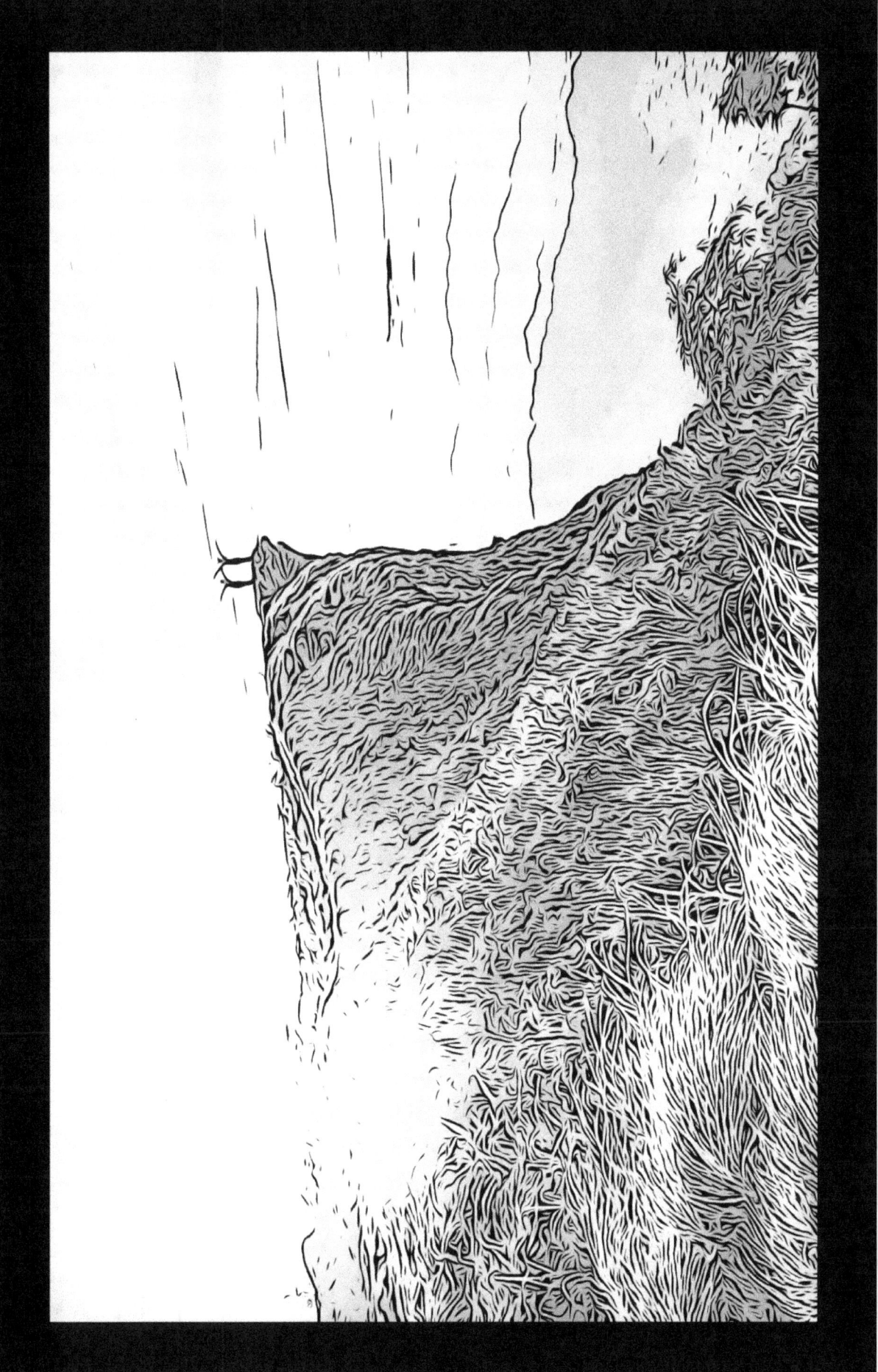

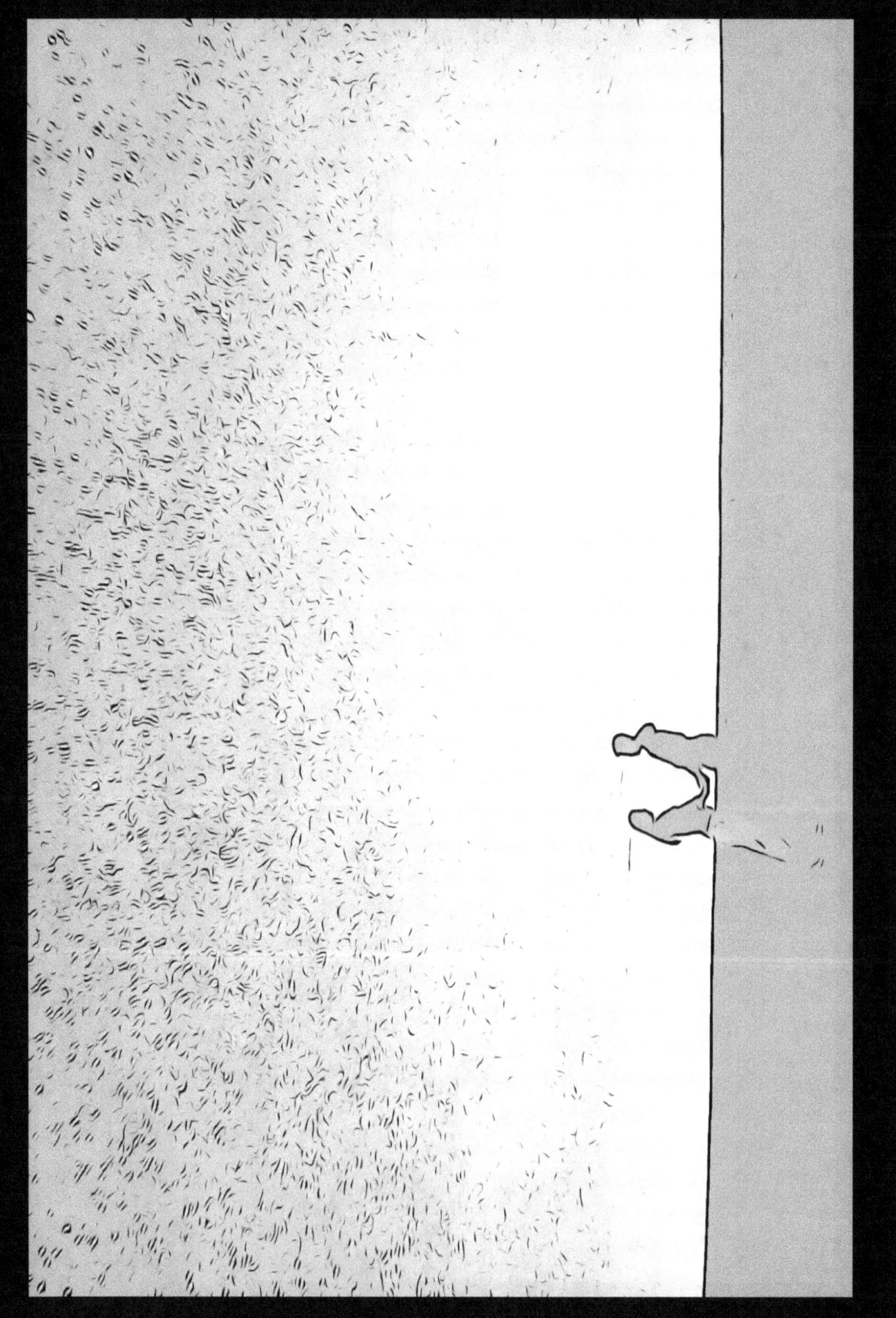

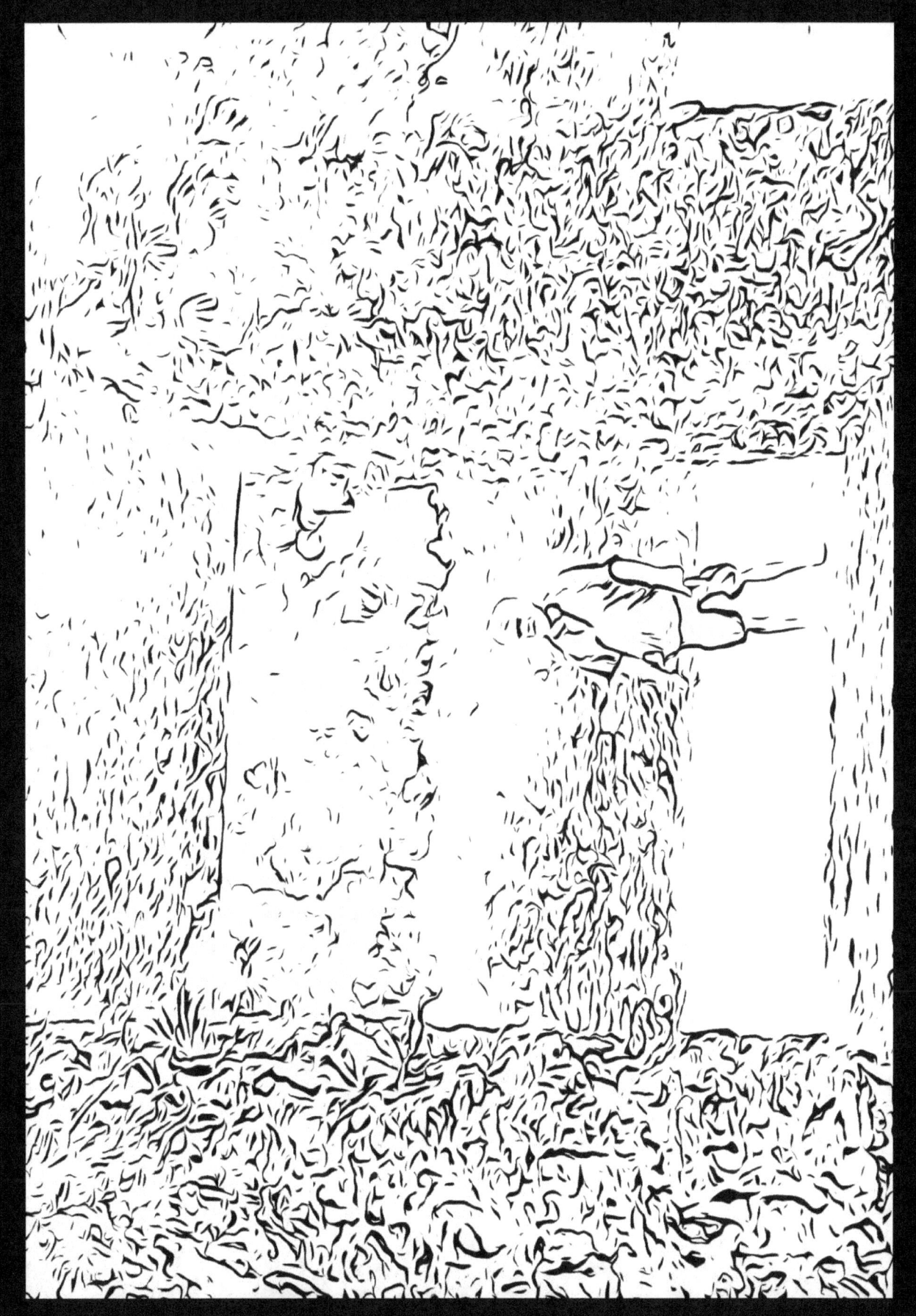

God blessed them and said to them, "Be fruitful and increase in number;
fill the earth and subdue it. Rule over the fish in the sea and the birds in
the sky and over every living creature that moves on the ground."
Genesis 1:28, NIV

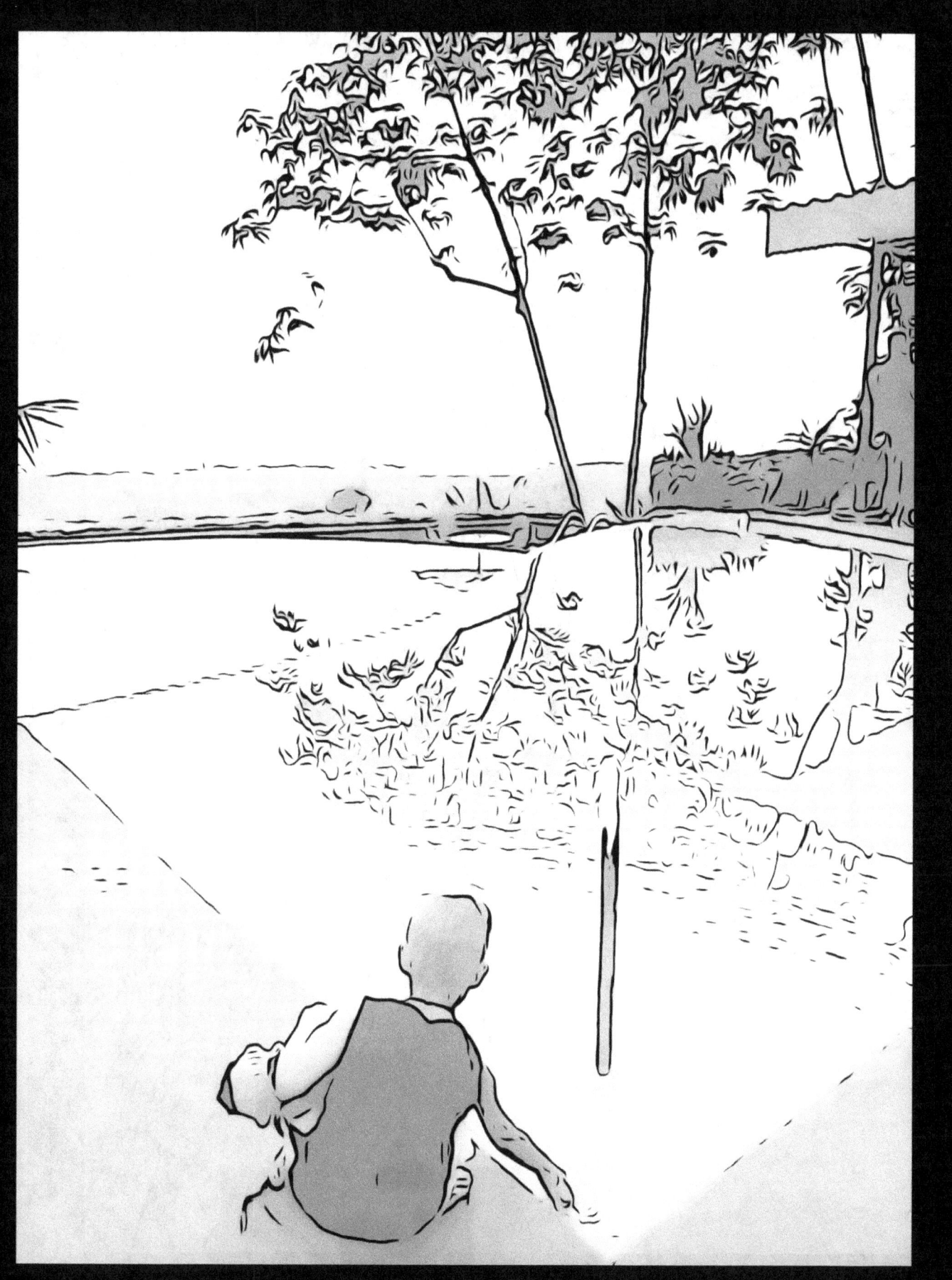

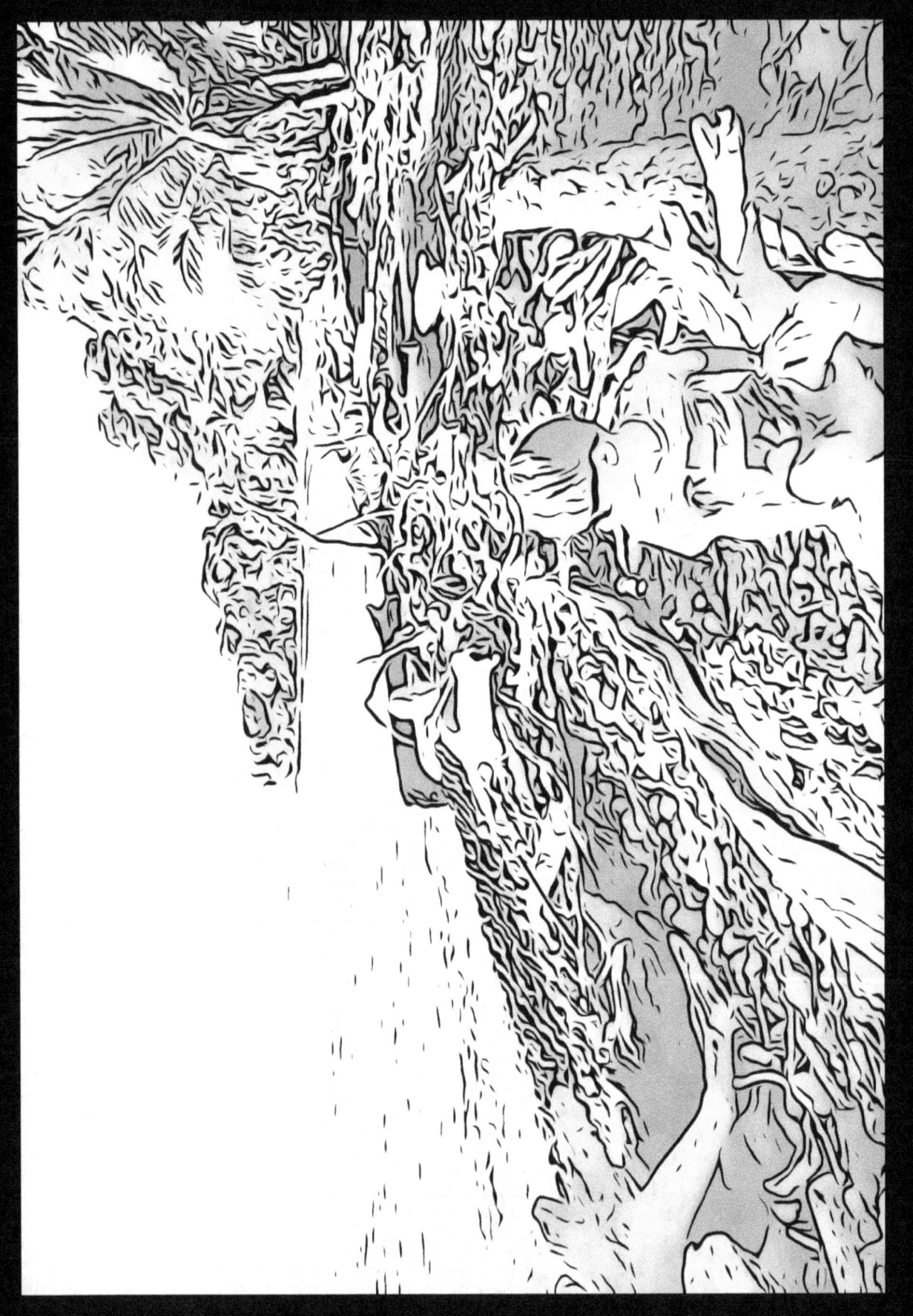

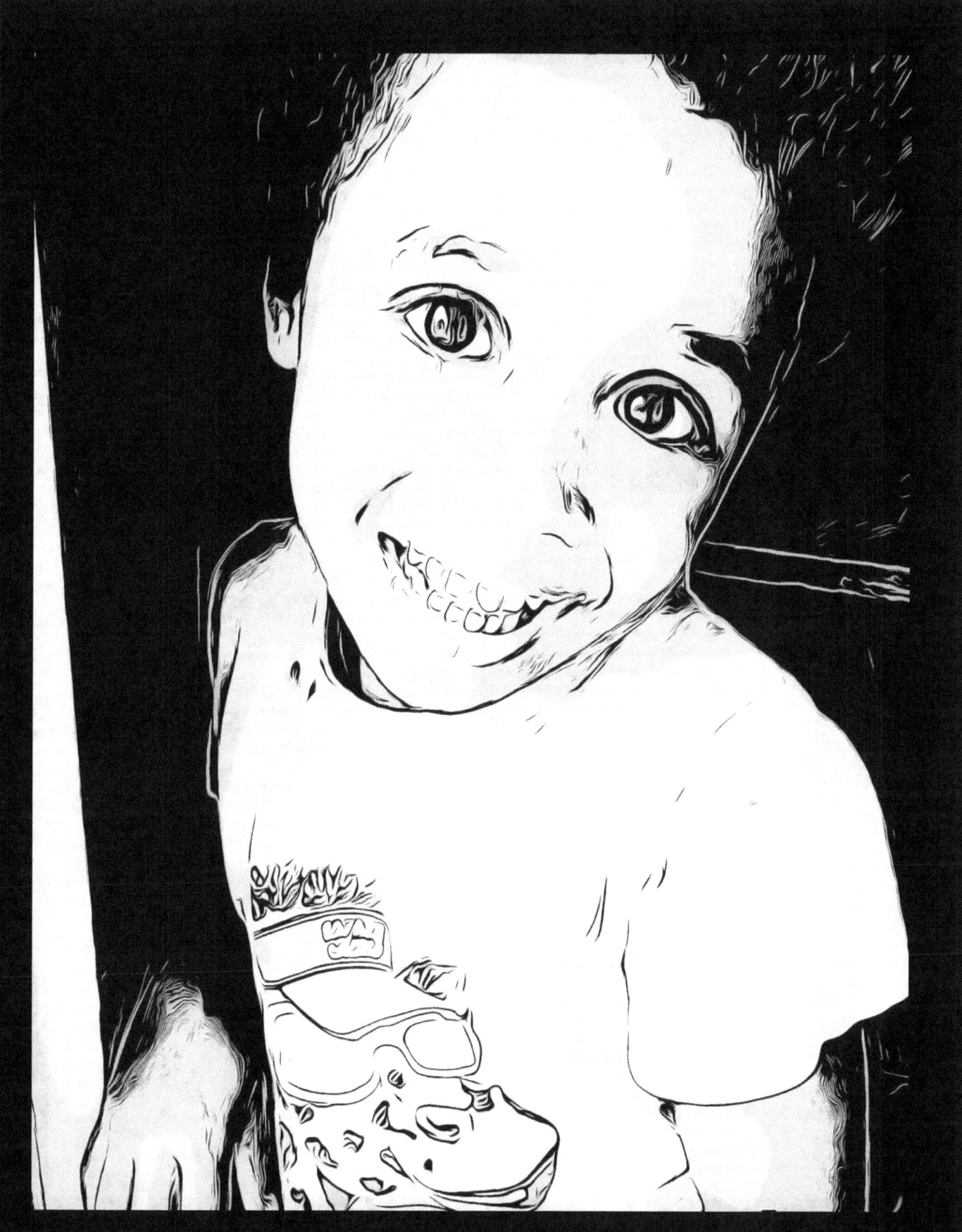

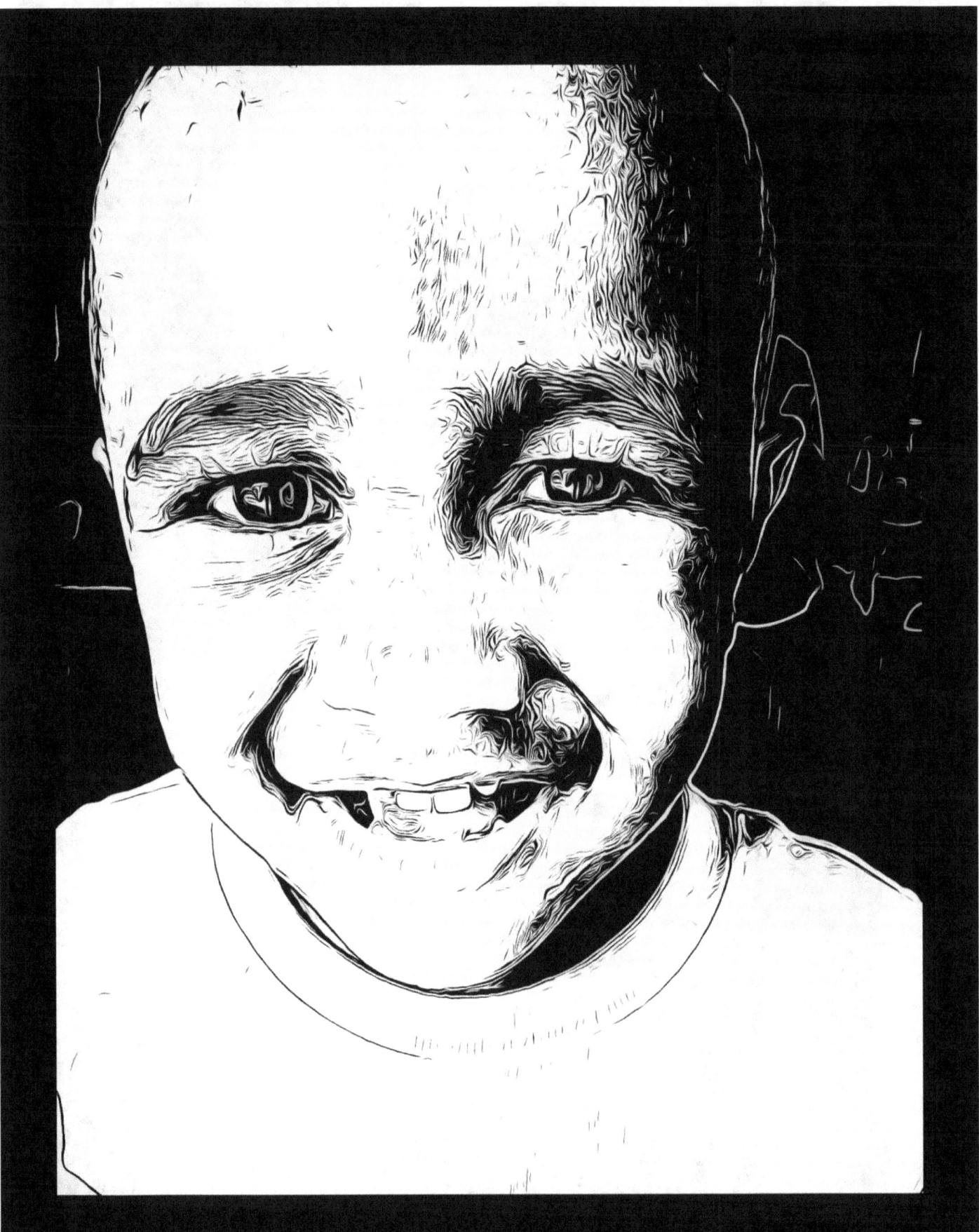

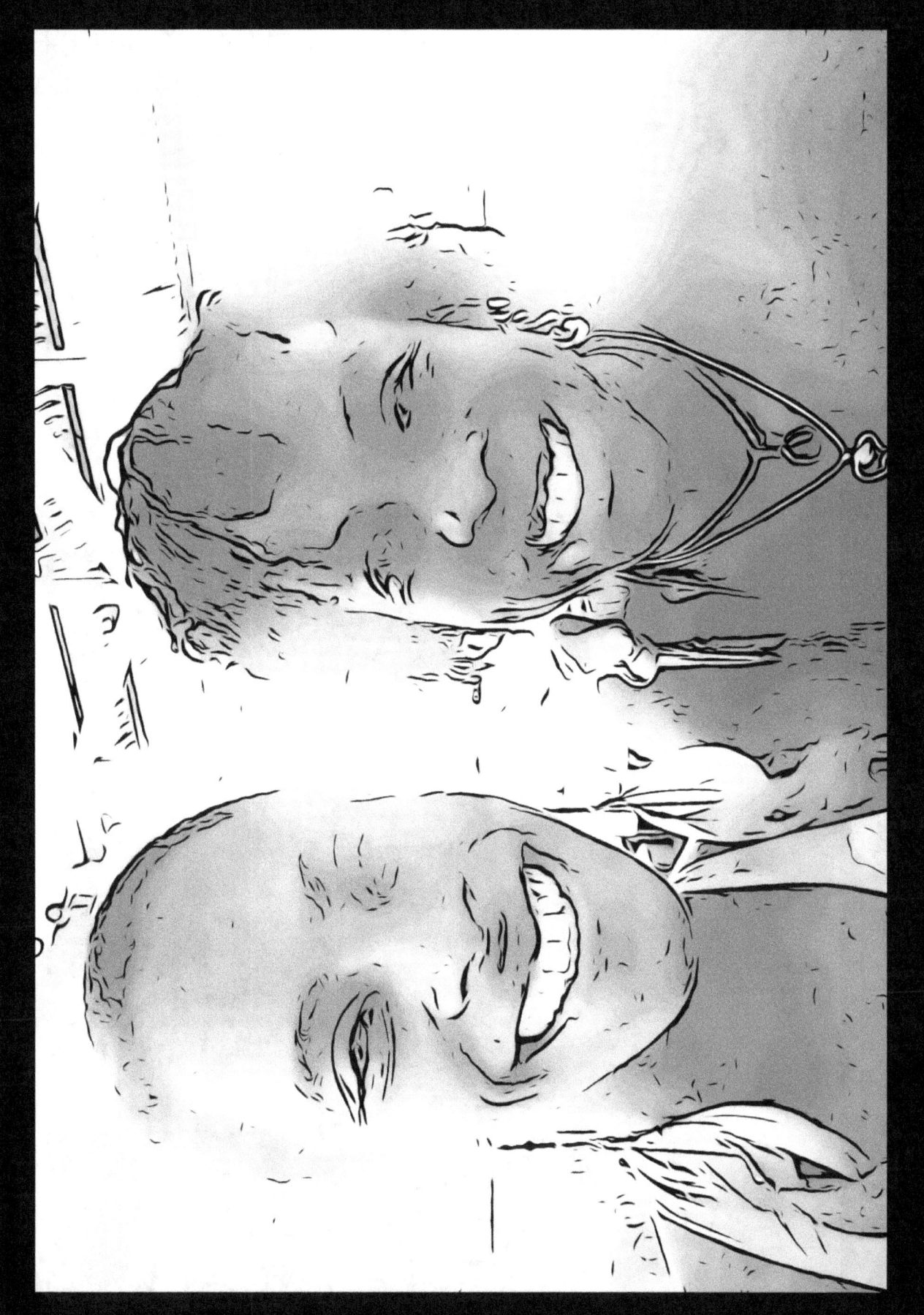

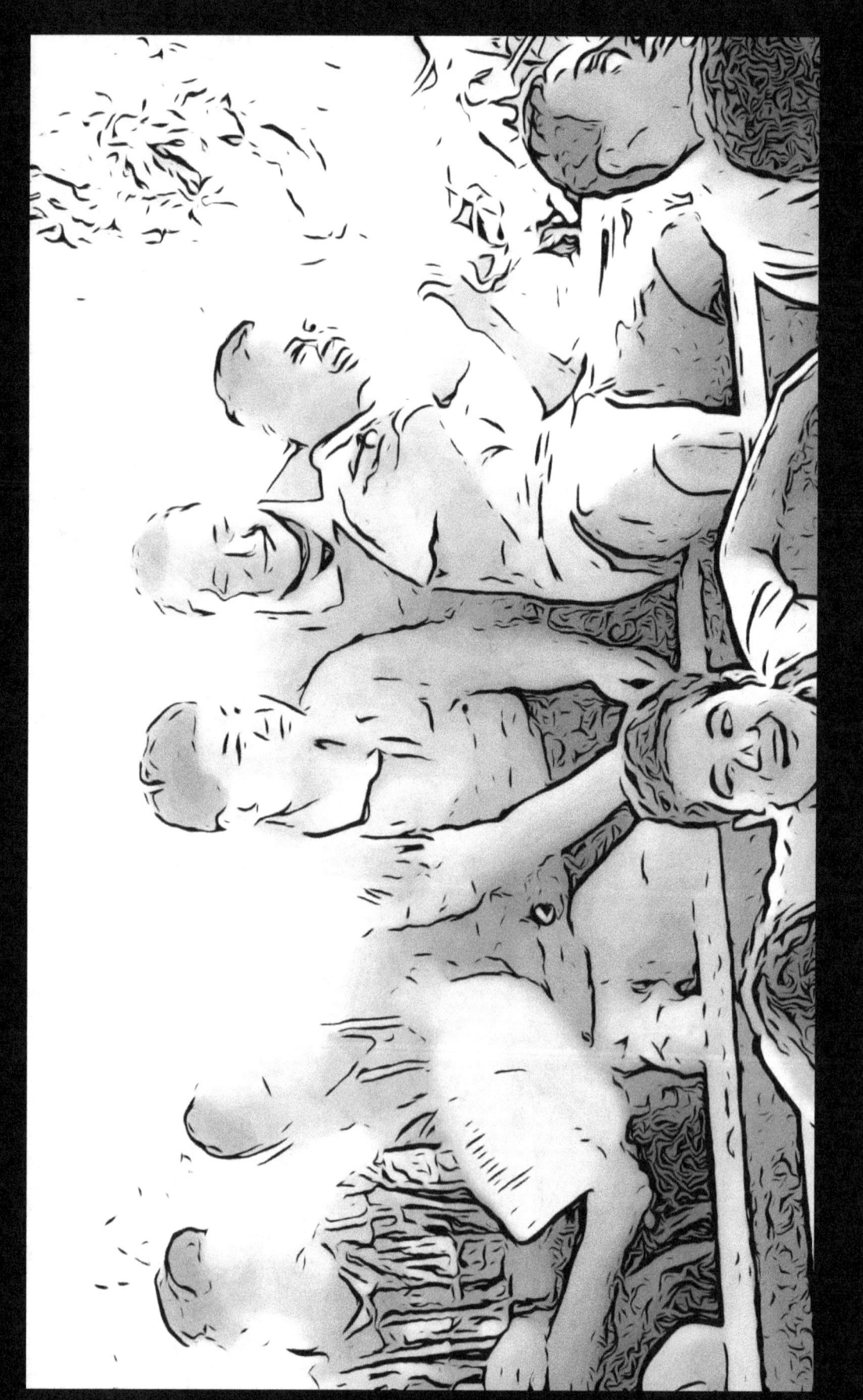

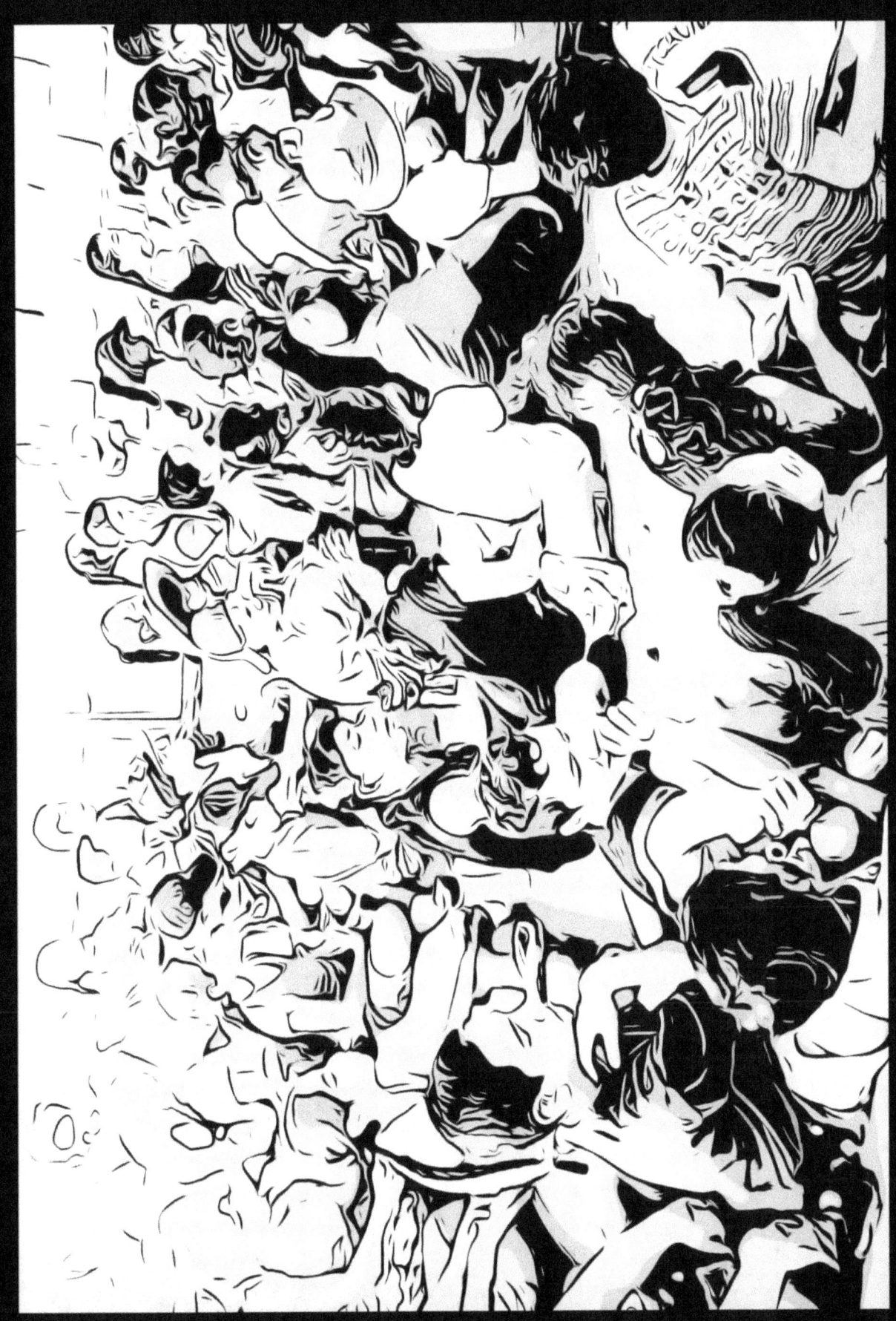

Then God said, "I give you every seed-bearing plant on the face of the whole earth and every tree that has fruit with seed in it. They will be yours for food. And to all the beasts of the earth and all the birds in the sky and all the creatures that move along the ground—everything that has the breath of life in it—I give every green plant for food." And it was so.
Genesis 1:29-30, NIV

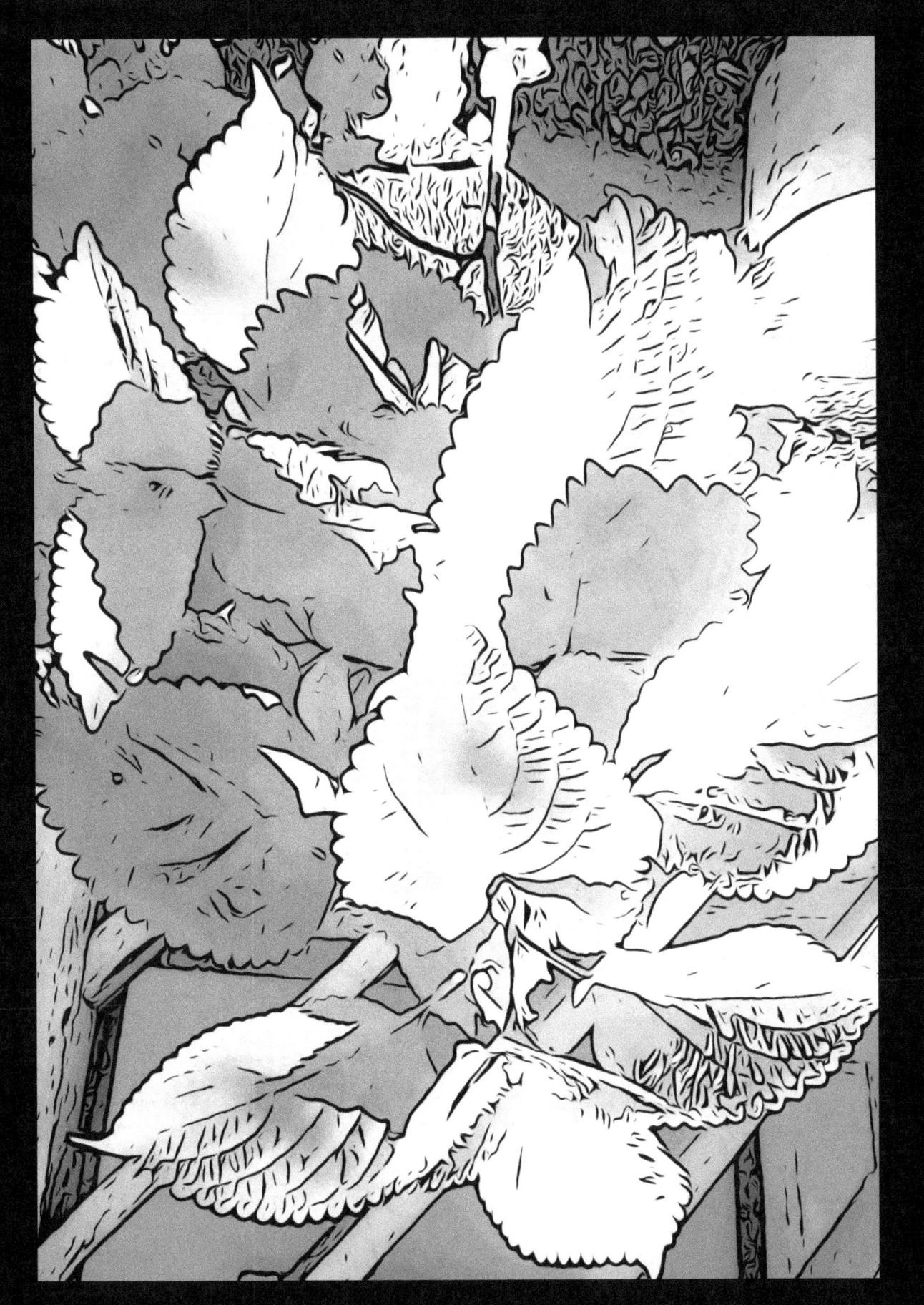

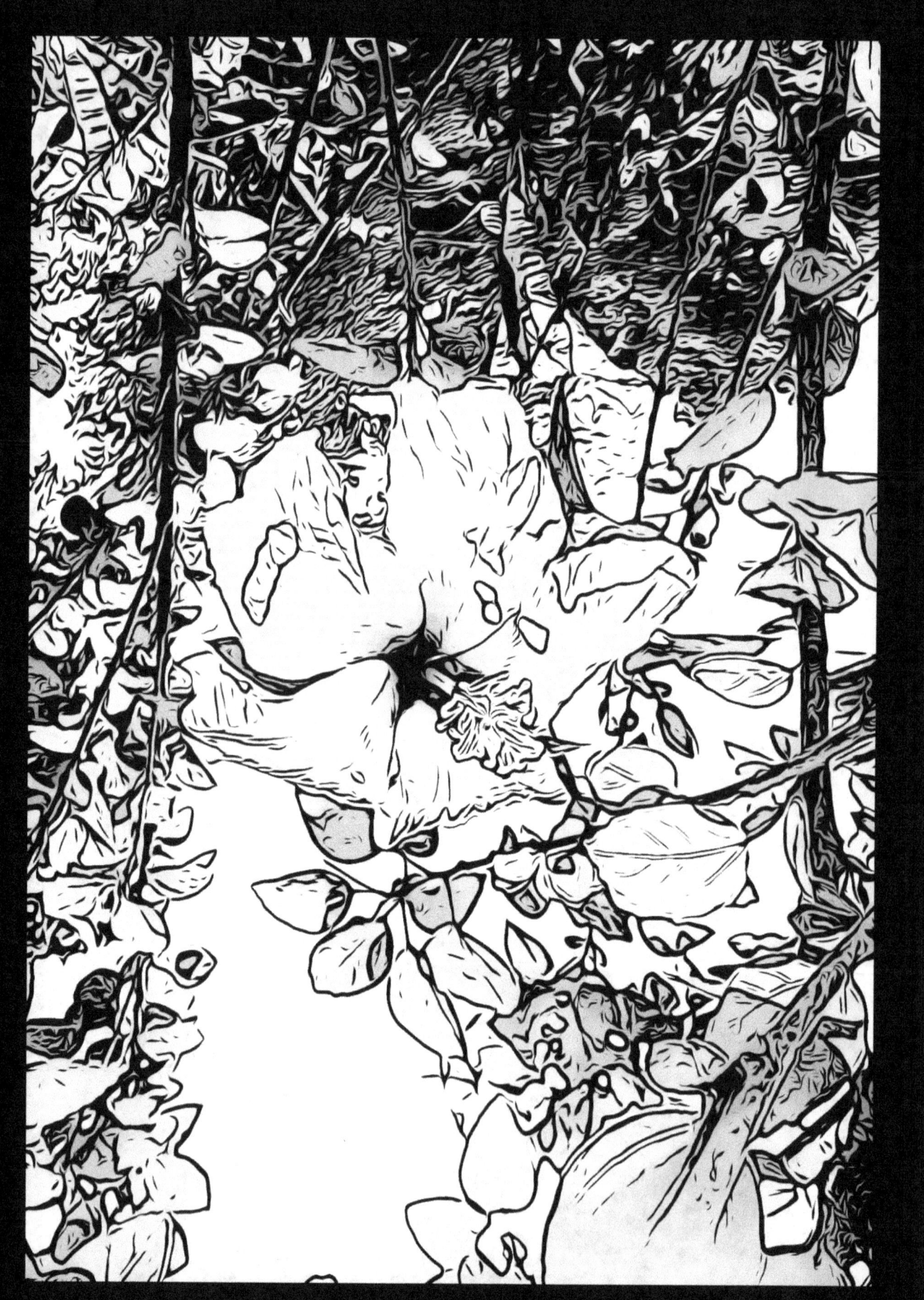

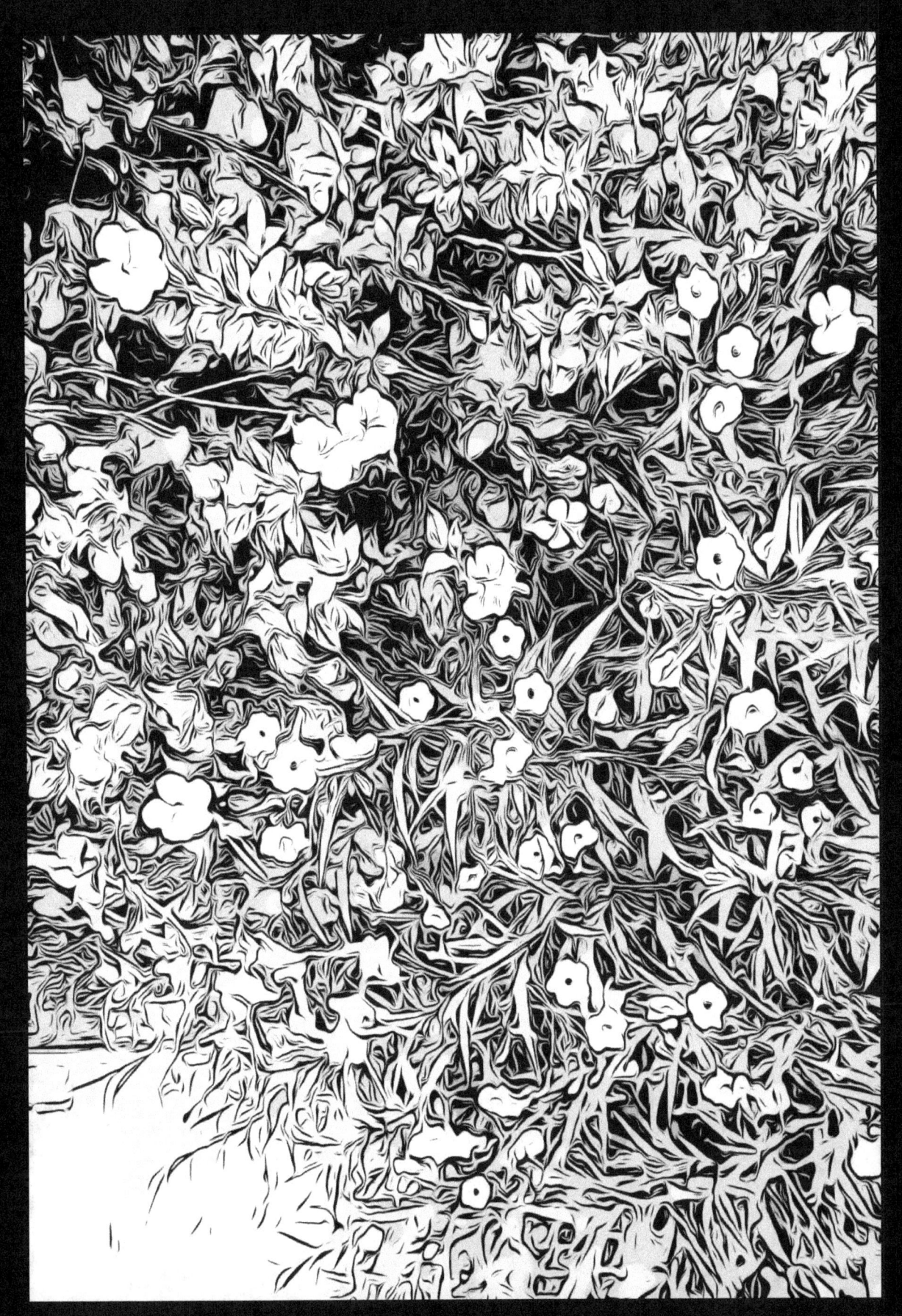

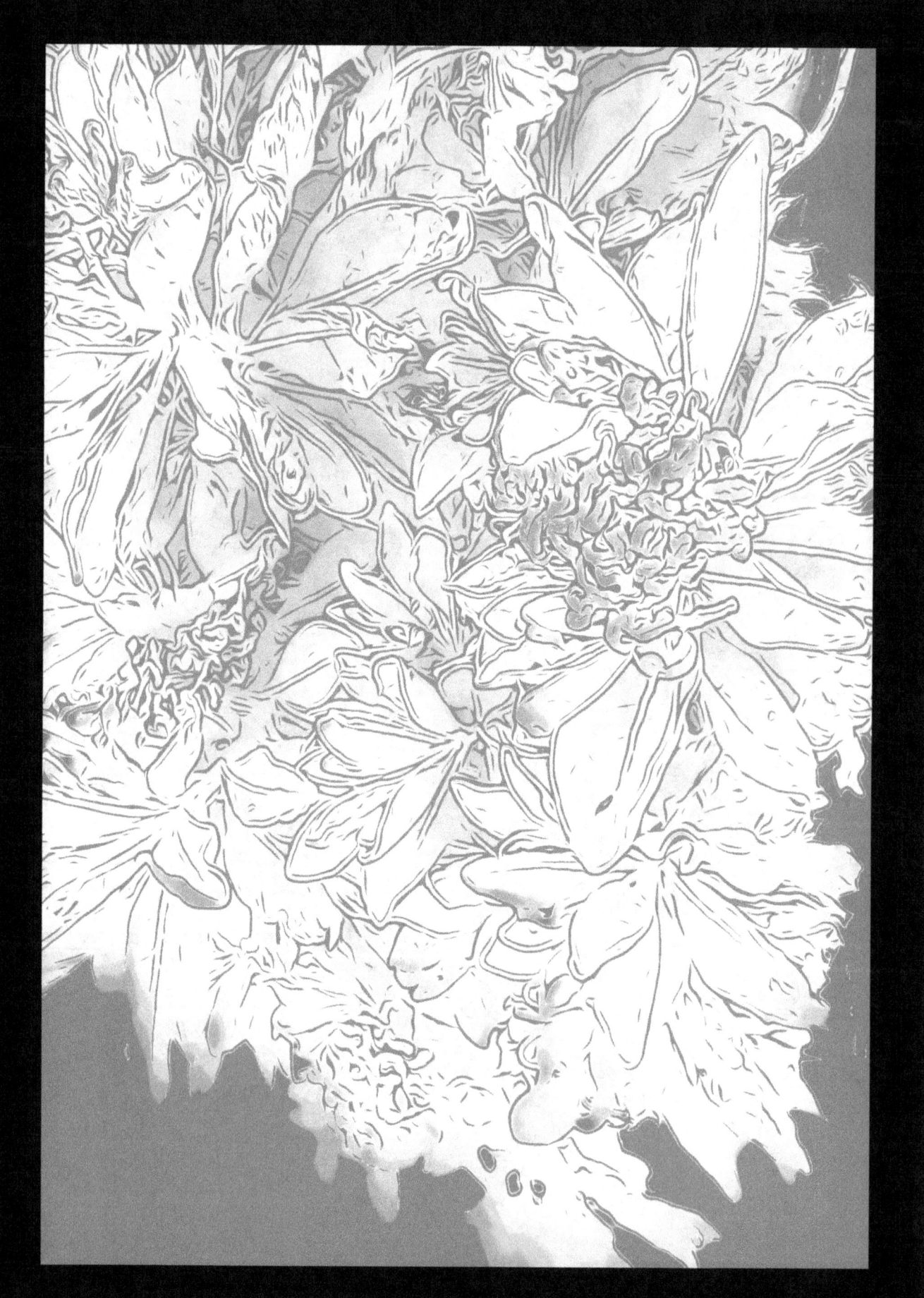

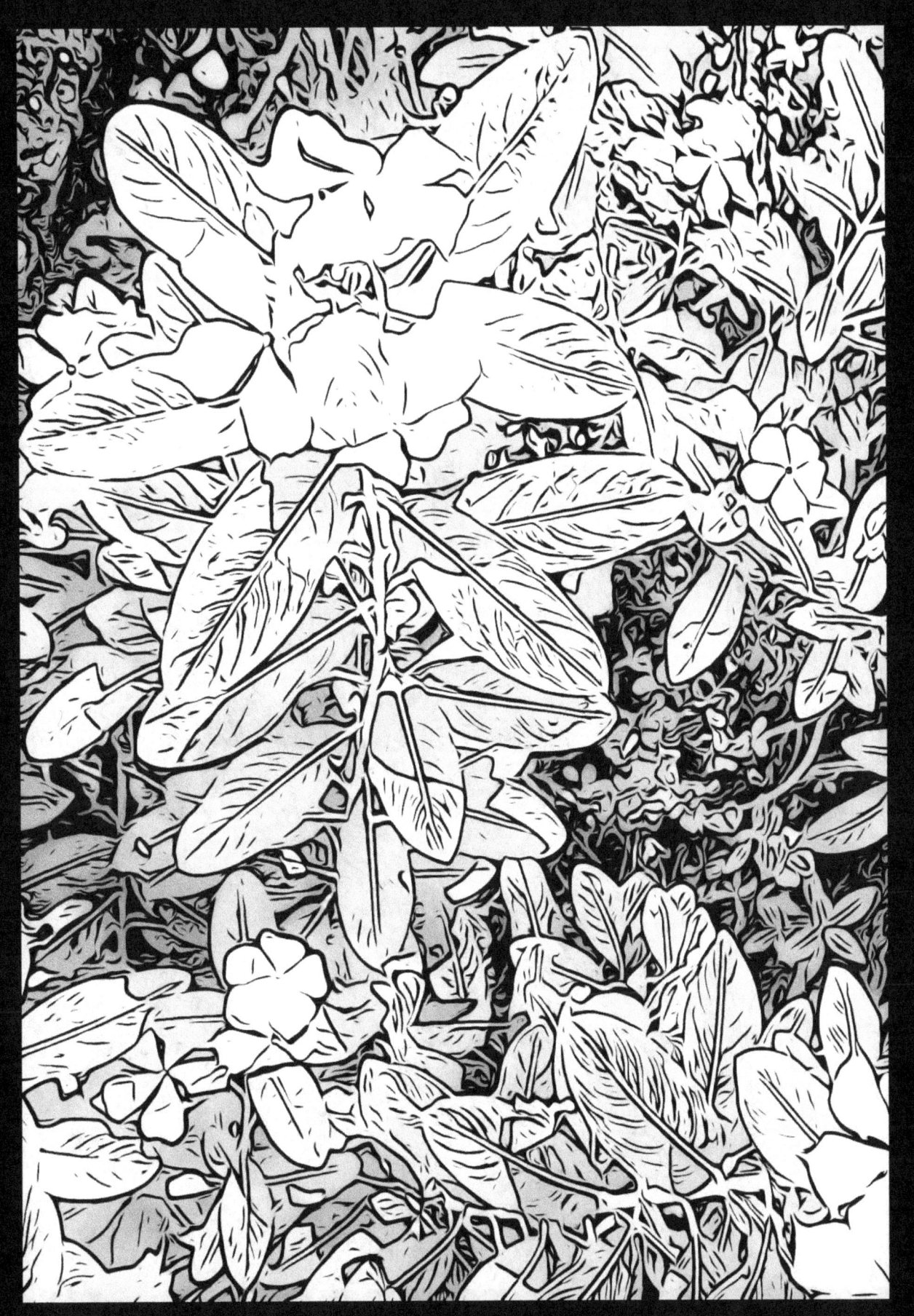

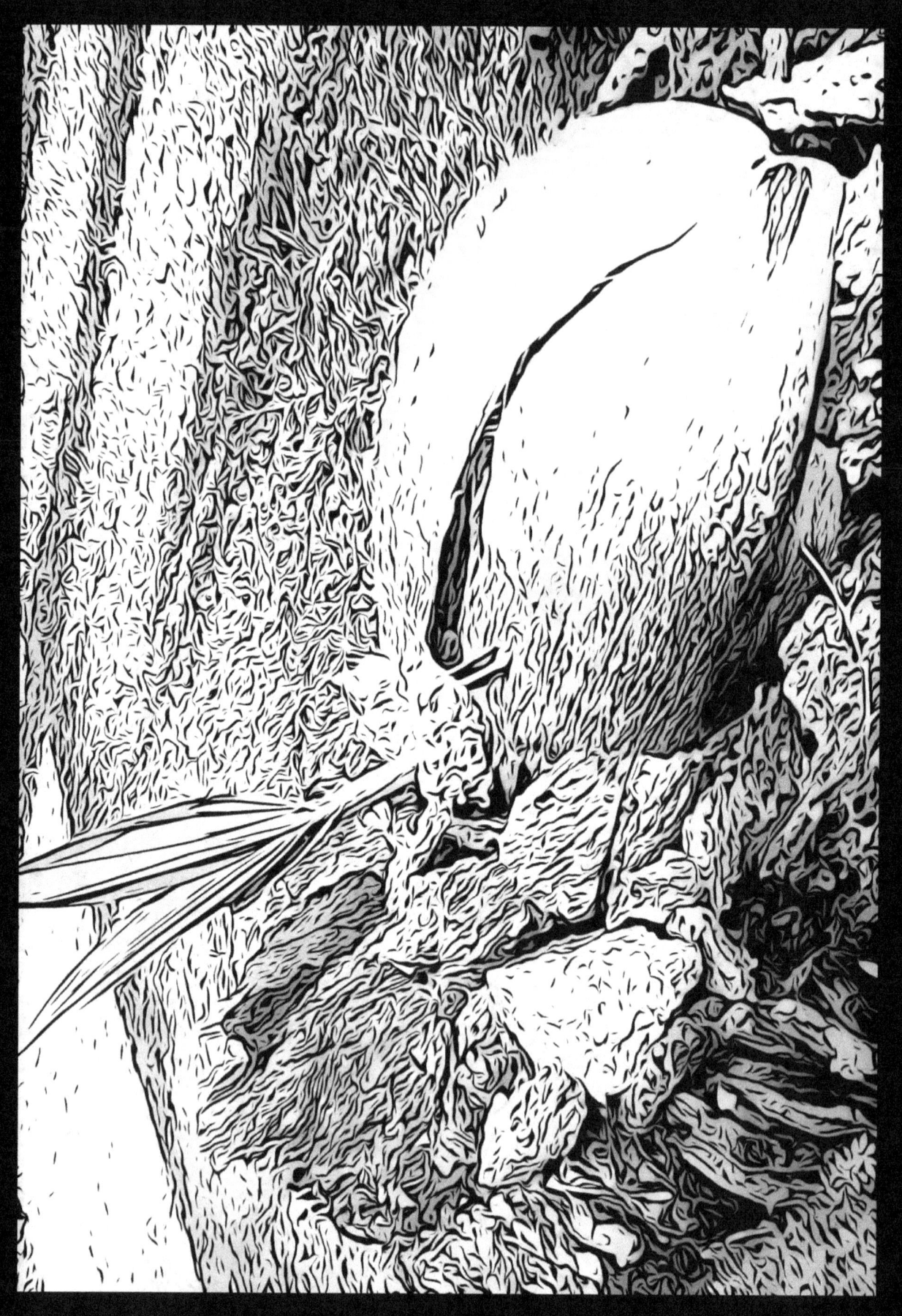

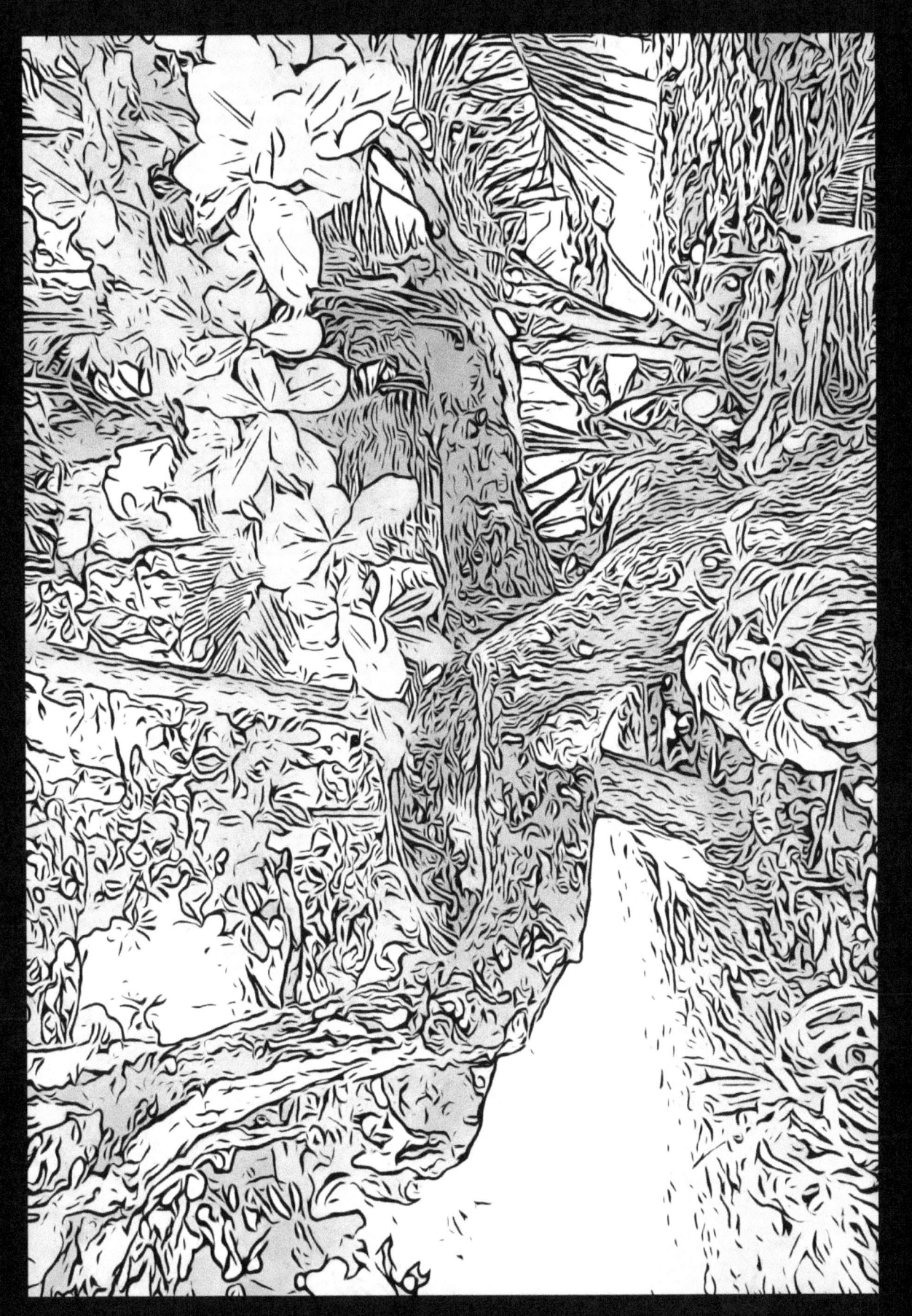

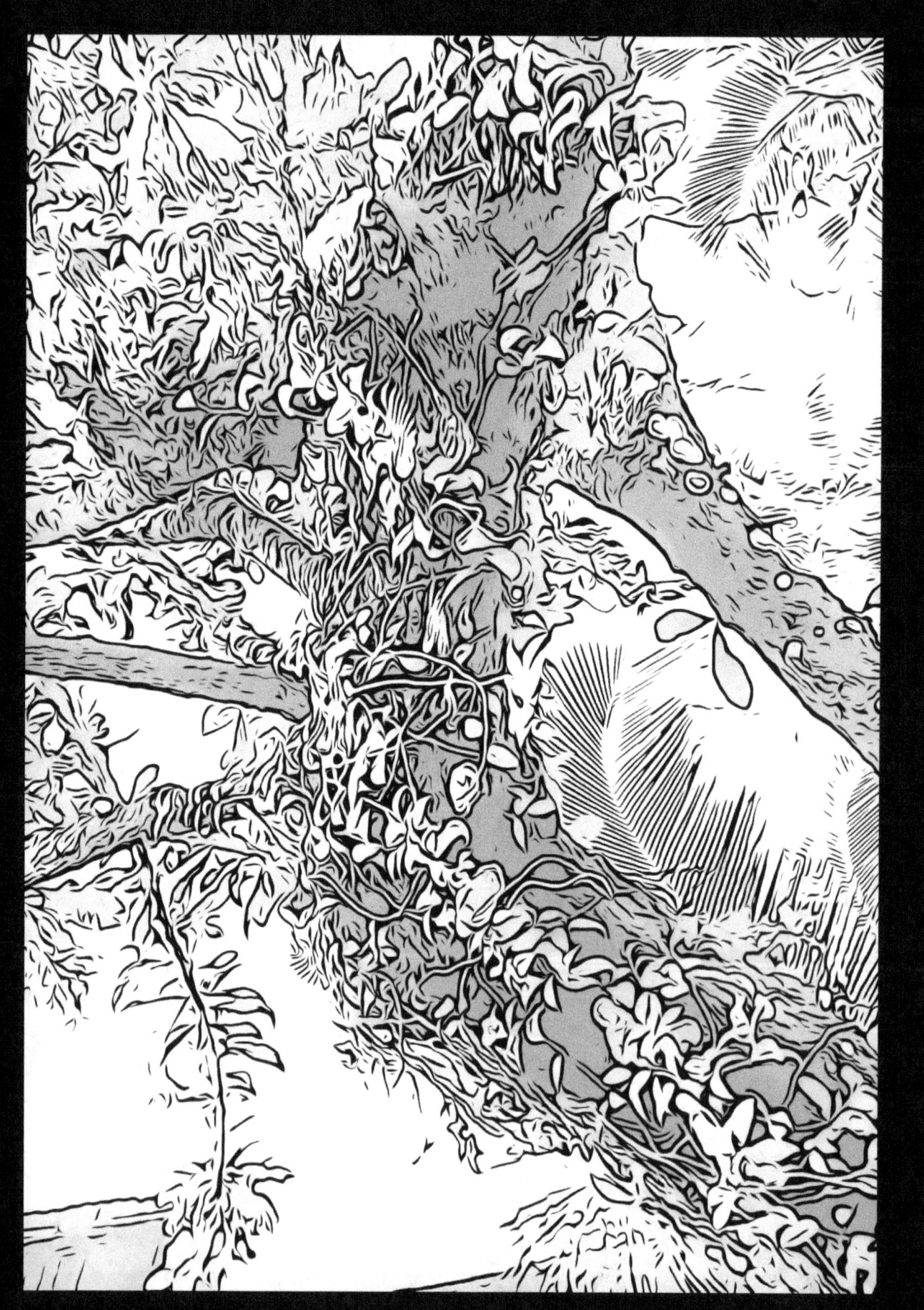

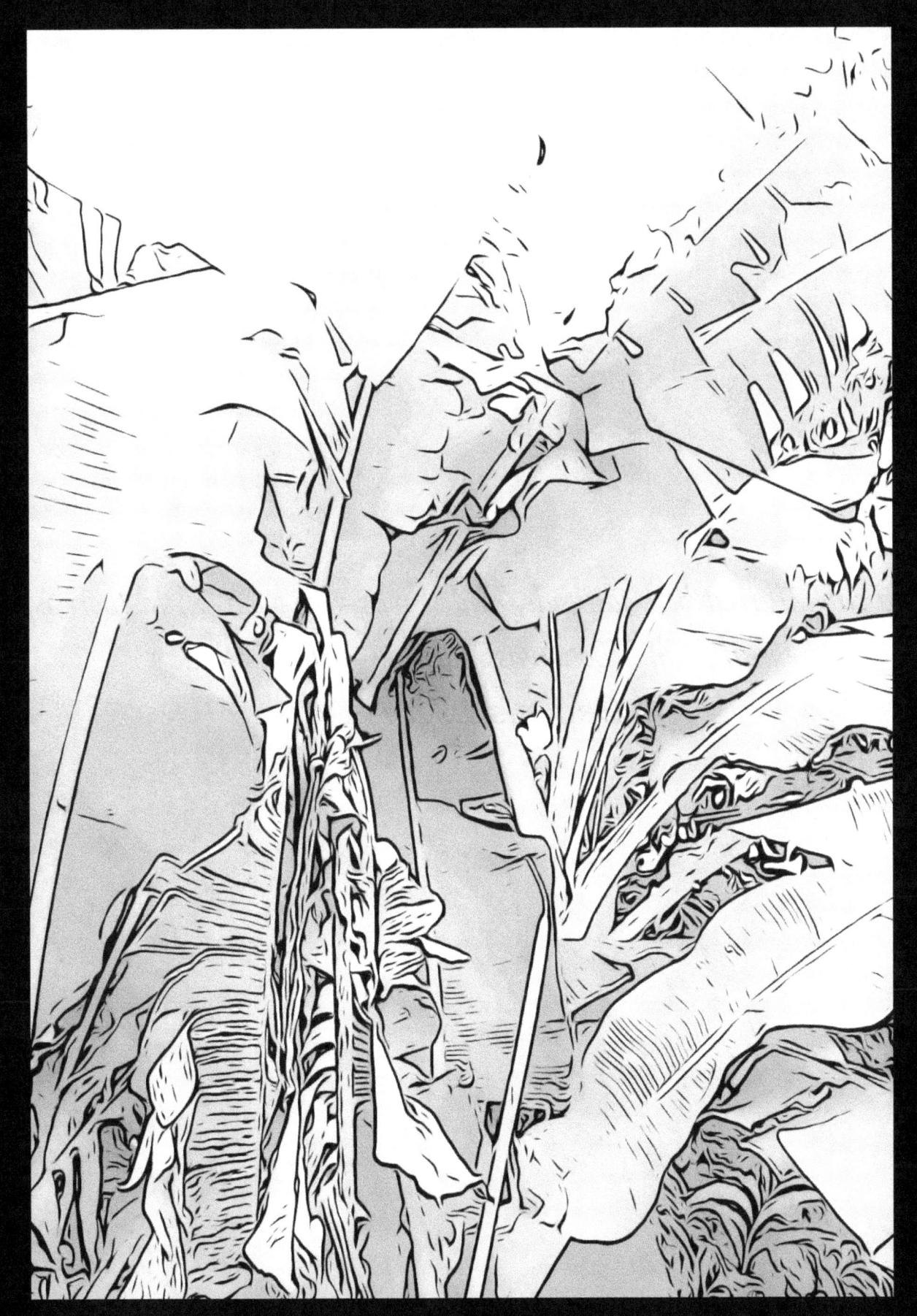

God saw all that he had made, and it was very good. And there was evening, and there was morning—the sixth day.
Genesis 1:31, NIV

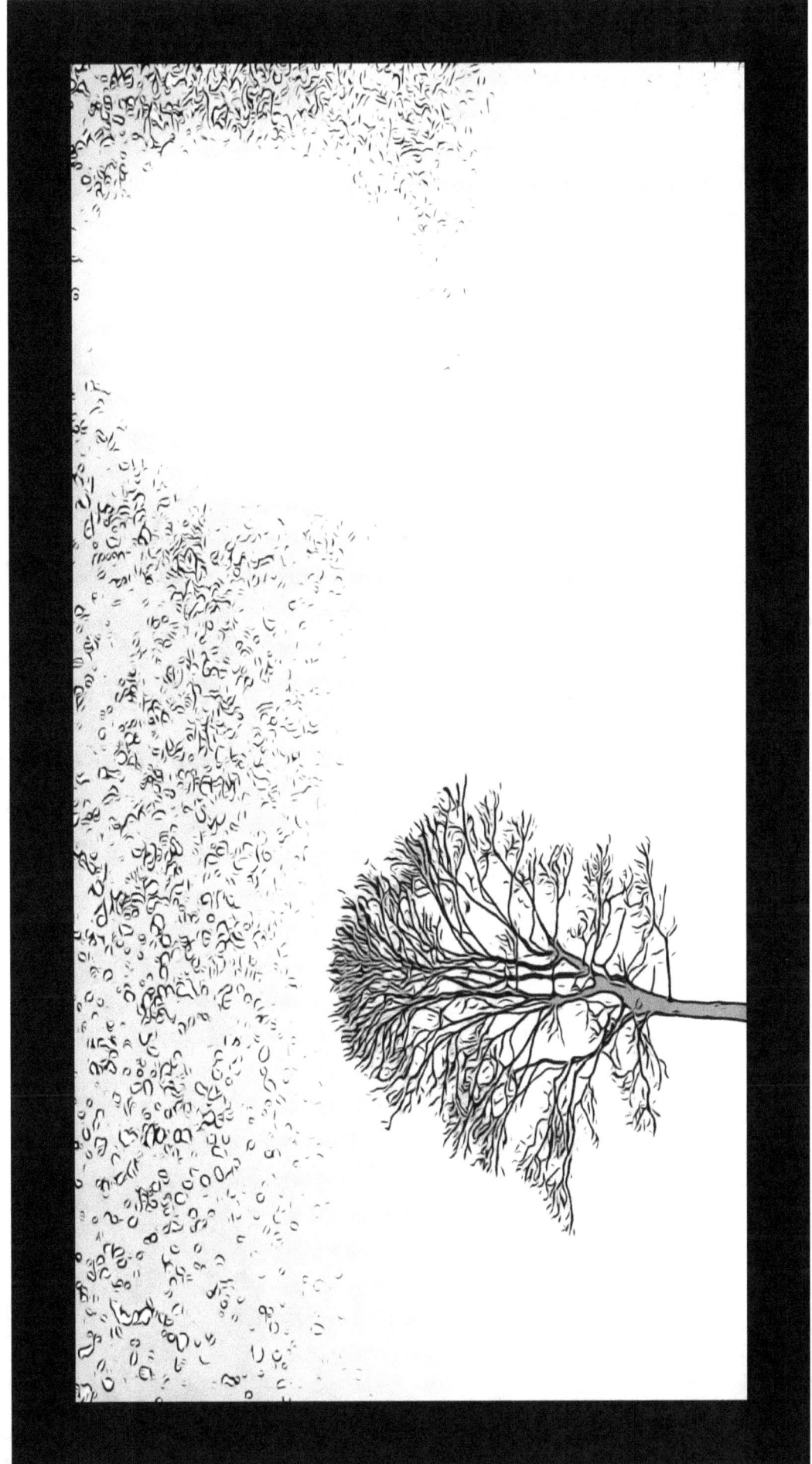

Thus the heavens and the earth were completed in all their vast array. By the seventh day God had finished the work he had been doing; so on the seventh day he rested from all his work. Then God blessed the seventh day and made it holy, because on it he rested from all the work of creating that he had done.

Genesis 2:1-3, NIV

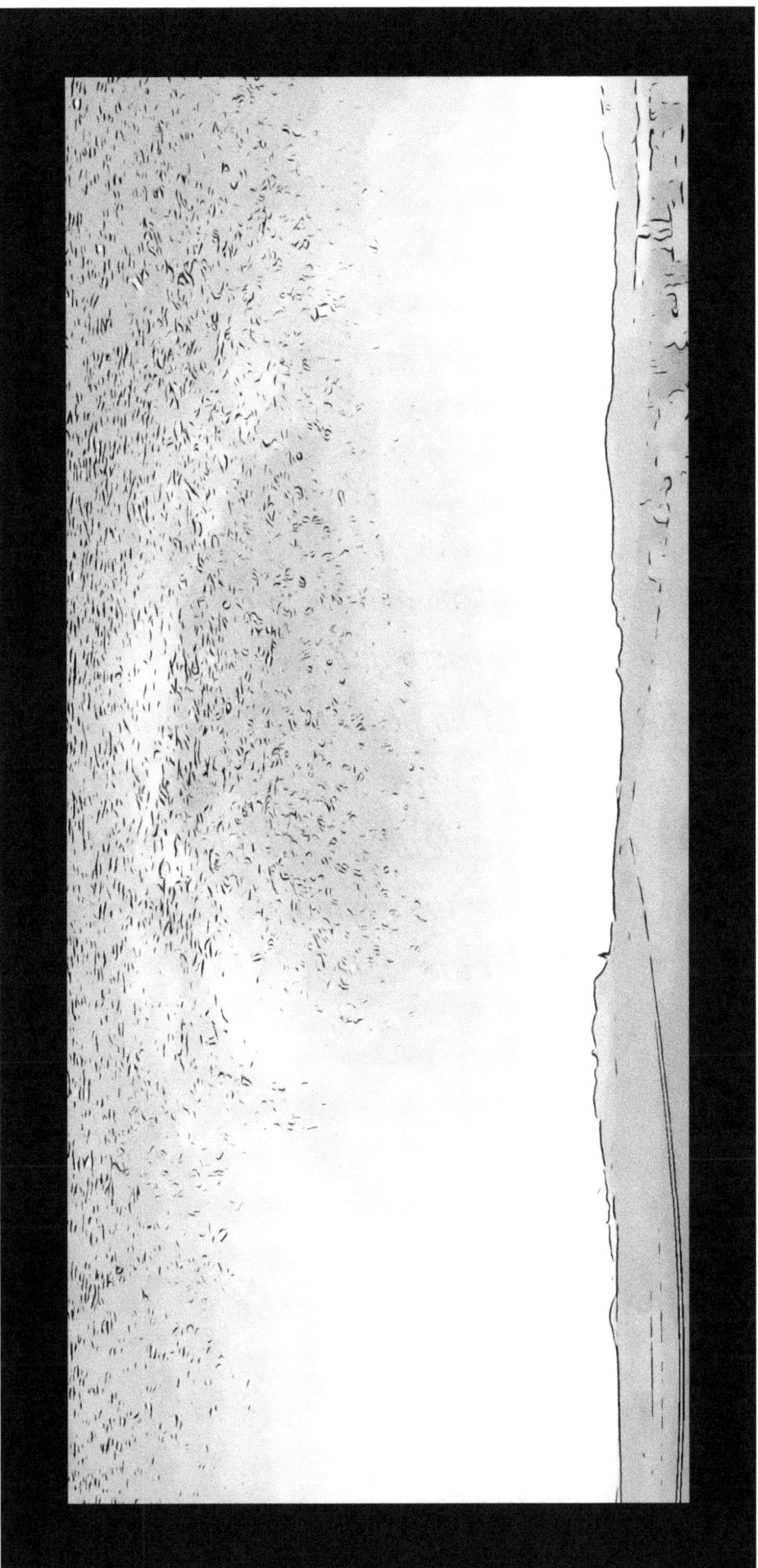

This is the account of the heavens and the earth when they were created, when the Lord God made the earth and the heavens. Now no shrub had yet appeared on the earth and no plant had yet sprung up, for the Lord God had not sent rain on the earth and there was no one to work the ground, but streams came up from the earth and watered the whole surface of the ground.

Genesis 2:4-6, NIV

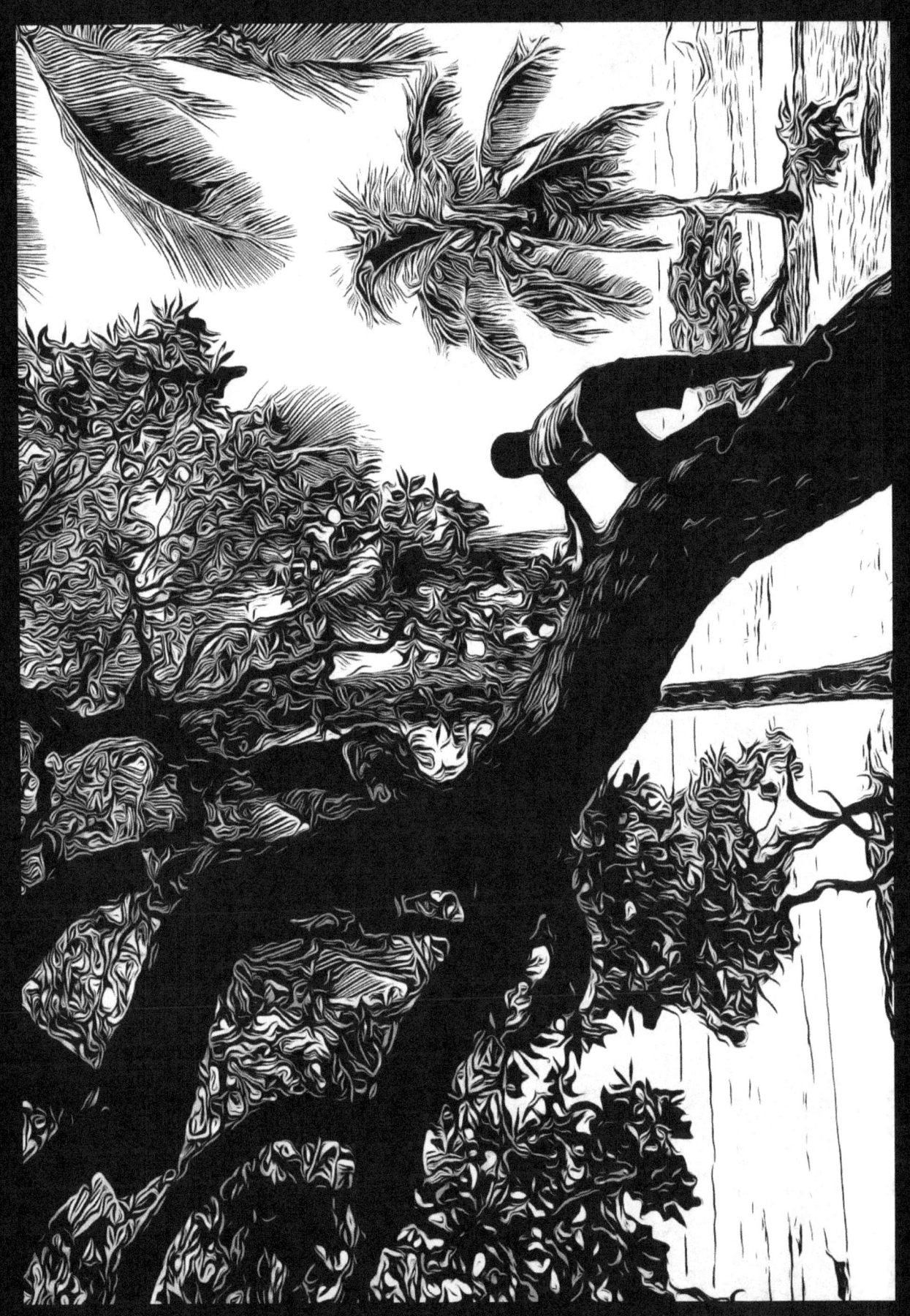

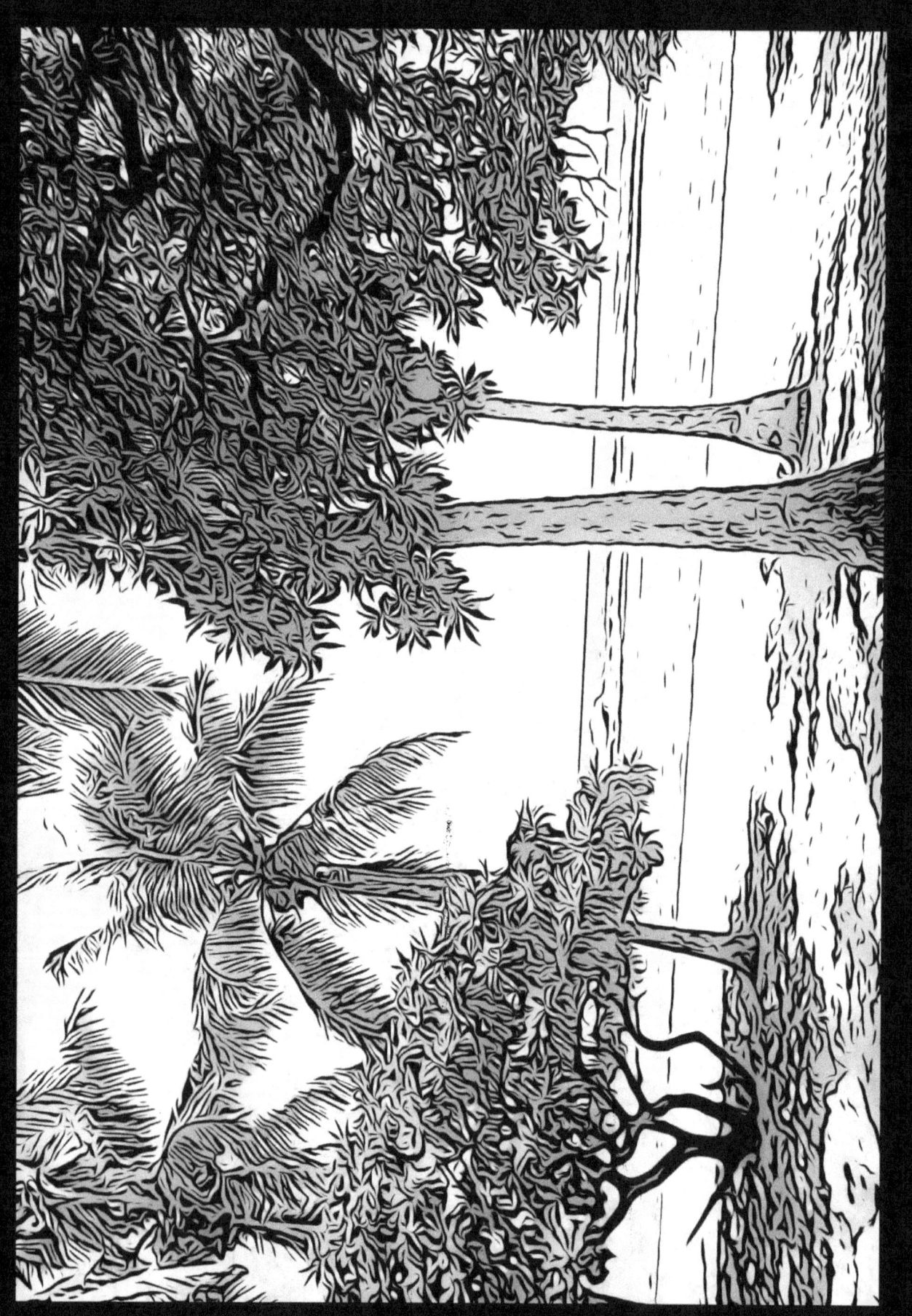

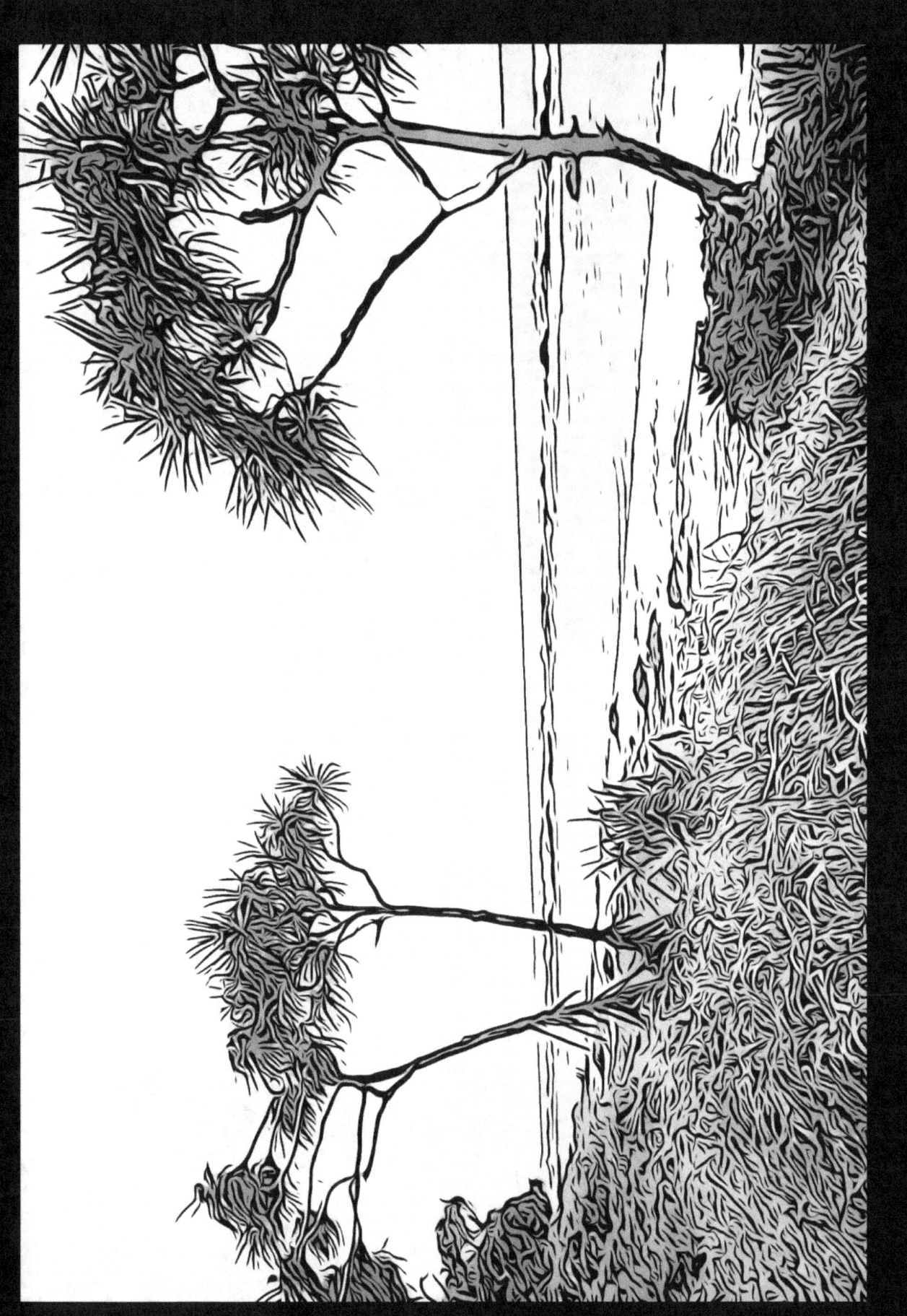

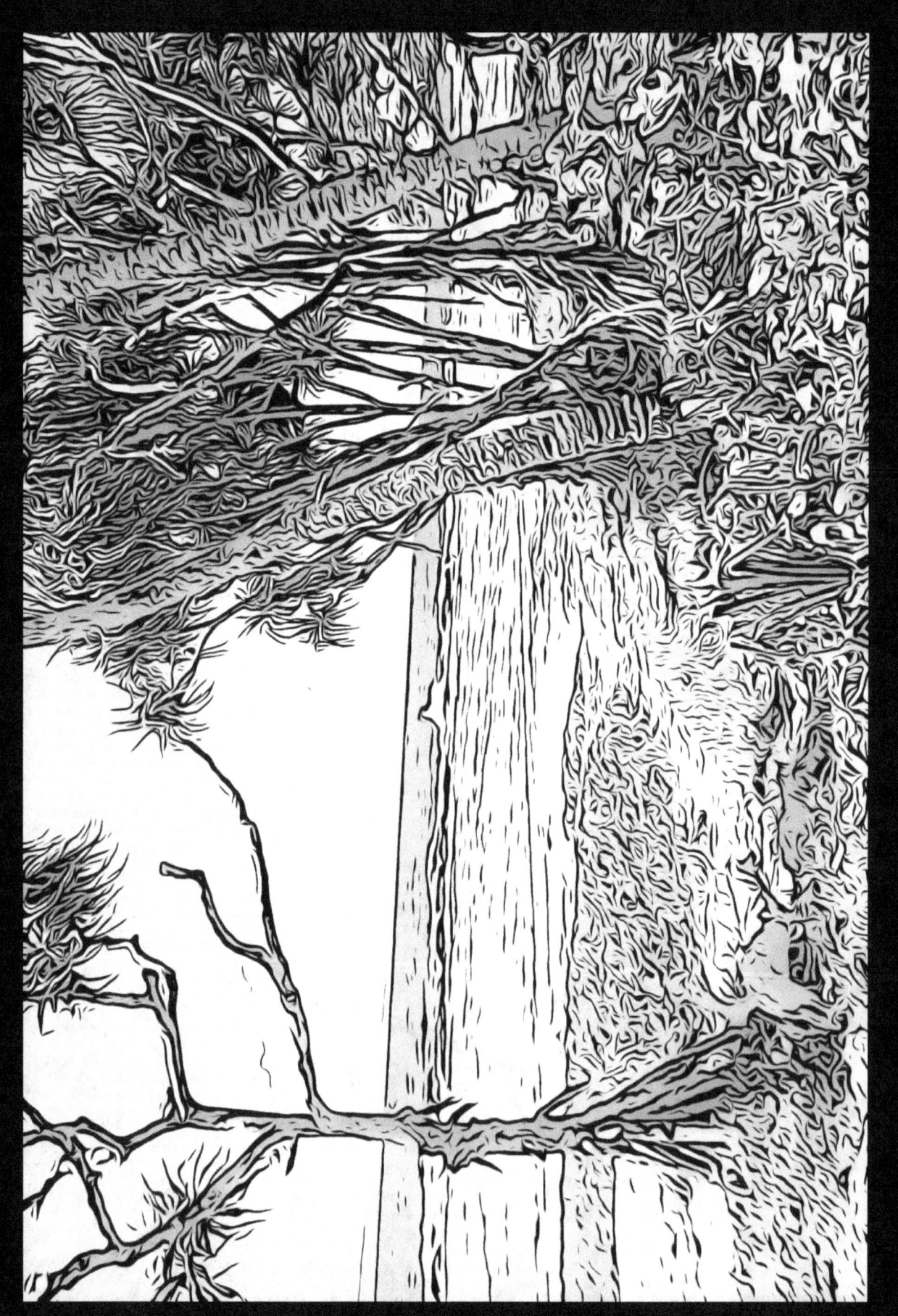

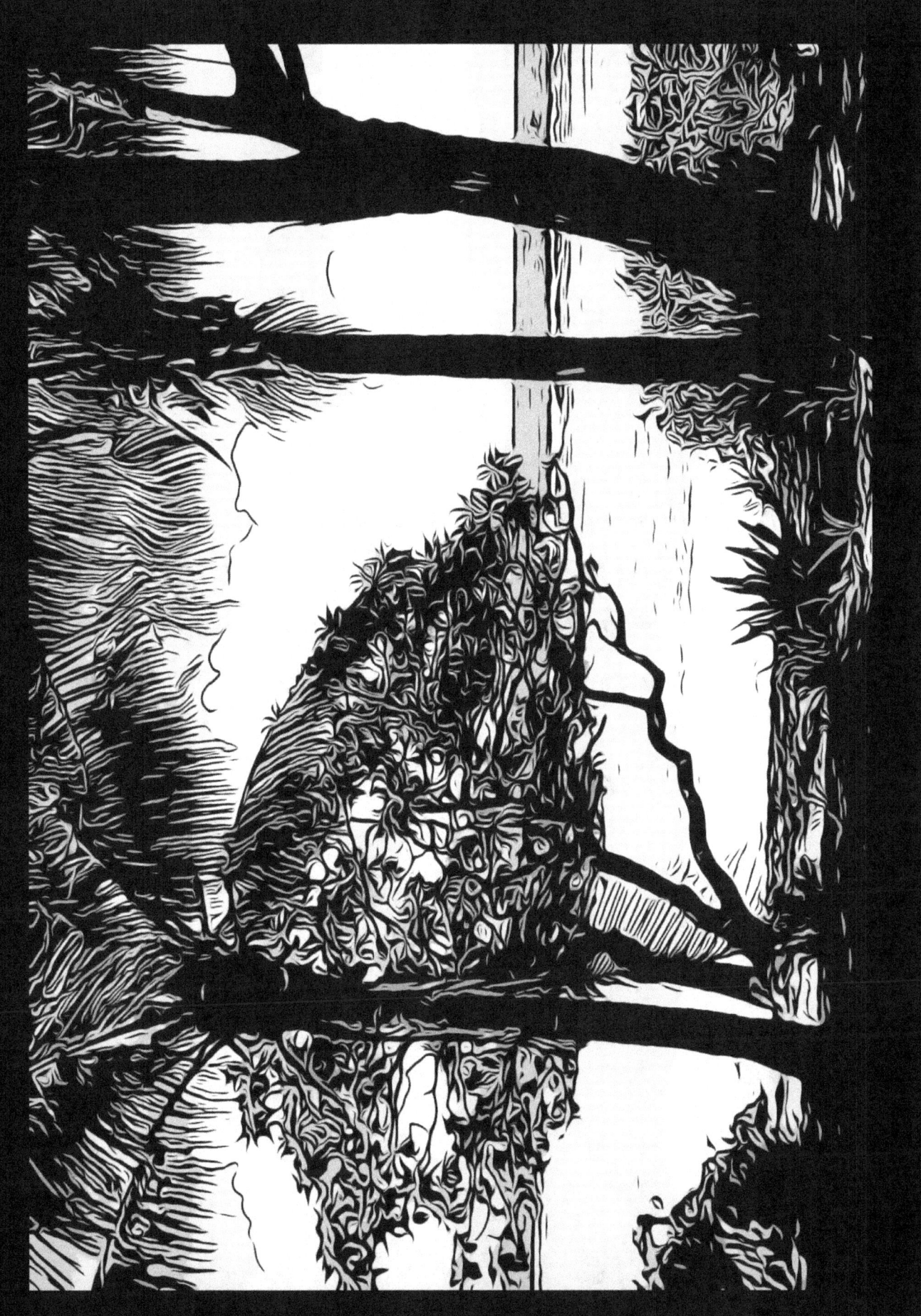

Now the Lord God had planted a garden in the east, in Eden; and there he put the man he had formed. The Lord God made all kinds of trees grow out of the ground—trees that were pleasing to the eye and good for food. In the middle of the garden were the tree of life and the tree of the knowledge of good and evil.

Genesis 2:8-9, NIV

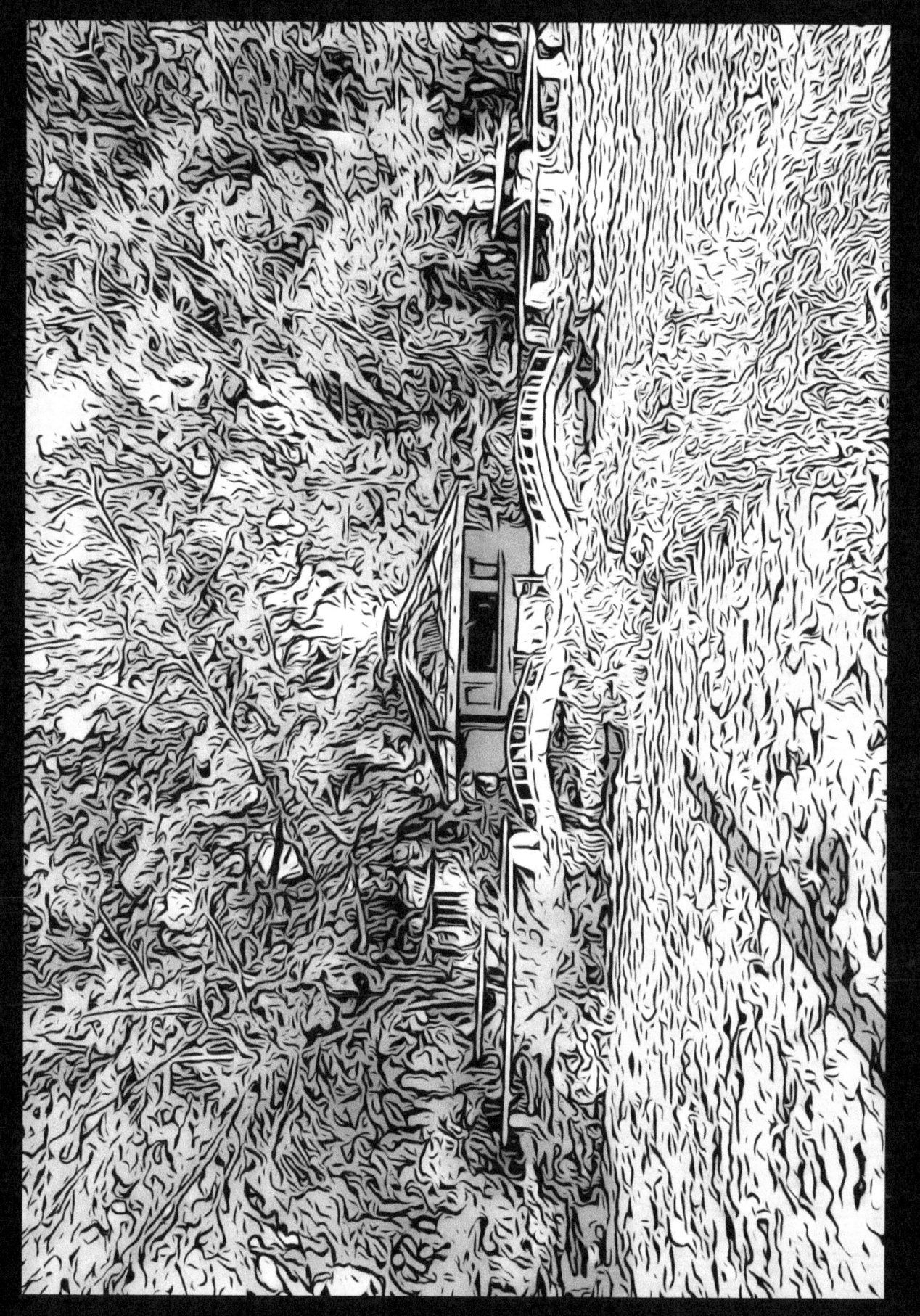

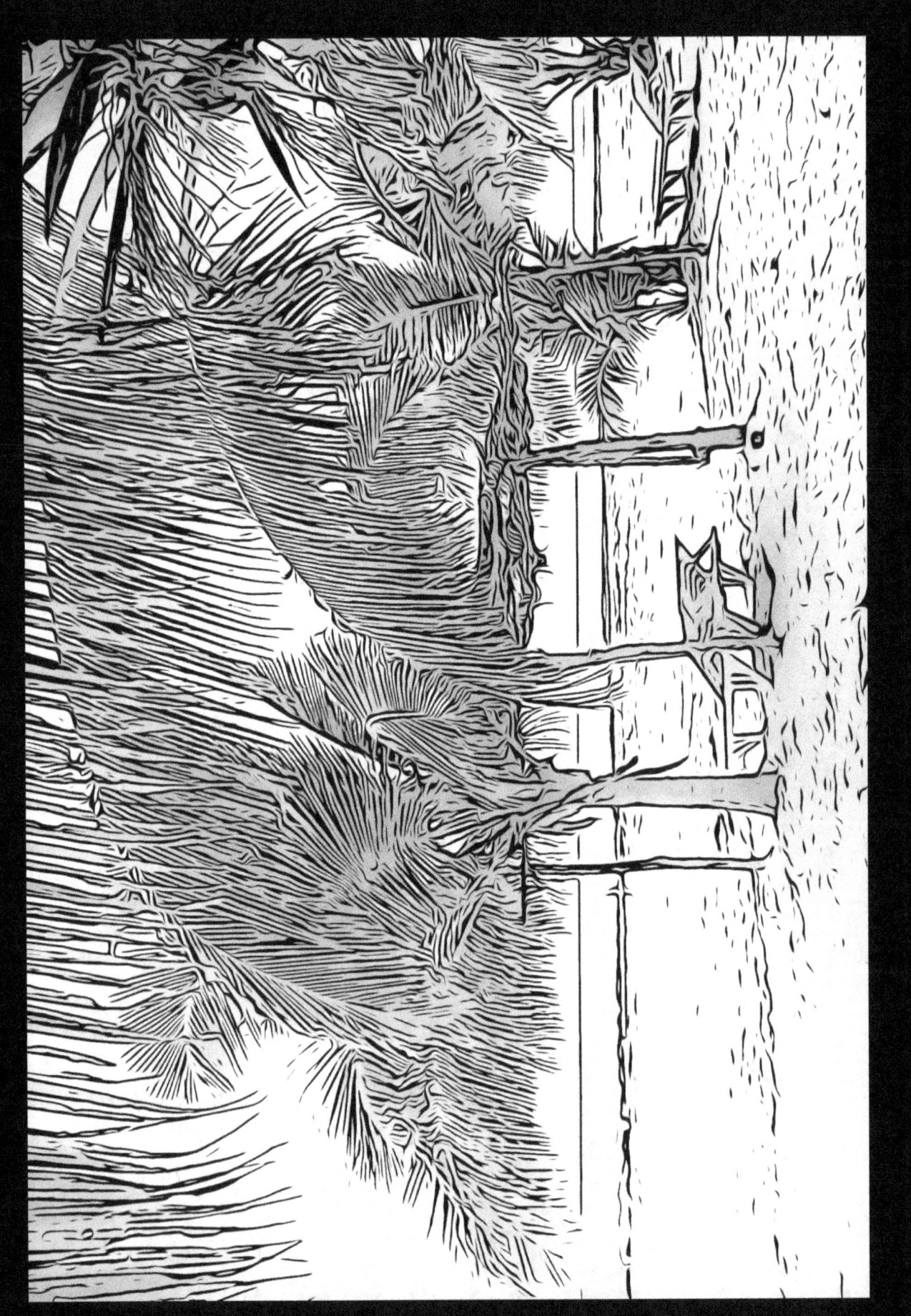

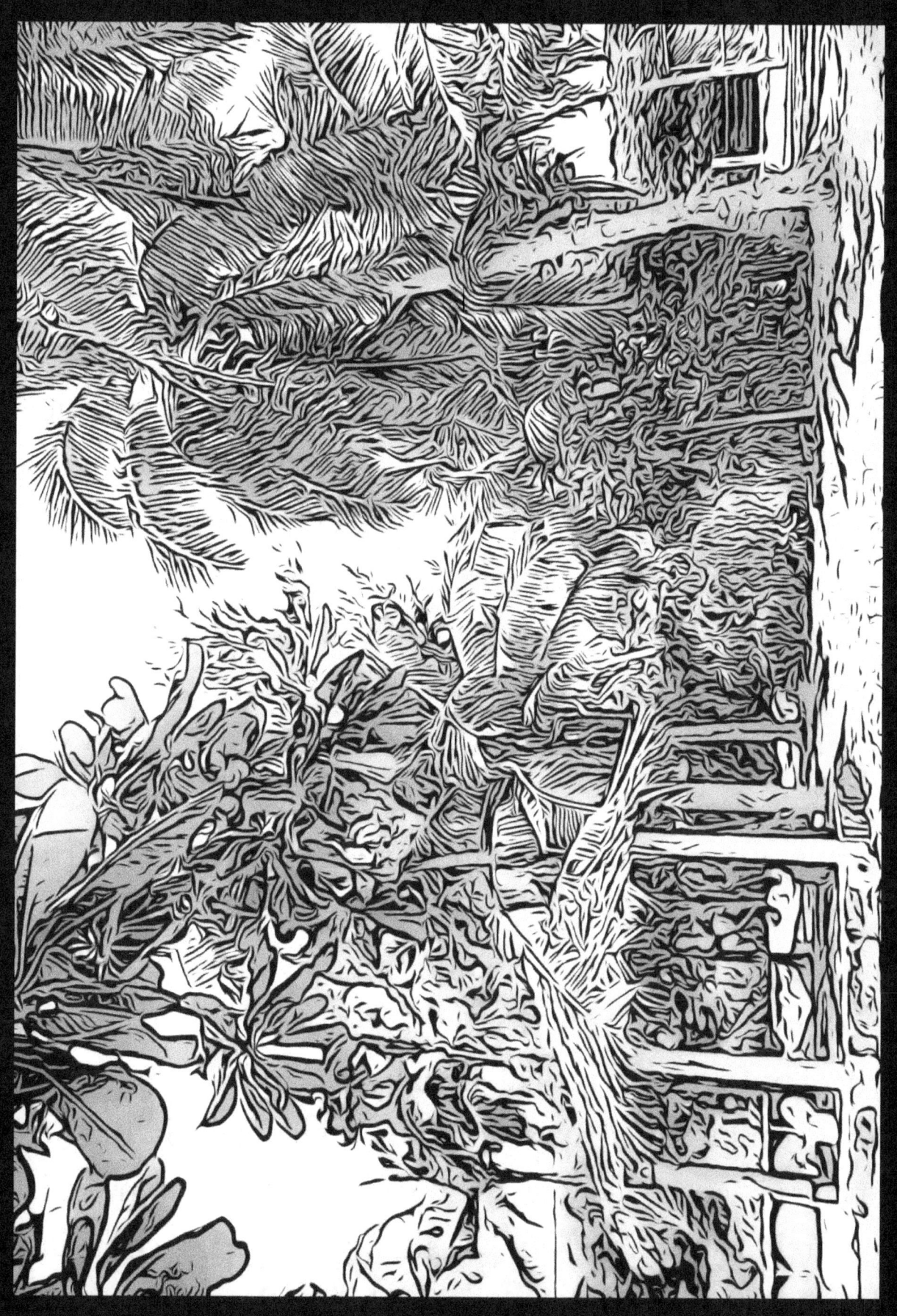

Part 2

Canvas of Adversity

If you are a beginner or a master, whatever task or project you choose and encounter, you open a new door of challenge and excitement, exploring a canvas of a adversity on your journey. It could be just a new hobby, a profession or a new idea or vision. Any occupation we choose we must full-heartedly embrace. Only then it becomes a rewarding golden opportunity. This includes endurances and sacrifices, and determines what are valuable assets that you will learn and accomplish. To take on adversity is to be brave and courageous, inner strength what is your benefit and uplift.

Dare to take a step into the unknown, willing to see beyond a momentarily limitation, to follow and look, search beyond the horizon. The process is like a baby or infant, that grows to maturity through the canvas or adversity in their lives.

Some start young, others when they are old; but in reality, age is completely irrelevant. Our dreams, joys, goals, commitments are what moves and drives our inner being to not give up, to not feel as if we are a failure, even if it take long, it is tough or looks impossible then we expect. Adversity taken even in the most littlest of steps, are the dynamic releasing power of adrenaline in our blood what is our sweet accomplishment. By doing this, we are climbing the mountain.

As an example, for the first time in my life, I started to write down my thoughts and feelings in poetry in my late fifties. I never enjoyed writing, not even any letters. Now my poetry became my secrets and fulfillment and over the years with lots of prayers, God created in my heart, a passion as an interest and love of dedication.

Eventually in my early beginnings I dared and shared my poetries and stories with loved one and friends, asking them for their feedback and opinions. People who love me were excited, other were smirking, "Ah, it's okay". They did not take my work seriously or valued them to the heart. While others gave them back with no comments.

The truth is, I hoped for positive approval, "Go on, it's a great beginning", but there was no encouragement. So I started to feel like a failure, got discouraged to show them to anybody and hid them for no one to see.

For around fifteen-years I was praying to God asking Him for His guidance. If he chooses to close the door and no one liked or approved my writings, then I would not force or push the gift He gave me to be recognized to continue.

This did not hinder me, my joy or my heart desire to continue to write. The love did not die, nor did I give up. In opposite, I became more productive in all these years, and today ended up with over a thousand poetries.

My emotions, energy, and passion for writing were like a glowing simmering fire, which I got a thrill and was more thankful then ever. I could not stop. My thoughts were like a river running to the ocean. I realized my writings I was experiencing, digesting, healing, and observing my life canvas where God was my mentor, inspiration, spirit, and partner. He taught me unbelievable valuable life lessons, to not write for approval or fame, to not become rich or be in the competitive power game becoming a bestselling author.

The gifts He planted silently in my soul was to be passionate and compassionate about my writings for myself to understand what adversity is all about. Through this, He blessed, healed, encouraged, and strengthened my spirit, to abundantly rejoice in Him, bringing us closer together.

Till today I experience the beauty of my own fulfilment, happiness, and satisfaction, and my conviction to trust His guidance what is a miracle between us.

It blessed me the most, and no one else. I accepted the marvellous plan of God's talents and adversity what He gave me. I needed to learn and go through to conquer my dramatic circumstances of tragedies and hardships filled with love, peace, and hope of my life canvas. He showed me that no one is a failure, if our motives are pure and right. Being an artist and achiever, means to conquer obstacles for your own sake. Fame is fleeting, but inner approval and contentment stays.

Over all these years God now had answered my prayers. It was He will use my experiences to help encourage and motivate other people so He can bless them too.

I am ready to walk, talk, and take on these next canvas of adversity in my life. God is watching as I am working day and night with love to publish as many poetries as I can. The outcome is in His hands. My thoughts and voice are only the messenger of His almighty creation. He is the real author in my mind.

When my husband and I went to Tonga as a missionary, we started the road of taking on the leap of hope of adversity. I had no clue that out of this choice and experience, my book Exhilarating Kingdom of Wonder was God's plan and will. Never would I have imagined that I could write or initiate these testimonies, of people and nature's miracles.

Now that I have finished this book in Costa Rica, I am reliving it all and inspired to add the documentation of art in the Canvas of Creation, which I had never planned as well. I believe by our actions and inner bold adversity, God moves our spirit. Our part is to listen and preparing our empty canvas page to start enthusiastically a new splendid vision, goal, and picture.

Canvas of Cloned

I am peaceful quiet in my soul.
I am content, accepting finally life's struggle,
highs and lows.
It took me a while, many years of trying
to stay in control or being in denial.

Finally it hit me: I accused myself for nothing.
Life with its chances. Opportunities come and go;
with failures, stress and, success, all puzzling.

People, generations, empires, money, health,
it is a constant evolution.
Rebirth of reaccepting yourself and your resolutions.
I have just a moment of living
before eternity is my solution.

Billions of people were born
and died before or after me.
Who am I in this history?
of molecules like a comet? Rising, shining, falling.

Today I am strong, tomorrow weak.
Loosing or winning my solitude.
I am finally peaceful, content in my soul.
I am who I am,
being in peace with myself,
approving of myself,
independent if I am loved or not at all.

I am a free person in my soul.
I am not a prisoner of anyone.
I am accountable to myself and my own consciousness
where I want to be, with whom,
and what to do.
It is my own responsibility.

I am peaceful, quiet in my soul.
I am not anymore,
a helpless ping-pong ball
for anyone to slap or move me
without my consent or control.

I embrace adversity and am creative in myself.
My actions are visible,
not a fairy-tale or flying fantasy elf.
I am not like a story a little gnome,
distorted or discontent.

I am myself,
unique and heavenly designed
and not artificial mankind cloned.

Finally, I chose to stand up for myself,
even if it took me a long while to learn.
I realized, because I am not cloned,
I don't need any approval, critique or injected sperm.

I become strong, independent,
wise and peaceful being on my own.
That's why I now face life with a peaceful soul.
As I have found faith in God,
new direction, priority, and goal.

I tell you honestly bold, what I like and not.
Respect my values, home, and my heart.

I will do the same to you
with joy and gladness,
self respecting each other's talents and space
is being individuality, what takes away tension and sadness.
DNA cloning; it is mixing in God's creation
and will bring no blessing,
only confusion and devastation.

Are you cloned?
Are you stoned?
If then, make yourself free
for a new destiny.

The canvas of your adversity
is to dare and break out of the cage of boundaries.
All power and talents are from God
that you are caring around with you.
Don't bury them.
See and grab and take your potential.
God will bless and walk you through.

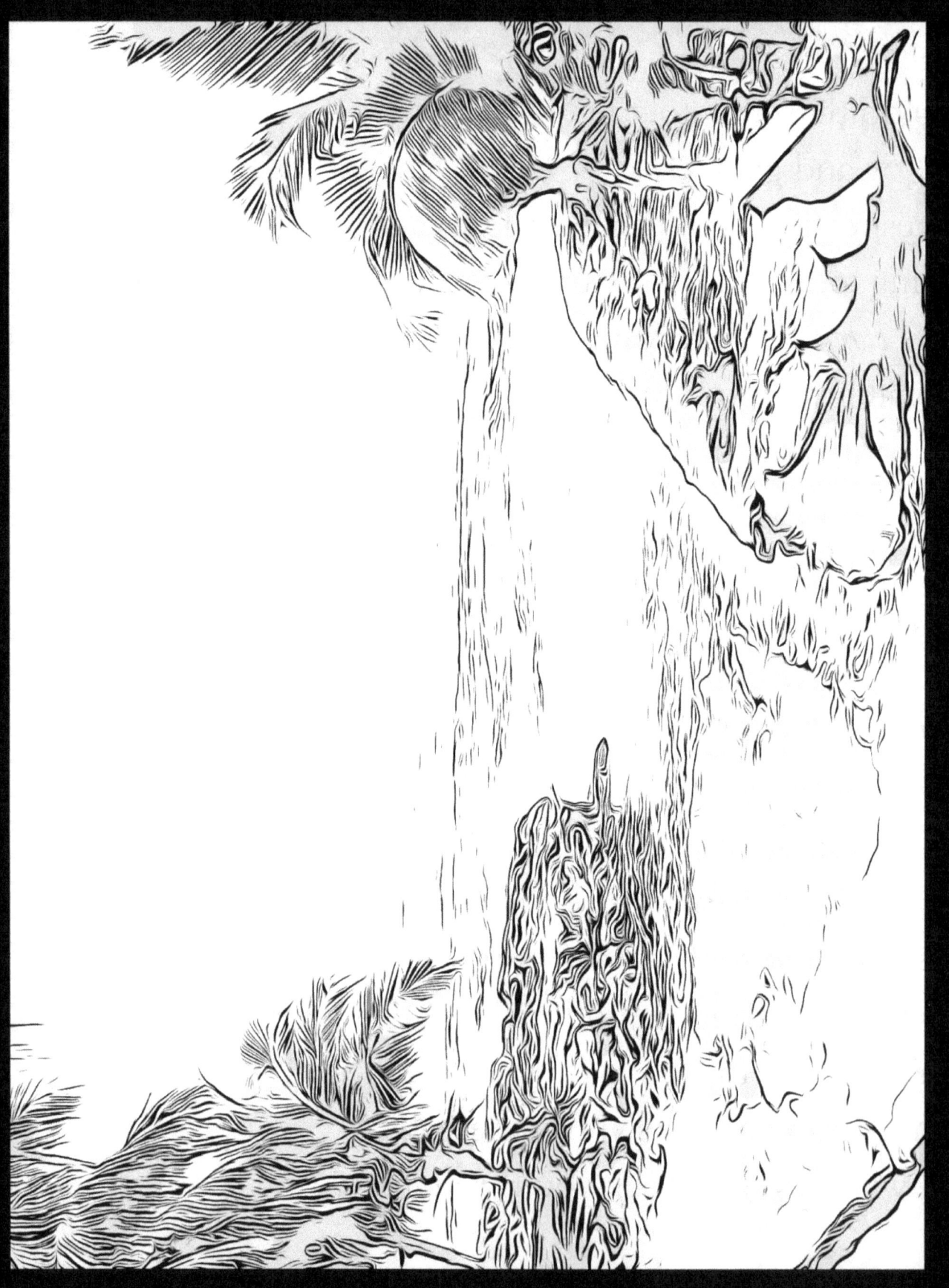

"Where were you when I laid the earth's foundation?
Tell me, if you understand.
Who marked off its dimensions? Surely you know!
Who stretched a measuring line across it?
On what were its footings set,
or who laid its cornerstone—
while the morning stars sang together
and all the angels shouted for joy?
"Who shut up the sea behind doors
when it burst forth from the womb,
when I made the clouds its garment
and wrapped it in thick darkness,
when I fixed limits for it
and set its doors and bars in place,
when I said, 'This far you may come and no farther;
here is where your proud waves halt'?

Job 38:4-11, NIV

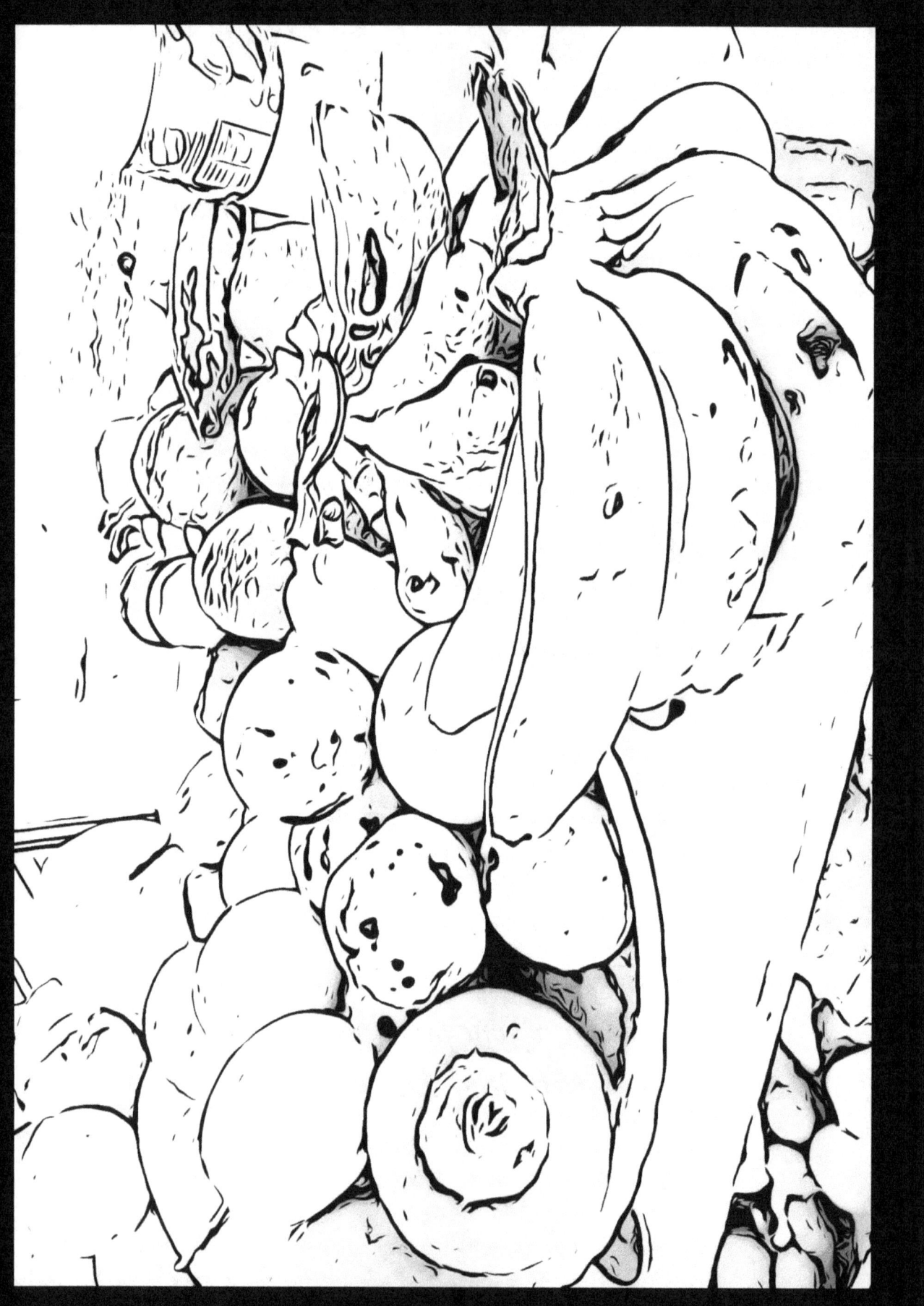

"Can you raise your voice to the clouds
and cover yourself with a flood of water?
Do you send the lightning bolts on their way?
Do they report to you, 'Here we are'?
Who gives the ibis wisdom[a]
or gives the rooster understanding?[b]
Who has the wisdom to count the clouds?
Who can tip over the water jars of the heavens
when the dust becomes hard
and the clods of earth stick together?
Job 38:34-38, NIV

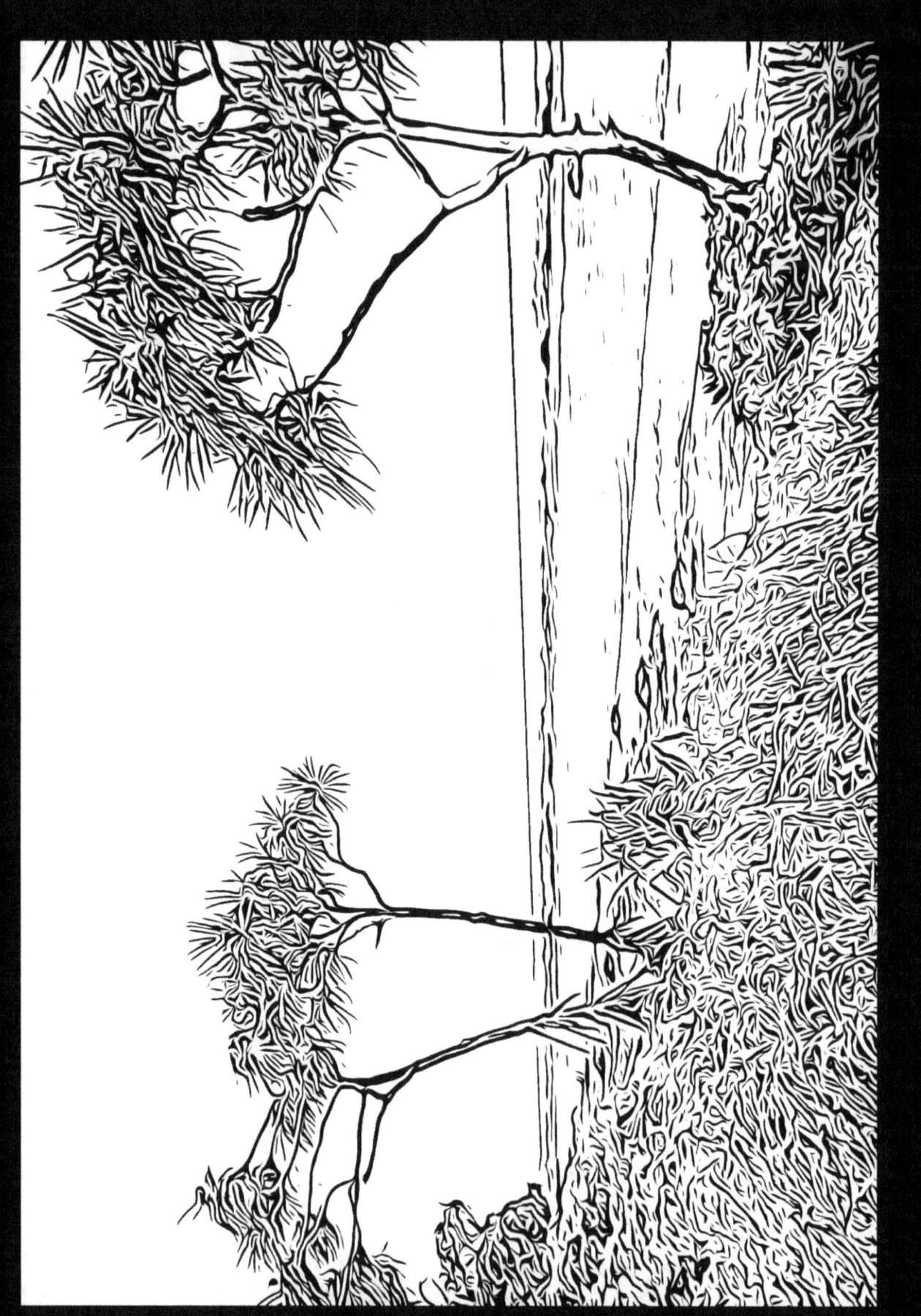

He spreads out the northern skies over empty space;
he suspends the earth over nothing.
He wraps up the waters in his clouds,
yet the clouds do not burst under their weight.
He covers the face of the full moon,
spreading his clouds over it.
He marks out the horizon on the face of the waters
for a boundary between light and darkness.
The pillars of the heavens quake,
aghast at his rebuke.
By his power he churned up the sea;
by his wisdom he cut Rahab to pieces.
By his breath the skies became fair;
his hand pierced the gliding serpent.

Job 26:7-13, NIV

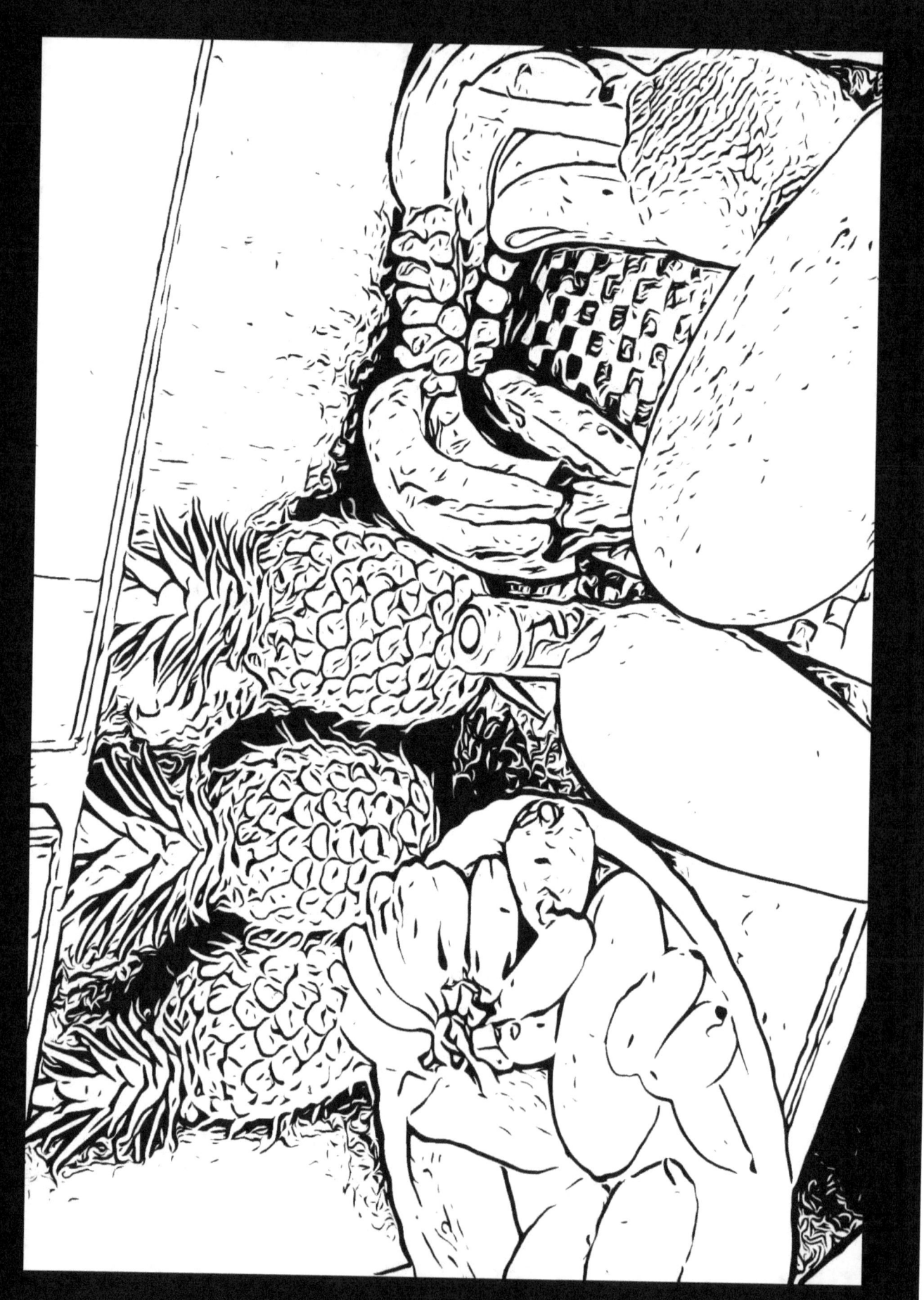

"What is the way to the abode of light?
And where does darkness reside?
Can you take them to their places?
Do you know the paths to their dwellings?
Surely you know, for you were already born!
You have lived so many years!
"Have you entered the storehouses of the snow
or seen the storehouses of the hail,
which I reserve for times of trouble,
for days of war and battle?
What is the way to the place where the lightning is dispersed,
or the place where the east winds are scattered over the earth?

Job 38:19-24, NIV

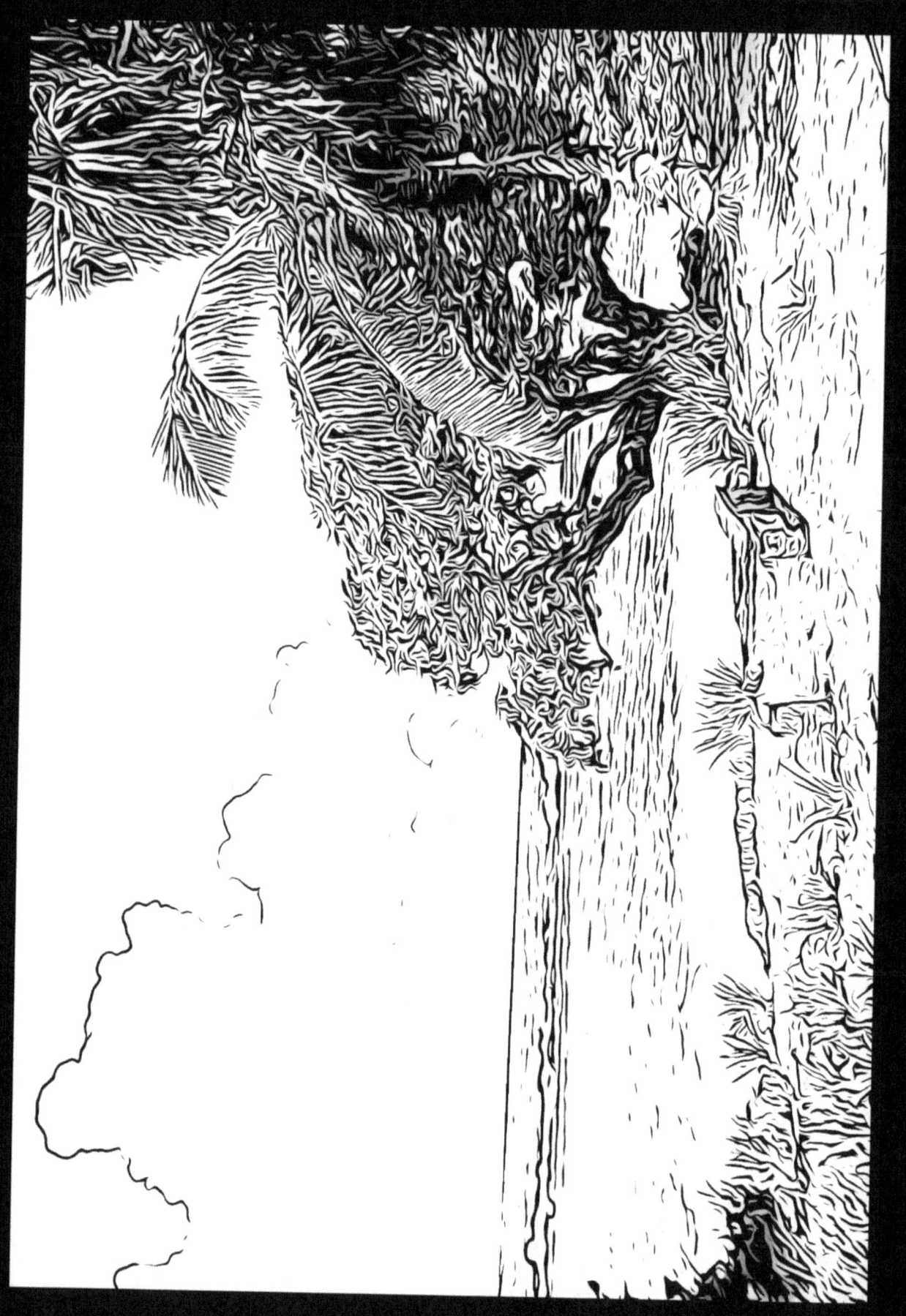

Who cuts a channel for the torrents of rain,
and a path for the thunderstorm,
to water a land where no one lives,
an uninhabited desert,
to satisfy a desolate wasteland
and make it sprout with grass?
Does the rain have a father?
Who fathers the drops of dew?
From whose womb comes the ice?
Who gives birth to the frost from the heavens
when the waters become hard as stone,
when the surface of the deep is frozen?
Job 38:25-30, NIV

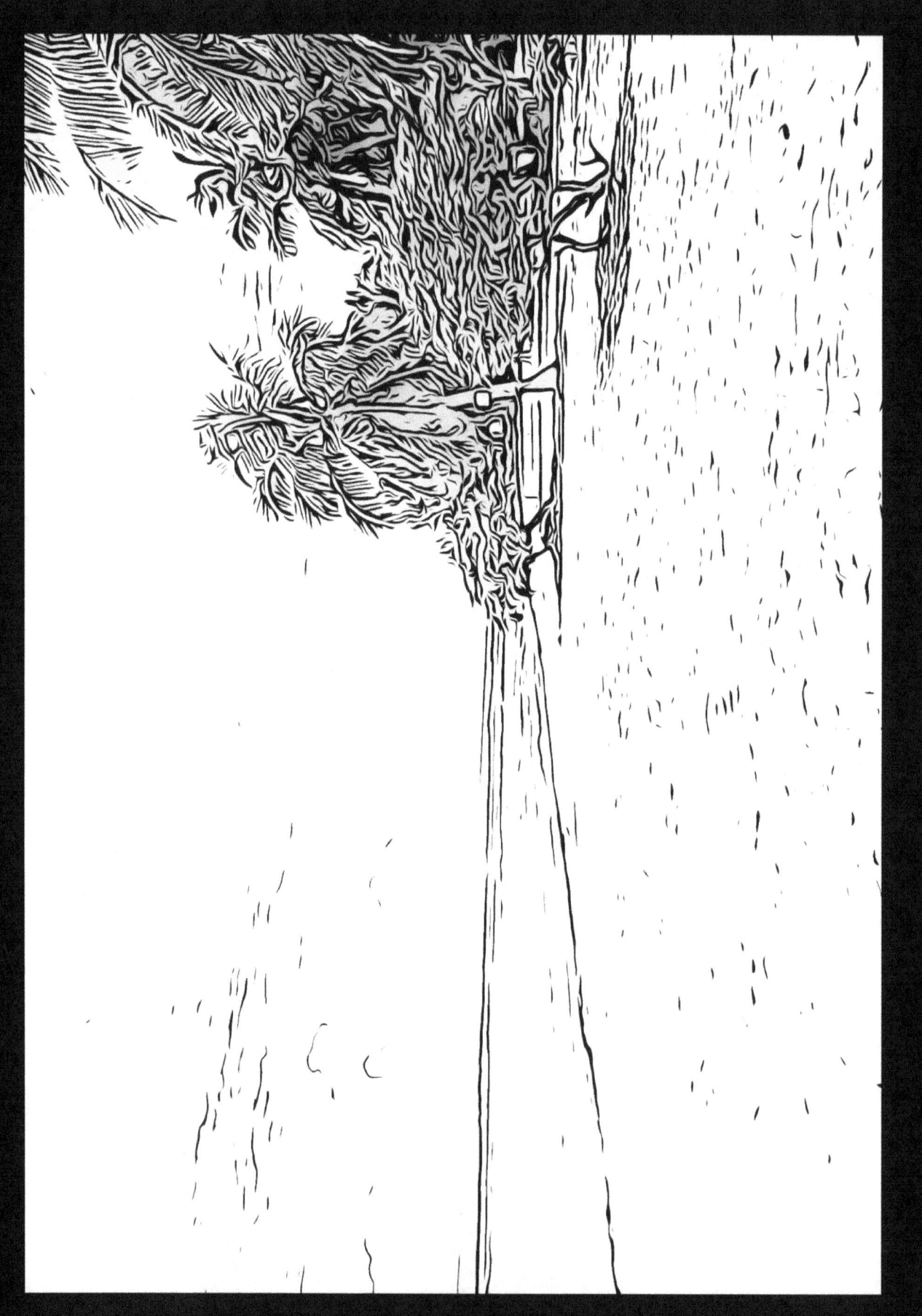

"God is exalted in his power.

Who is a teacher like him?

Who has prescribed his ways for him,

or said to him, 'You have done wrong'?

Remember to extol his work,

which people have praised in song.

All humanity has seen it;

mortals gaze on it from afar.

How great is God—beyond our understanding!

The number of his years is past finding out.

"He draws up the drops of water,

which distill as rain to the streams[a];

the clouds pour down their moisture

and abundant showers fall on mankind.

Who can understand how he spreads out the clouds,

how he thunders from his pavilion?

See how he scatters his lightning about him,

bathing the depths of the sea.

This is the way he governs[b] the nations

and provides food in abundance.

He fills his hands with lightning

and commands it to strike its mark.

His thunder announces the coming storm;

even the cattle make known its approach.

Job 36:22-33, NIV

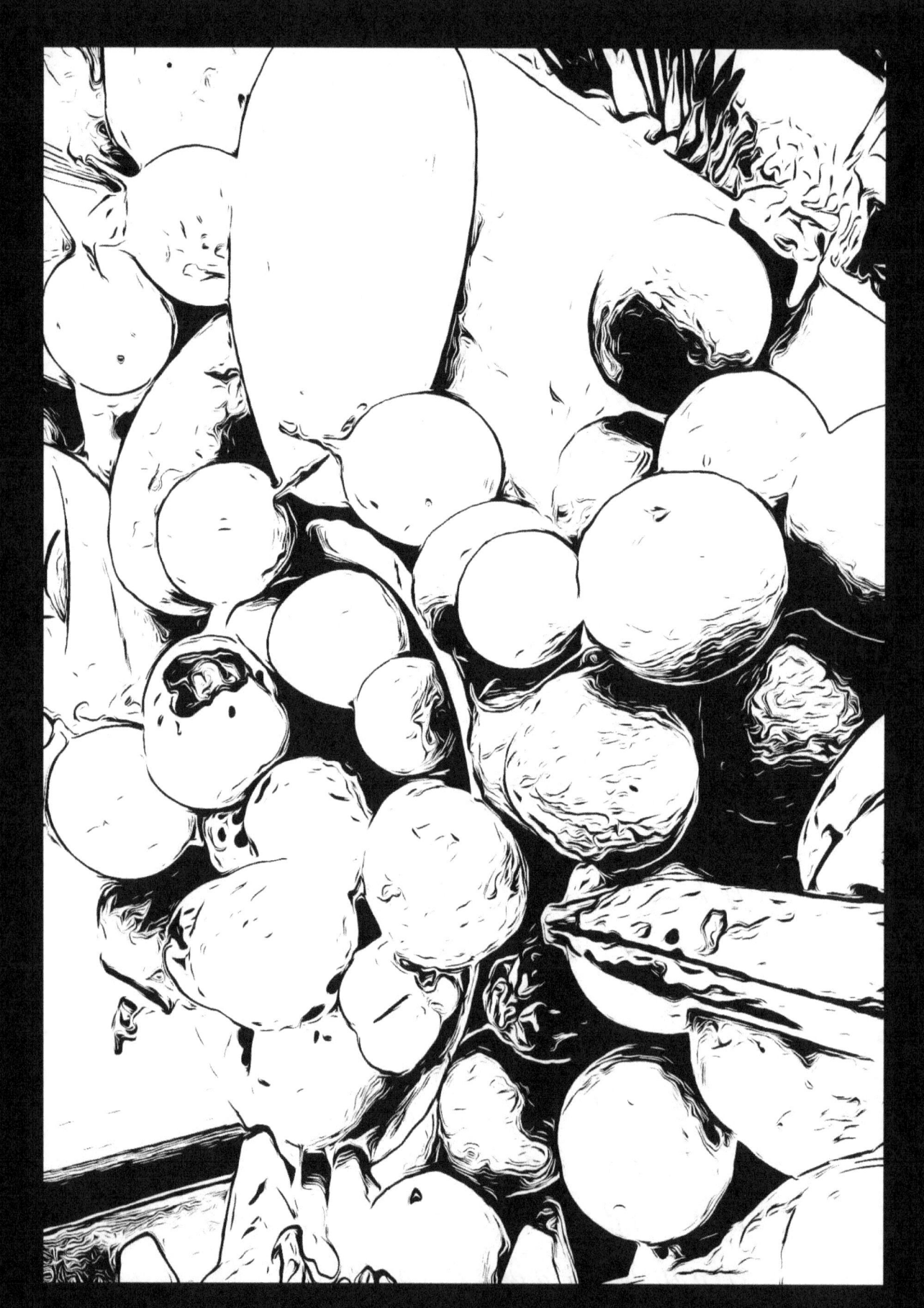

"But ask the animals, and they will teach you,
or the birds in the sky, and they will tell you;
or speak to the earth, and it will teach you,
or let the fish in the sea inform you.
Which of all these does not know
that the hand of the Lord has done this?
In his hand is the life of every creature
and the breath of all mankind.
Does not the ear test words
as the tongue tastes food?
Is not wisdom found among the aged?
Does not long life bring understanding?
"To God belong wisdom and power;
counsel and understanding are his.

Job 12:7-13, NIV

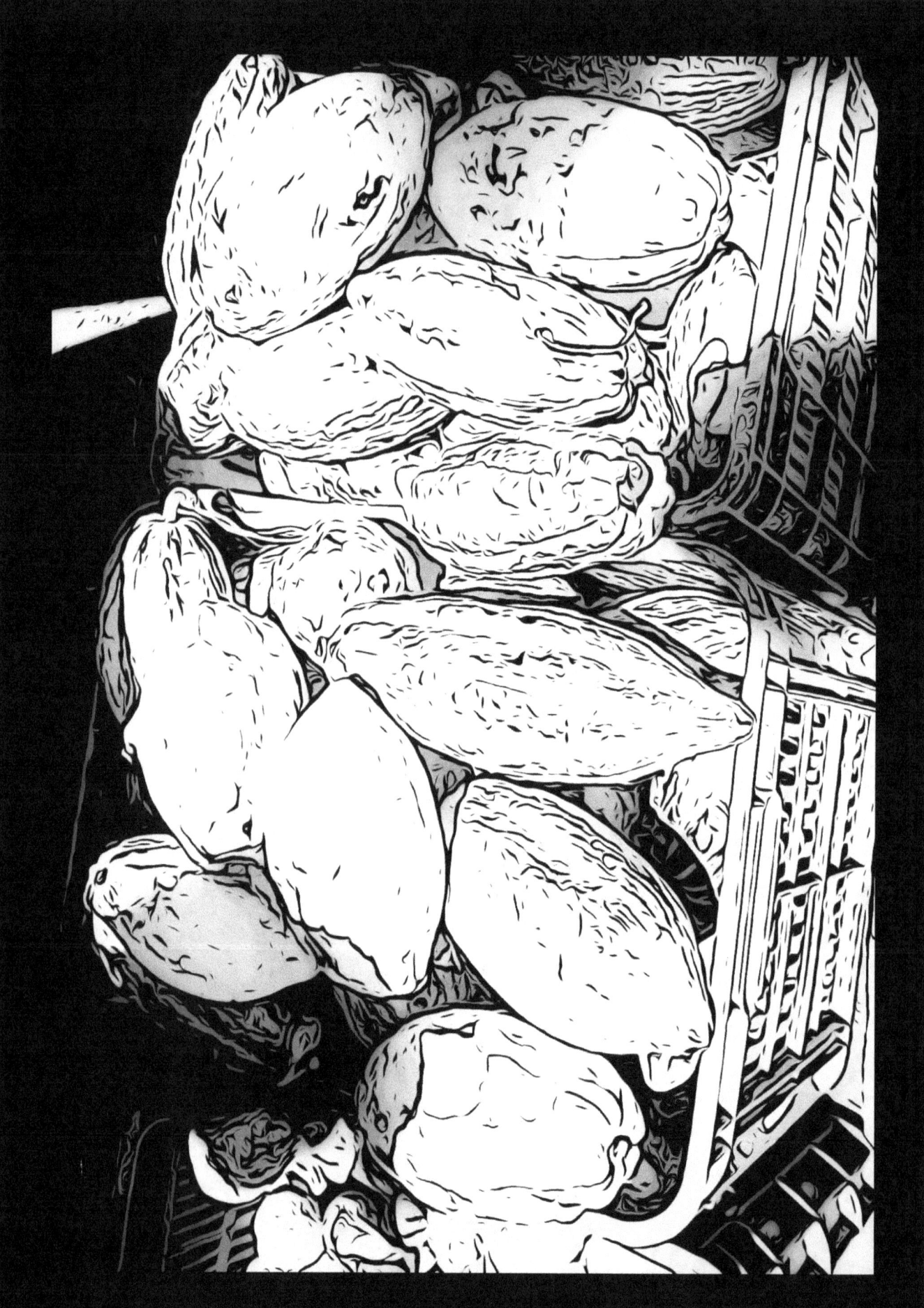

"To God belong wisdom and power;
counsel and understanding are his.
What he tears down cannot be rebuilt;
those he imprisons cannot be released.
If he holds back the waters, there is drought;
if he lets them loose, they devastate the land.
To him belong strength and insight;
both deceived and deceiver are his.
Job 12:13-16, NIV

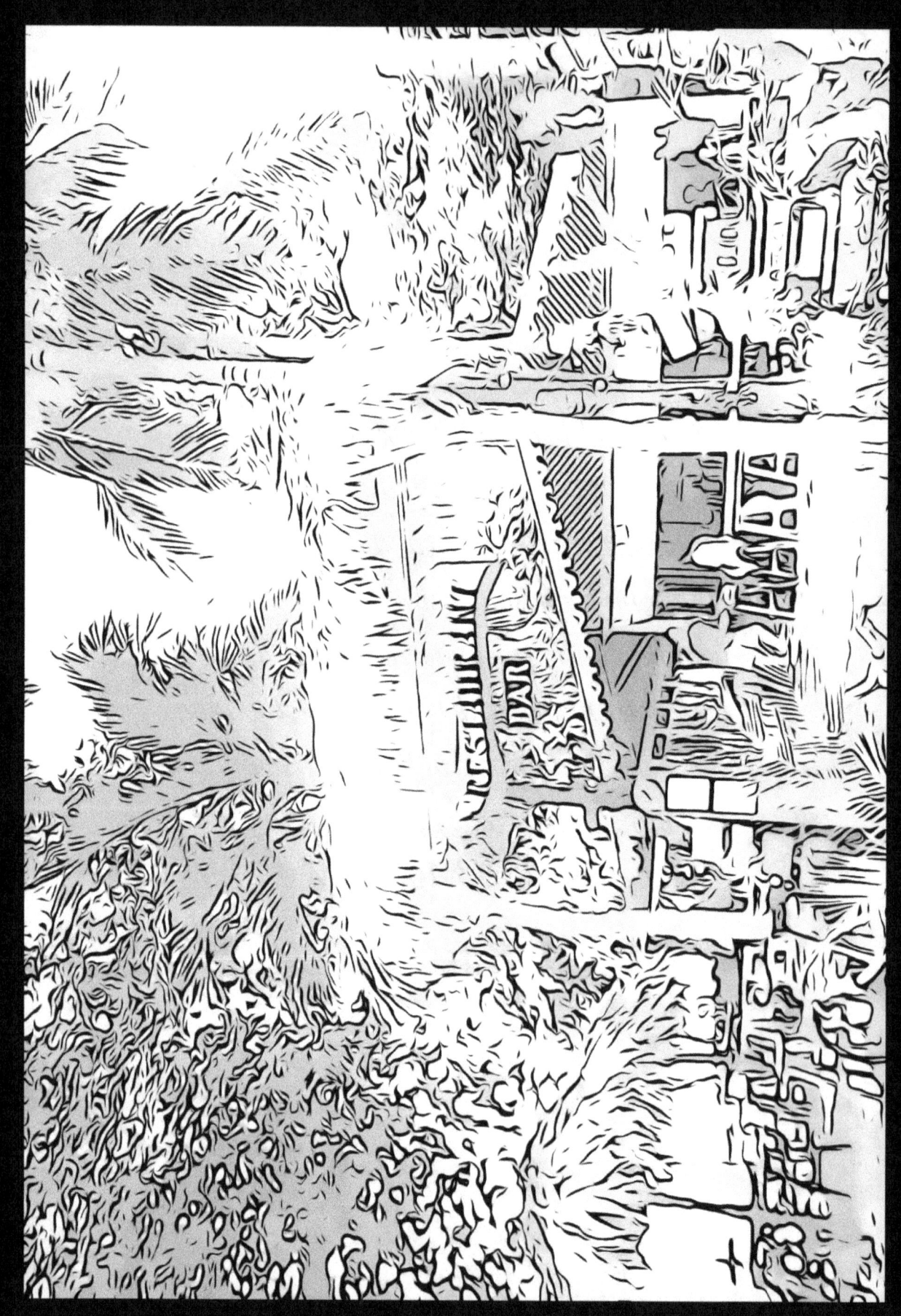

God's voice thunders in marvelous ways;
he does great things beyond our understanding.
He says to the snow, 'Fall on the earth,'
and to the rain shower, 'Be a mighty downpour.'
So that everyone he has made may know his work,
he stops all people from their labor.
Job 37:5-7, NIV

The breath of God produces ice,
and the broad waters become frozen.
He loads the clouds with moisture;
he scatters his lightning through them.
At his direction they swirl around
over the face of the whole earth
to do whatever he commands them.
He brings the clouds to punish people,
or to water his earth and show his love.
Job 37:10-13, NIV

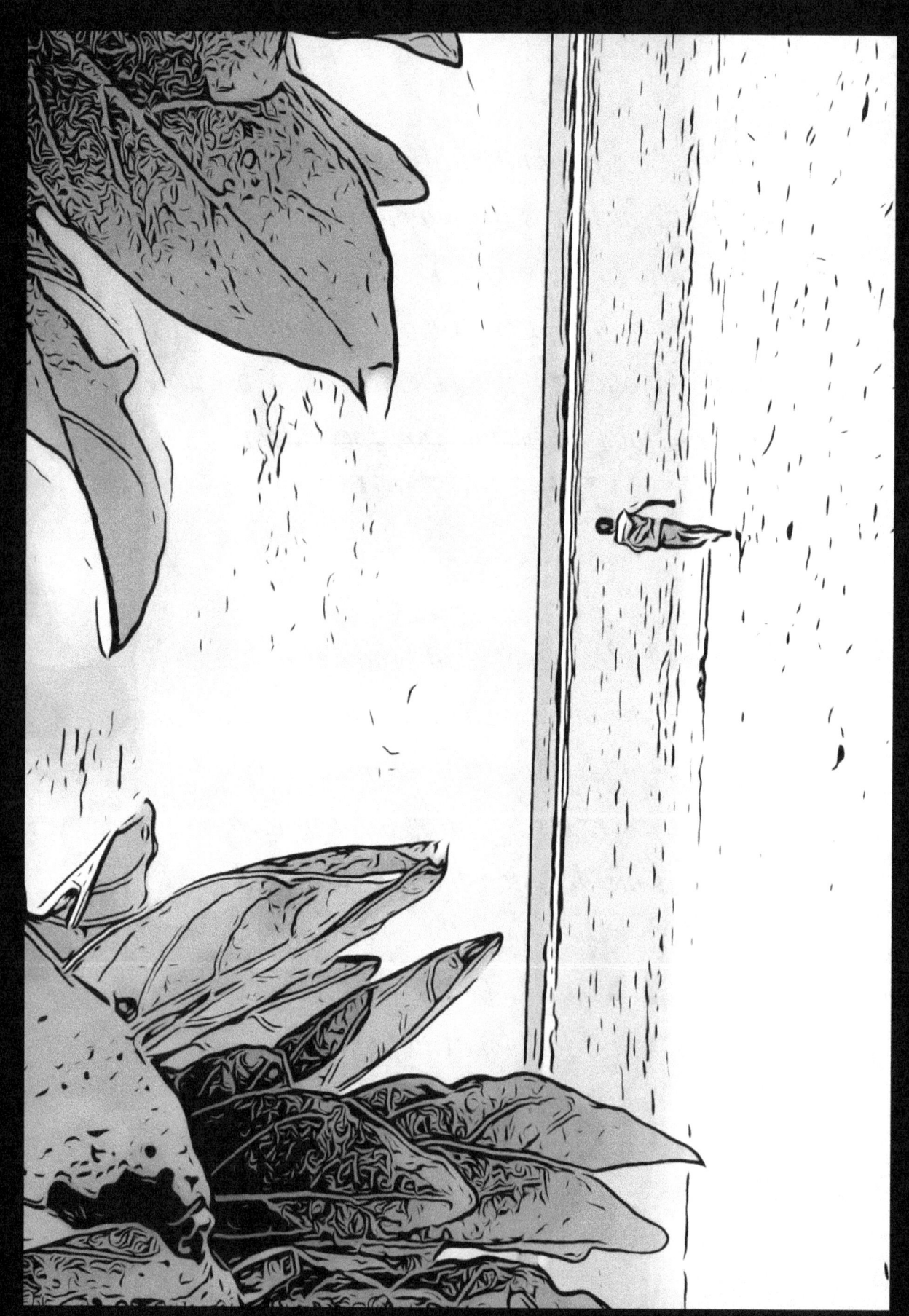

Now no one can look at the sun,
bright as it is in the skies
after the wind has swept them clean.
Out of the north he comes in golden splendor;
God comes in awesome majesty.
The Almighty is beyond our reach and exalted in power;
in his justice and great righteousness, he does not oppress.
Therefore, people revere him,
for does he not have regard for all the wise in heart?
Job 37:21-24, NIV

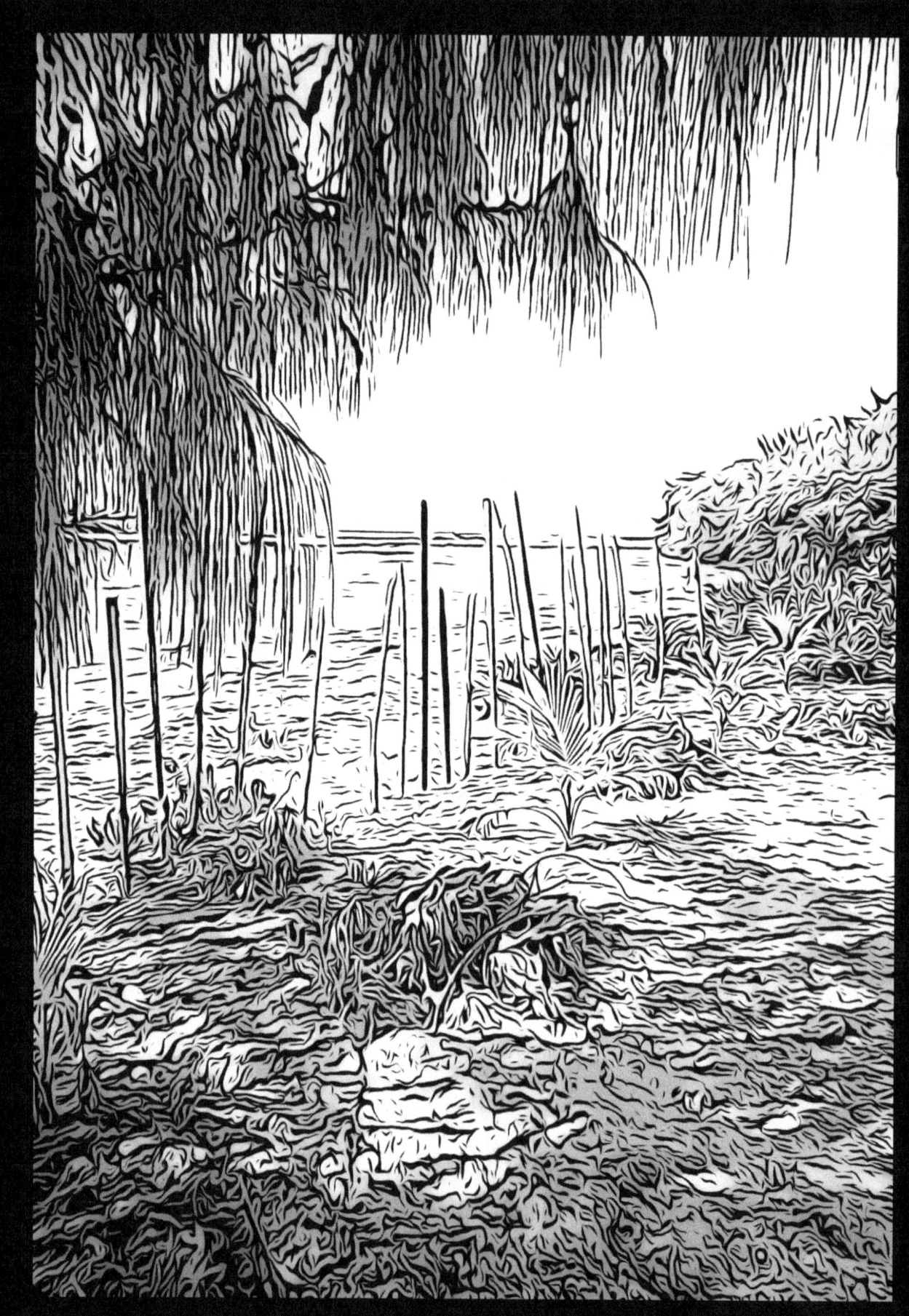

"Submit to God and be at peace with him;
in this way prosperity will come to you.
Accept instruction from his mouth
and lay up his words in your heart.
If you return to the Almighty, you will be restored:
If you remove wickedness far from your tent…
Job 22:21-23, NIV

…then the Almighty will be your gold,
the choicest silver for you.
Surely then you will find delight in the Almighty
and will lift up your face to God.
You will pray to him, and he will hear you,
and you will fulfill your vows.
What you decide on will be done,
and light will shine on your ways.
Job 22:25-28, NIV

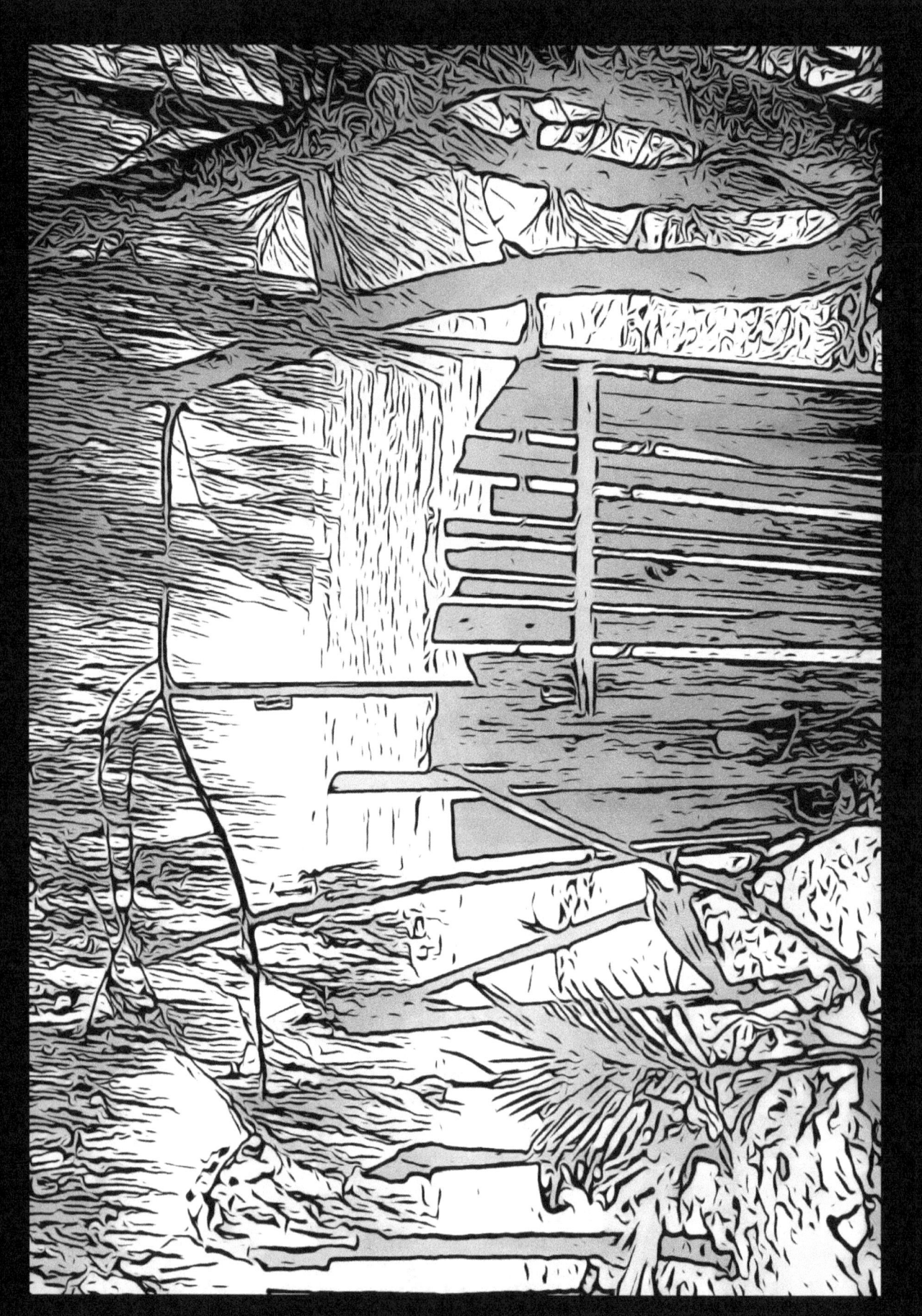

Part 3
Canvas of Love

The canvas of pure innocent love, where can we see or find it? Or can we feel and experience the truth and sincerity that love becomes our rejoicing inner sanctuary. The canvas of rainbow, colours of adoring and appreciating each and any little details of people and our surroundings, with full kindness and warm-hearted thanksgiving. The canvas of honouring respecting, protecting, and giving, because real love has never heard or harmed with a continuous committed ongoing plan.

A canvas of love is manifested in our soul and heart to accept and submit and fear God. Not fear in the human understanding, of being scared or worried. To fear God is a surrender of His will and authority. The canvas of creation and nature, is God's testimony of His supreme power, of love to us all. True love that I'm talking about is not the attraction of physical enjoyment: sex, lust or falling in love, it is what is a canvas of mankind's interpretation of love. I am talking about an unexplained supernatural love, what we all have in our inner core.

God the designer, artist of creation, has given us billions of example in His paintbrush when He draws on His canvas on Heaven on Earth making mankind to perfection. His love that He created everywhere: in every colour, shadow, forms, who flies, crawls or swims. On every mountain and in every fields of meadows, trees, leaves or flowers, in the morning or evening, sunrise or moon shadows, in the formation of stars and universe, in the sun, rain or storm, His master hands and mind created for us, His healthy love.

Love is to be able to breath, walk around, see, touch, and feel, when our hearts are open and soft, embracing the small and big wonders of lakes, rivers and seas. Love is peace and joy and praising to dwell on the good and beauty of mankind and God's canvas of creation. You love when your heart goes out with warmth and compassion. You love when a smile or joy radiates. When you see and hold your loved one with rejoicing, then you know the secret of real love.

Love has uncountable sources, styles, meanings, purpose, values or faces. The quality of love must be laid out with blessings. Love is observing the smallest detail and beauty of people and nature with sincerity. Love is when you are happy to give, share, care, and know when you are needed.

God gave Love to us, the spiral and backbone of our existence. If we loose this love of simplicity, then our lives are empty. False attractions, false temptations, false promises of happiness, we then fallow and are on the search lifelong hoping that something or someone will make us happy, instead of looking inside of ourselves for the inner joy and peace what is the seed of love and understanding.

To end this book in Costa Rica, *Canvas of Creation*, I'd love to share the beautiful real love of care in action. Tropical wind and humidity is very difficult for my personal weak body. So since I am here, I have to be extremely careful. But, obviously this is not enough, because it hit me and I got very sick. Three days I patiently endured the illness, hoping it would calm down and I would recover, but that hope was slowly fading.

There were a few other long-term guests just like me, we all enjoyed watching and talking to each other daily. All of us are retired, having fun in the sun, even though I work many days, from morning to night. They observed and realized that something was not right with me. I was sitting constantly looking pale and quite on my verandah in a big chair

I did not work or move, just like a little bird with clipped wings who was hurt. They saw that I had no energy, sitting only watching the crashing ocean waves. Silently, I prayed for myself to get better, but my medication did not help. I felt lonely, tired, and exhausted 'till my grateful neighbours came to get me.

Mike my edit, made vegetable soup. The Italian, former nurse lady, and Jose, a teacher and principle, looked after me and took charge. Like old wise pelicans, they huffed and puffed, taking me in their big wings while I was in blankets well covered.

They talked out loud and argued back and forth and the commotion went on for awhile. They then decided for me to go to the doctor and to move quickly. Like a little helpless child I quietly followed their plan. They called a taxi. Jose became my interpreter. From Spanish to English and off we went to the local medical centre. Just to be precautious and go for a checkup. They were overbooked, so we had to go 20 km to the hospital out of our way.

Out there, thinking I would go in quickly in and out. But Jose committed and waited four hours. To my amazement he was a stranger to me, but stayed patiently to bring me home safely with a smile. But my results were not good. So the doctor decided and continued to proscribe medication and care for many hours for a quick recover. I was exhausted, but convinced Jose to go home, as the doctor said he would order a taxi for me later. So weak and cold I was in all the air condition, but I was happy that I found help at the right moment.

Later to my absolute surprise and shock, I saw Aroceli the hotel owner, standing at the door. She realized I did not come home yet and was worried. She took a bus for over half an hour and walked a long distance to find me in the hospital. She doesn't speak English but our looks, smiles, and hearts made the love connection. She waited another five-hours outside in the dark until twelve midnight when she finally took me to my protected home by taxi.

In the dark of the car we held our hands. Her love was to assure me that I am not alone. She like Jose, protected and cared enough to give me the gift of love. She was happy to reach out, as I was happy to take their gift of her love. In the taxi before I arrived in my hotel room, we both prayed with joy with hugs and gave thanks in our own languages to God and His marvellous ways that He shares love.

Hot soups and caring continued for the following days and I felt so thankful and that I was embraced by kindness and love. This small testimony is just a touch of colour from my paintbrush of my canvas of love. To finish my canvas I will put the past, present, and future with all details and wonder so al of us will never forget that love has the last word to give and reign.

To count our smallest blessings, but to give our Godly big love is God's commandant what we should do with no hesitation. Godly love is an art, the canvas, a picture, what only he can plan in our heart if we ask Him to do so. So, our duty and rejoicing is to give Him our canvas of love with praising.

All our brushes, all our colours, all our heart desires let Him help us to be the canvas of love creator and part of our lives. Praise creation and the creator to see the depths of beauty and praise and see true love in each other.

Canvas of Glass Bowl

What I really like, is my joy of poetry,
because it is my life canvas reality.
I imagine that it looks like a glass bowl
from outside gorgeous fragile,
colourful, perfect and whole.

I love you, I love you, life long,
but sometimes I hate you, I hate you.
Both words are emotions, truthfully
they are opposites of each other
and their meanings are very strong.

Wherever you stand,
be sure you know why they are like a rainbow,
like a spectrum of feelings,
full to see and hear in display.
To really love a person is a mindset each on its own.
Individually, you have power and control
to decide to give love and put it unconditionally
in your heart's thrown.

Real love is not at all blinded like attraction will do.
Truthfully, honest love makes you glass clear aware,
what is needed to give at first,
before you receive that function,
don't be confused or let frustration get through.

If we question our own love to a person,
we need to be careful to assess exactly why,
what are my reasons, my motives.
The awareness to think and do so,
and what makes me happy or unsecure,
to love truly, maybe I am afraid or shy?

The question is…
What holds me back and is disturbing my inner being?
Is it instinct, facts or my hopeful feeling?

I love you, I hate you,
can be easily said with no meaning
thrown in joy or anger in the air.
But it can affect another person's life
for good when in despair.
Real love has to go through fire tests and trials,
so we do not give up is a strength of it
and hope that it will go on a unlimited miles.

Your true love is a commitment to not go astray
and to keep pure love in your
soul without revenge or punishment
when it is not responded back to you or in delay.
Free love and true love is a twister,
a blessing, a hardship all together,
because it hurts or has fear to lose or give up
that person through deaths or divorce forever.

Pain and joy are so closely related together;
a turbulence we never could solve or escape,
a God-given destiny in our daily endeavor.
Through life we learn to cope
and to learn to experience and give and take.
But our mindset about this is the key factor
to move or feel, to heal, to laugh or to break.

Love is loyal, love is honesty.
To be loved is an honor,
a gift in a person's life; it is the biggest treasure.
To know someone stands unconditionally
behind, next or in front of you. As your security,
protection, and shelter in unity.

Oneness of mind and soul,
when we were young,
we wished so often to have a glass bowl.
Without us, what will the future become?
When we are old and wise,
we look back into the glass bowl
and do know if we were weak or strong
or what we have done, right or wrong.

If you loved someone or someone hates you,
it is like heaven or hell as close or far away from each other
and that is a decision like a gate we must go through.
Your mind is your glass bowl, your initiator,
your own atomic bomb creator or reactor.
So, wake up, don't fall in the worldly trap.
It will seduce, influence, and force,
to put your mindset to their needs and liking,
until they turn around against you,
then you'll see and feel the double-minded striking.

Don't trust naively and innocently,
the big slogan that love making enjoying is freely.
Everything has a price to pay. By doing it you wont away.
Everything is self-afflicted or matures.
Quitting, staying, for good or bad, or you lose or choose.

So, wisdom is what?
And who do we love or hate?
Listen to your mind and your soul carefully,
before you say something to someone
you love or hate truthfully.
A mind, a soul, a love, is as fragile as a glass bowl
if you consciously step on and break it,
you may fix it, but it never will be the same,
beautiful, trustworthy, flawless, and whole.

So, be careful that you keep it in safety;
choose to have love and give abundantly
from your soul and mind truthfully.

A beautiful poetry about reality,
that I always believed in,
where two people or a family,
men and wives or children can experience,
can share and can give love abundantly.

True love is still existing in our world,
even we don't see it sometimes clearly
or if we don't want it anymore.
But true love will always stay
and is designed from God definitely for eternity.

The heavens declare the glory of God;
the skies proclaim the work of his hands.
Day after day they pour forth speech;
night after night they reveal knowledge.
They have no speech, they use no words;
no sound is heard from them.
Yet their voice goes out into all the earth,
their words to the ends of the world.
In the heavens God has pitched a tent for the sun.
It is like a bridegroom coming out of his chamber,
like a champion rejoicing to run his course.
It rises at one end of the heavens
and makes its circuit to the other;
nothing is deprived of its warmth.
Psalm 19:1-6, NIV

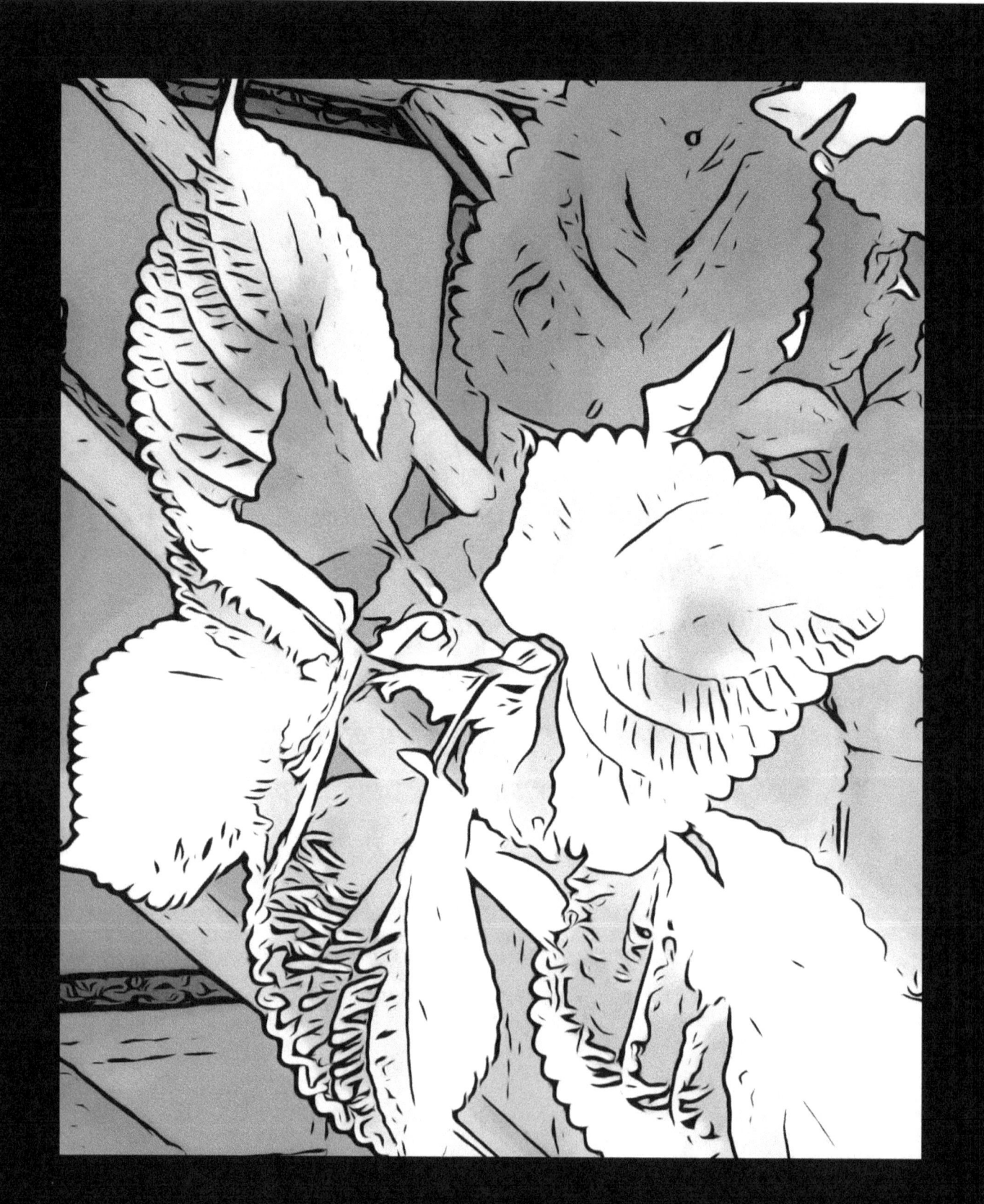

The law of the Lord is perfect,
refreshing the soul.
The statutes of the Lord are trustworthy,
making wise the simple.
The precepts of the Lord are right,
giving joy to the heart.
The commands of the Lord are radiant,
giving light to the eyes.
The fear of the Lord is pure,
enduring forever.
The decrees of the Lord are firm,
and all of them are righteous.
Psalm 19:7-9, NIV

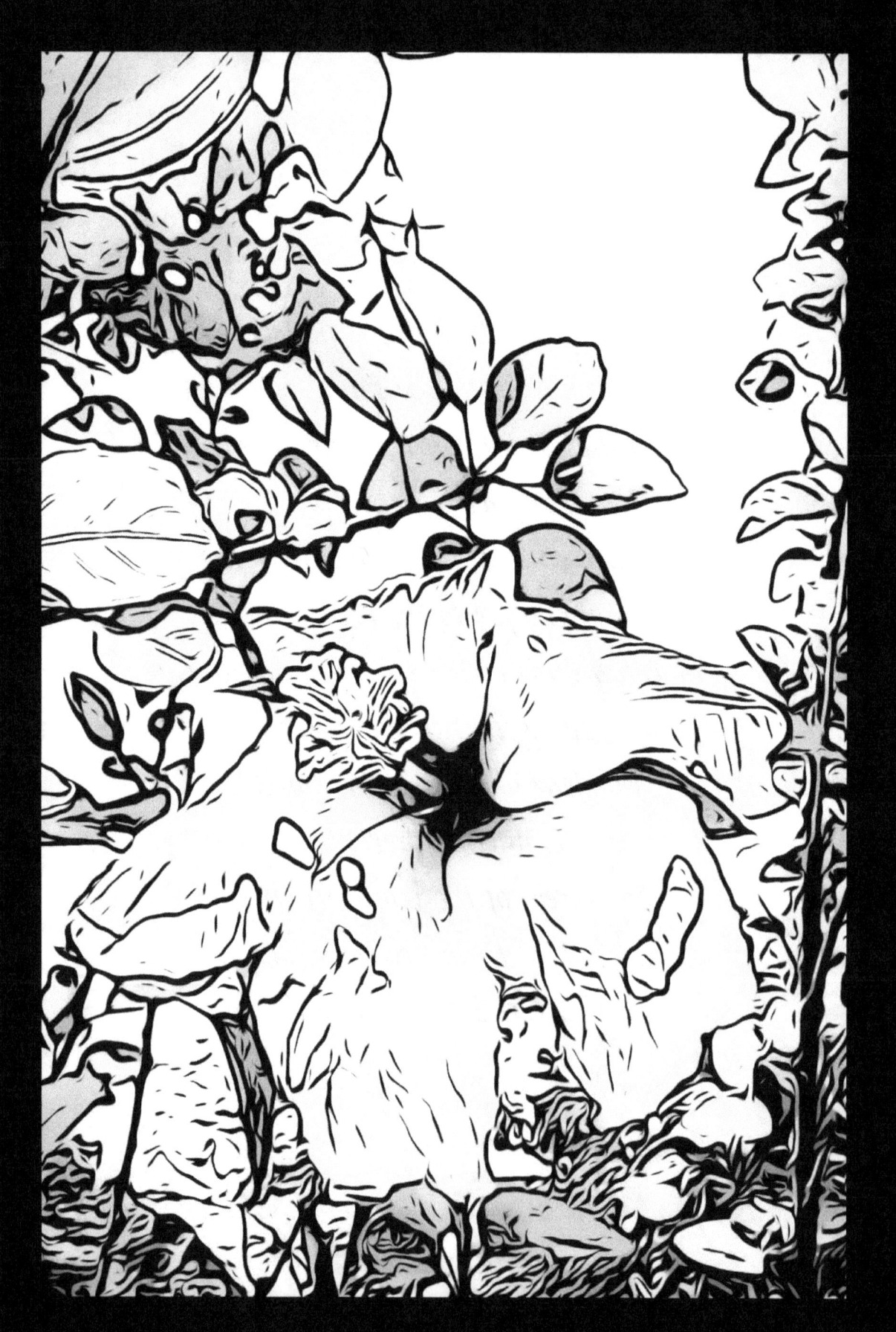

In God, whose word I praise,
in the Lord, whose word I praise—
in God I trust and am not afraid.
What can man do to me?
I am under vows to you, my God;
I will present my thank offerings to you.
For you have delivered me from death
and my feet from stumbling,
that I may walk before God
in the light of life.
Psalm 56:9-13, NIV

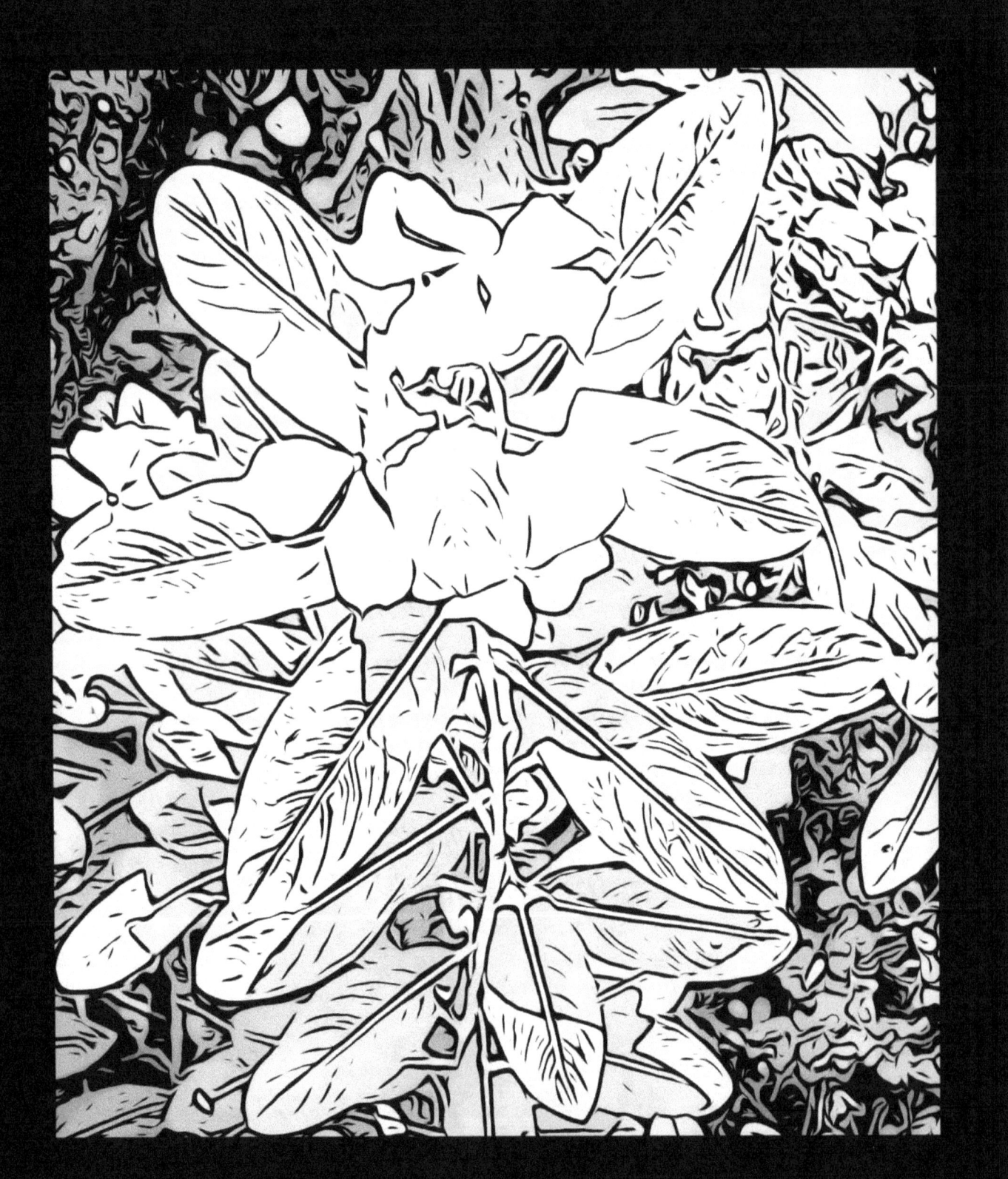

Declare his glory among the nations,
his marvelous deeds among all peoples.
For great is the Lord and most worthy of praise;
he is to be feared above all gods.
For all the gods of the nations are idols,
but the Lord made the heavens.
Splendor and majesty are before him;
strength and glory are in his sanctuary.
Ascribe to the Lord, all you families of nations,
ascribe to the Lord glory and strength.
Psalm 96:3-7, NIV

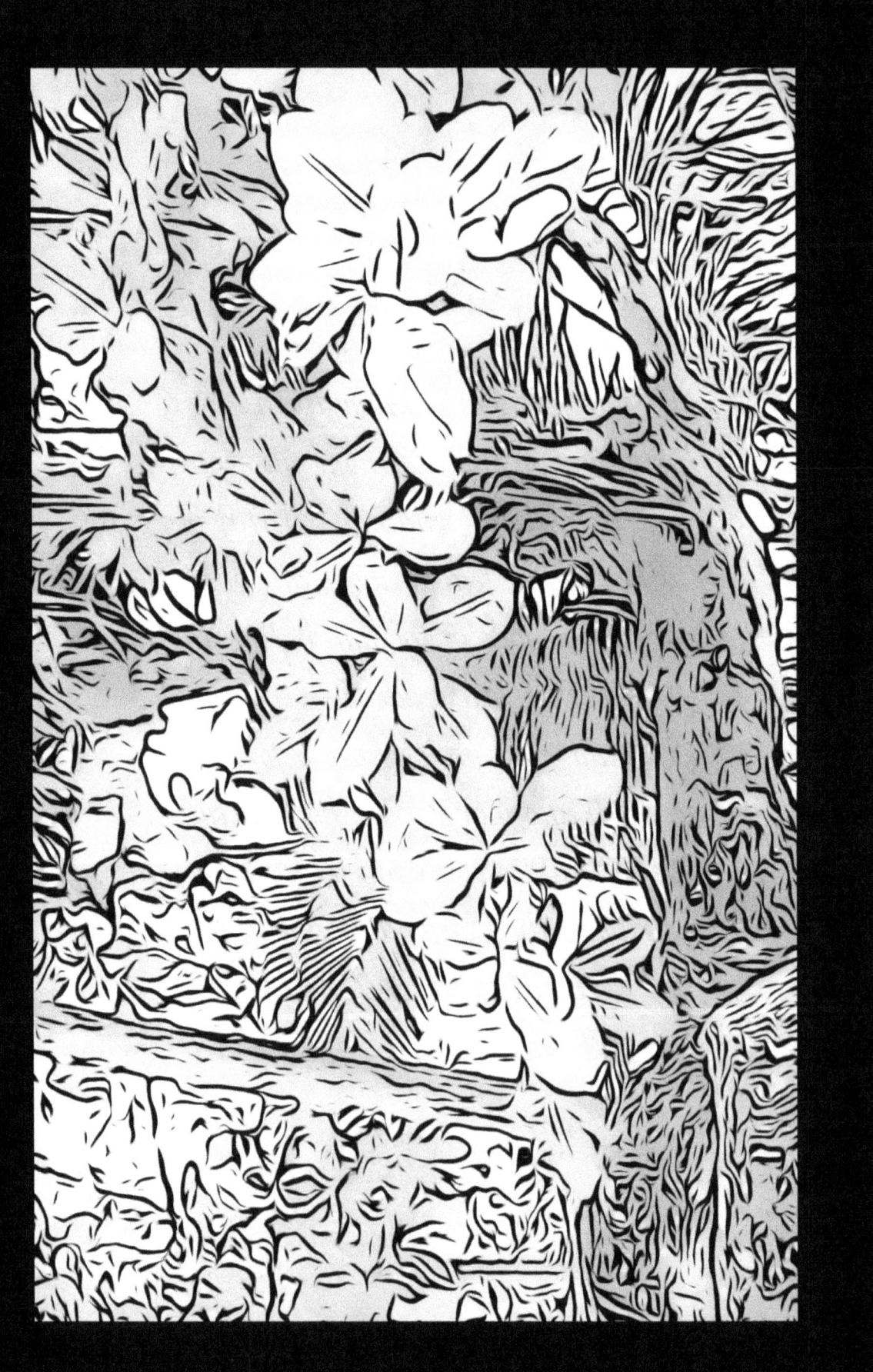

How many are your works, Lord!
In wisdom you made them all;
the earth is full of your creatures.
There is the sea, vast and spacious,
teeming with creatures beyond number—
living things both large and small.
There the ships go to and fro,
and Leviathan, which you formed to frolic there.
All creatures look to you
to give them their food at the proper time.
When you give it to them,
they gather it up;
when you open your hand,
they are satisfied with good things.
When you hide your face,
they are terrified;
when you take away their breath,
they die and return to the dust.
When you send your Spirit,
they are created,
and you renew the face of the ground.
Psalm 104:24-30, NIV

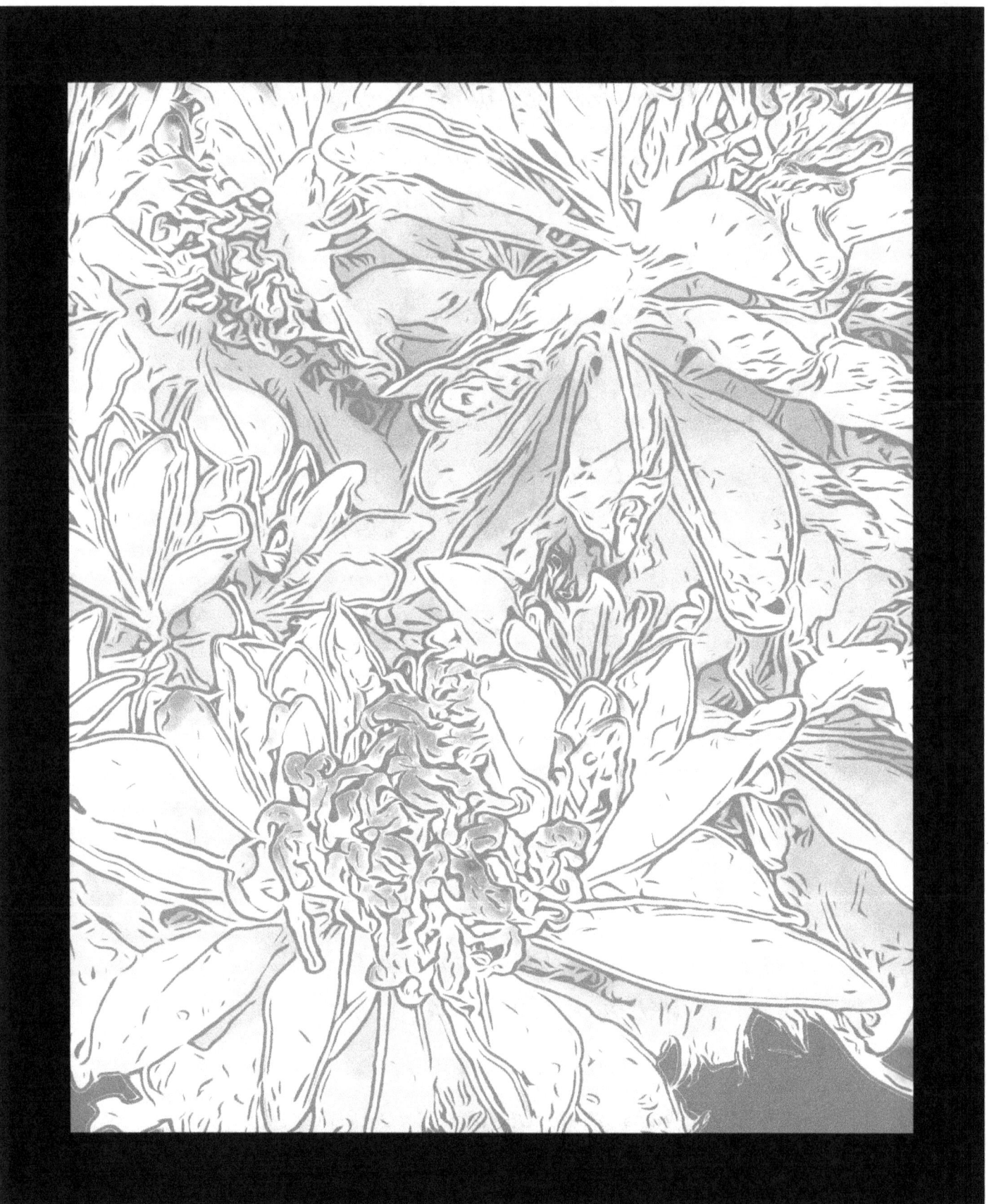

Teach me your way, Lord,
that I may rely on your faithfulness;
give me an undivided heart,
that I may fear your name.
I will praise you, Lord my God, with all my heart;
I will glorify your name forever.
For great is your love toward me;
you have delivered me from the depths,
from the realm of the dead.
Psalm 86:11-13, NIV

I will extol the Lord at all times;
his praise will always be on my lips.
I will glory in the Lord;
let the afflicted hear and rejoice.
Glorify the Lord with me;
let us exalt his name together.
Psalm 34:1-3, NIV

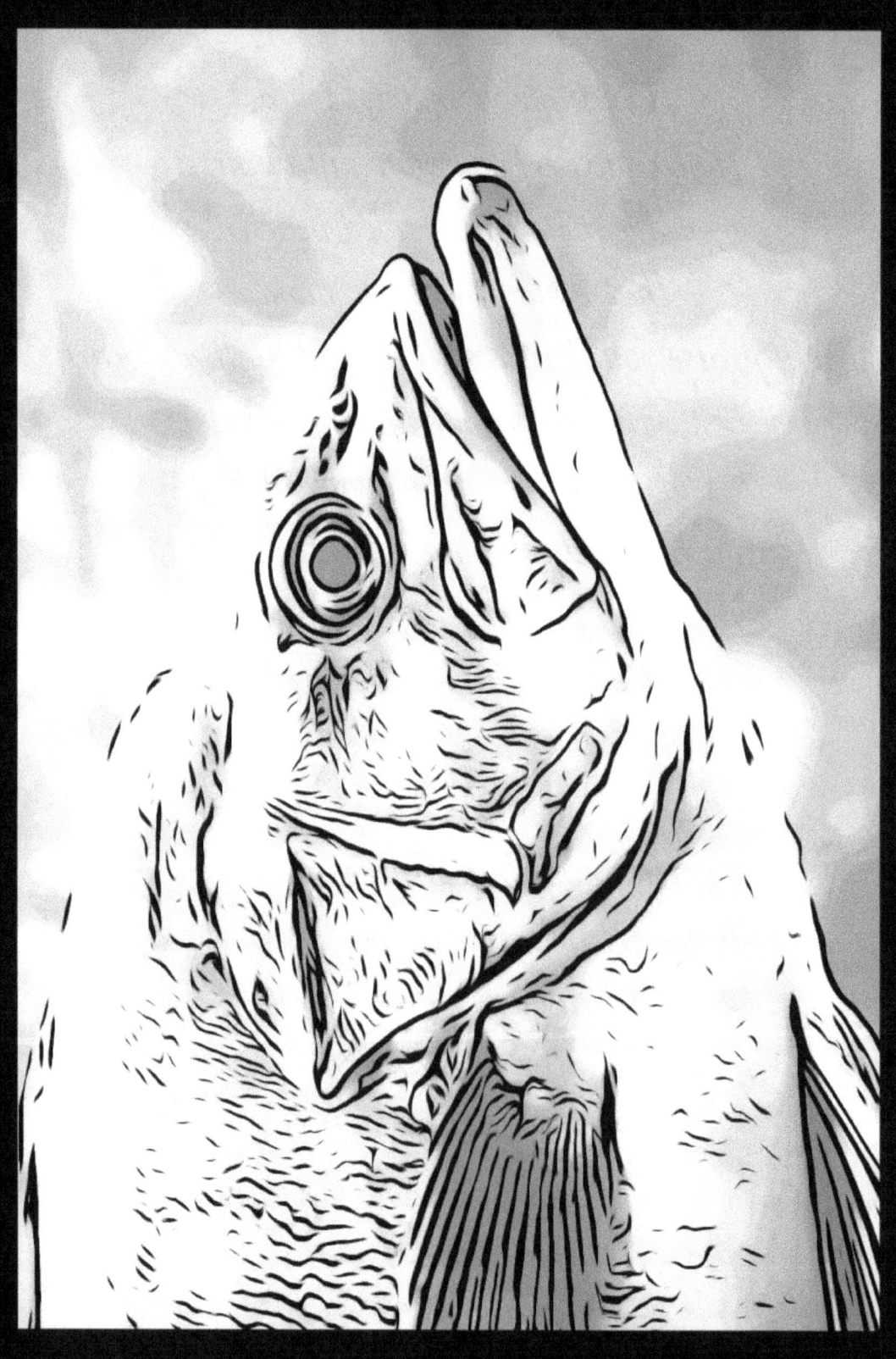

Truly my soul finds rest in God;
my salvation comes from him.
Truly he is my rock and my salvation;
he is my fortress, I will never be shaken.
Psalm 62:1-2, NIV

Because your love is better than life,
my lips will glorify you.
I will praise you as long as I live,
and in your name I will lift up my hands.
I will be fully satisfied as with the richest of foods;
with singing lips my mouth will praise you.
Psalm 63:3-5, NIV

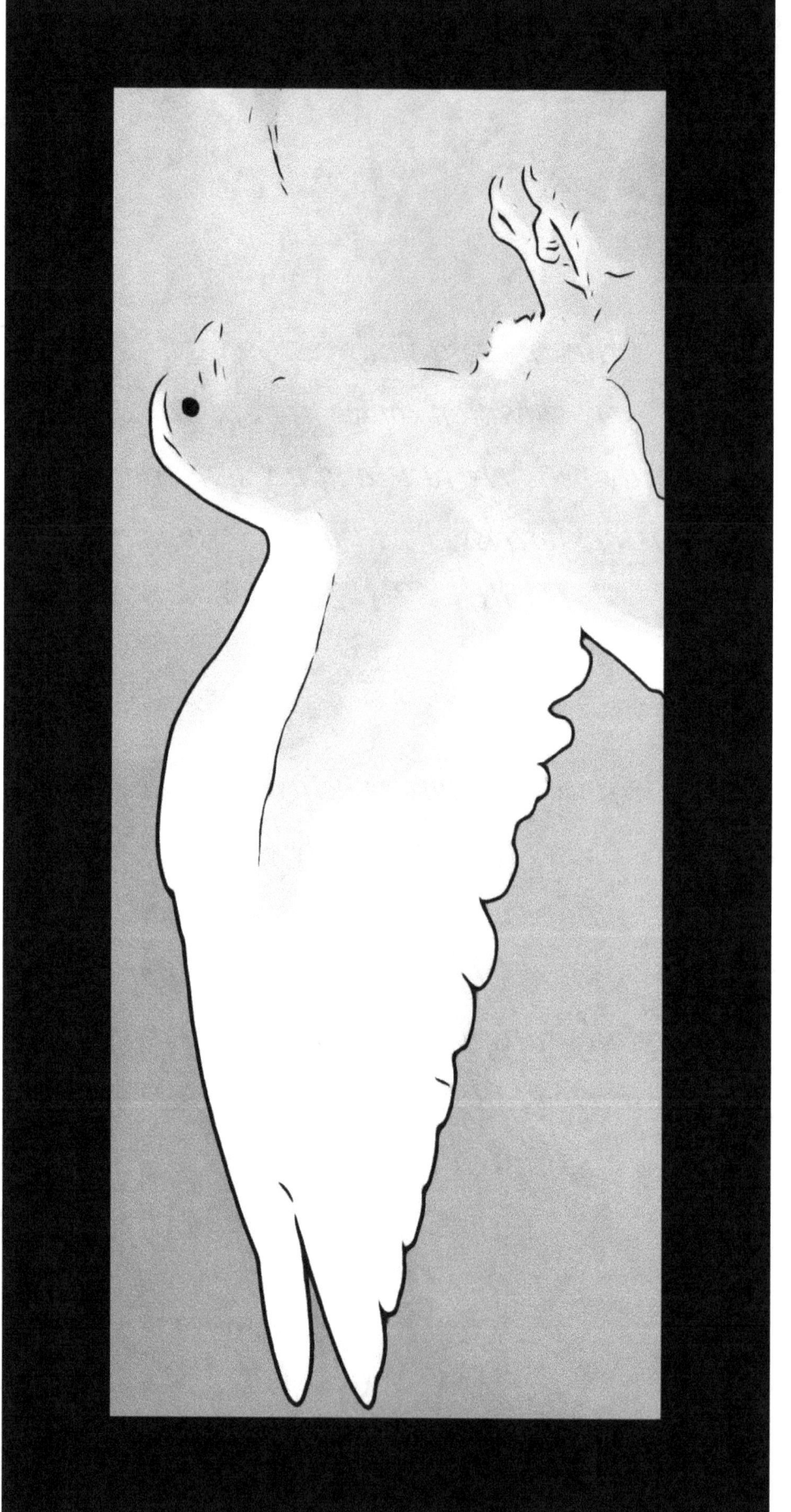

As for God, his way is perfect:
The Lord's word is flawless;
he shields all who take refuge in him.
For who is God besides the Lord?
And who is the Rock except our God?
It is God who arms me with strength
and keeps my way secure.
He makes my feet like the feet of a deer;
he causes me to stand on the heights.
He trains my hands for battle;
my arms can bend a bow of bronze.
You make your saving help my shield,
and your right hand sustains me;
your help has made me great.
Psalm 18:30-35, NIV

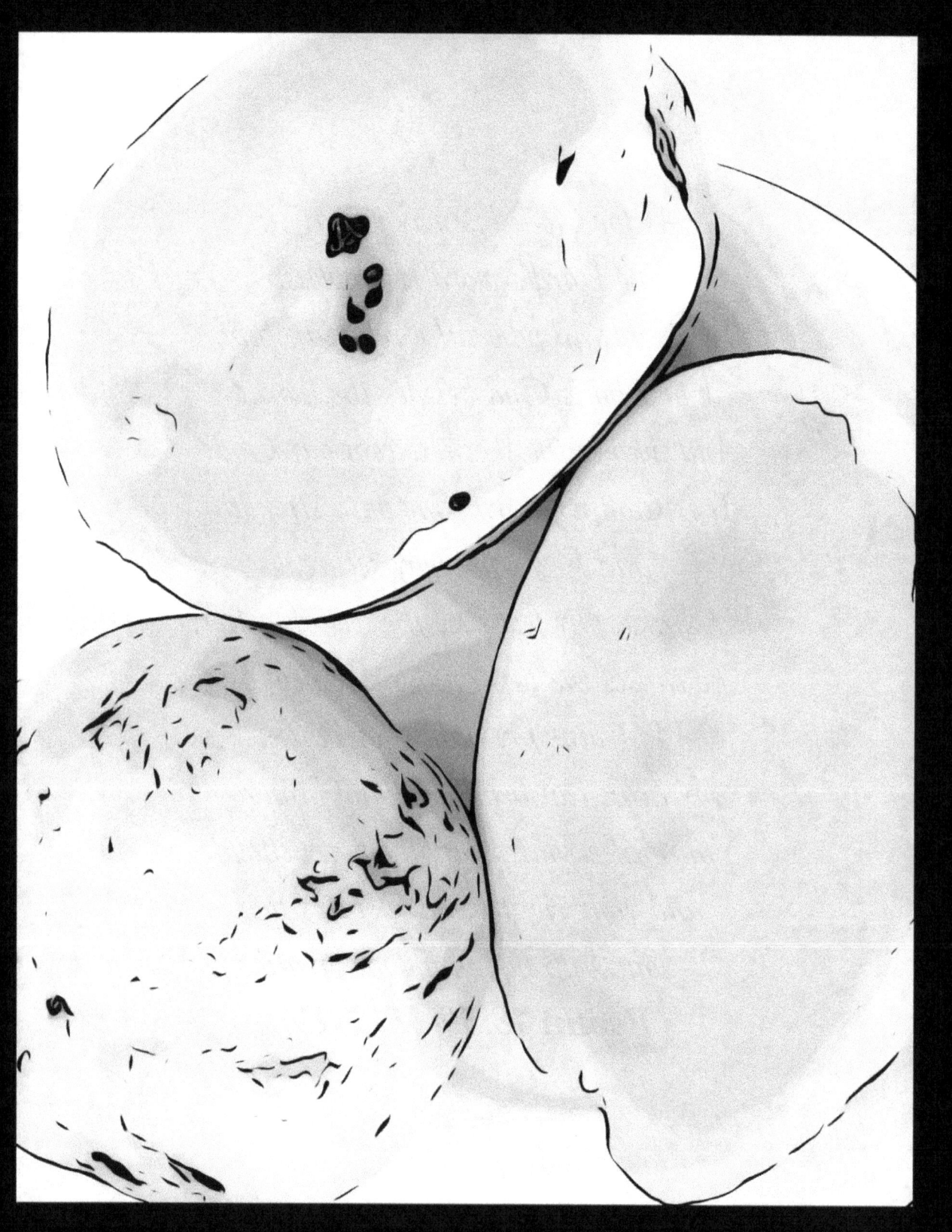

Blessed is the nation whose God is the Lord,
the people he chose for his inheritance.
From heaven the Lord looks down
and sees all mankind;
from his dwelling place he watches
all who live on earth—
he who forms the hearts of all,
who considers everything they do.
No king is saved by the size of his army;
no warrior escapes by his great strength.
A horse is a vain hope for deliverance;
despite all its great strength it cannot save.
But the eyes of the Lord are on those who fear him,
on those whose hope is in his unfailing love,
to deliver them from death
and keep them alive in famine.
We wait in hope for the Lord;
he is our help and our shield.
In him our hearts rejoice,
for we trust in his holy name.
May your unfailing love be with us, Lord,
even as we put our hope in you.
Psalm 33:12-22, NIV

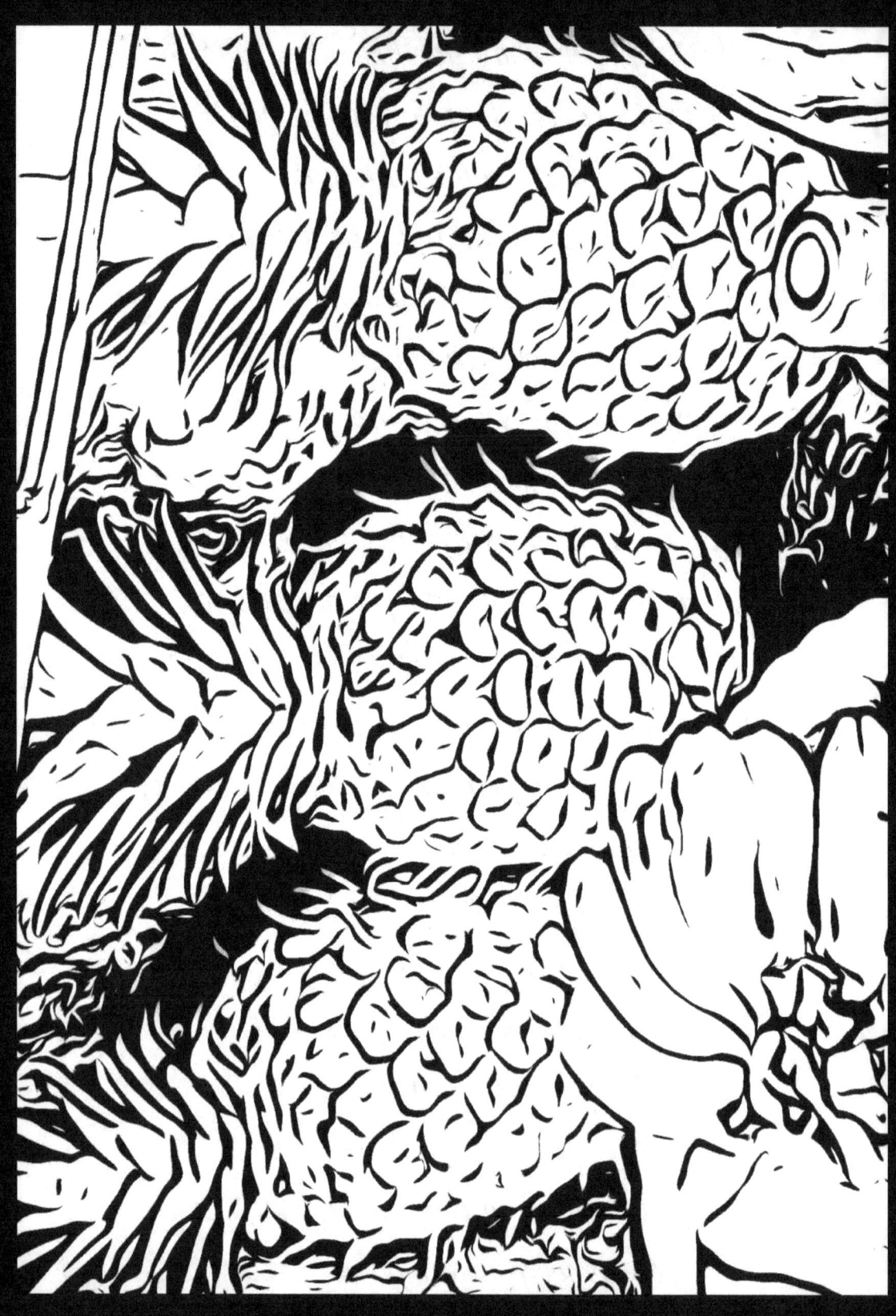

Part 4
Canvas of Art of Man

Praise the Lord.

Praise the Lord from the heavens; praise him in the heights above. Praise him, all his angels; praise him, all his heavenly hosts. Praise him, sun and moon; praise him, all you shining stars. Praise him, you highest heavens and you waters above the skies. Let them praise the name of the Lord, for at his command they were created, and he established them for ever and ever—he issued a decree that will never pass away. Praise the Lord from the earth, you great sea creatures and all ocean depths, lightning and hail, snow and clouds, stormy winds that do his bidding, you mountains and all hills, fruit trees and all cedars, wild animals and all cattle, small creatures and flying birds, kings of the earth and all nations, you princes and all rulers on earth, young men and women, old men and children. Let them praise the name of the Lord, for his name alone is exalted; his splendor is above the earth and the heavens.

Psalm 148:1-13, NIV

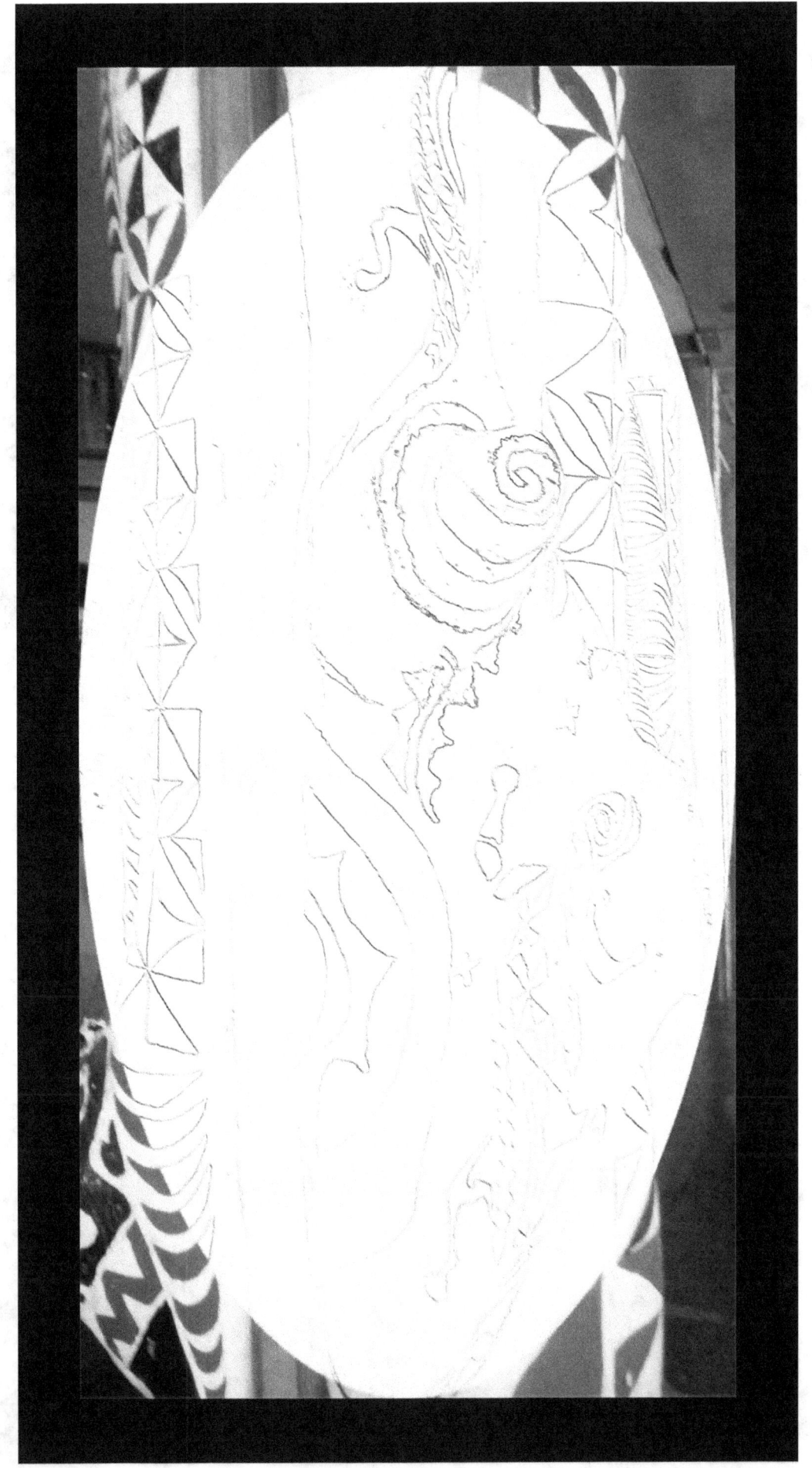

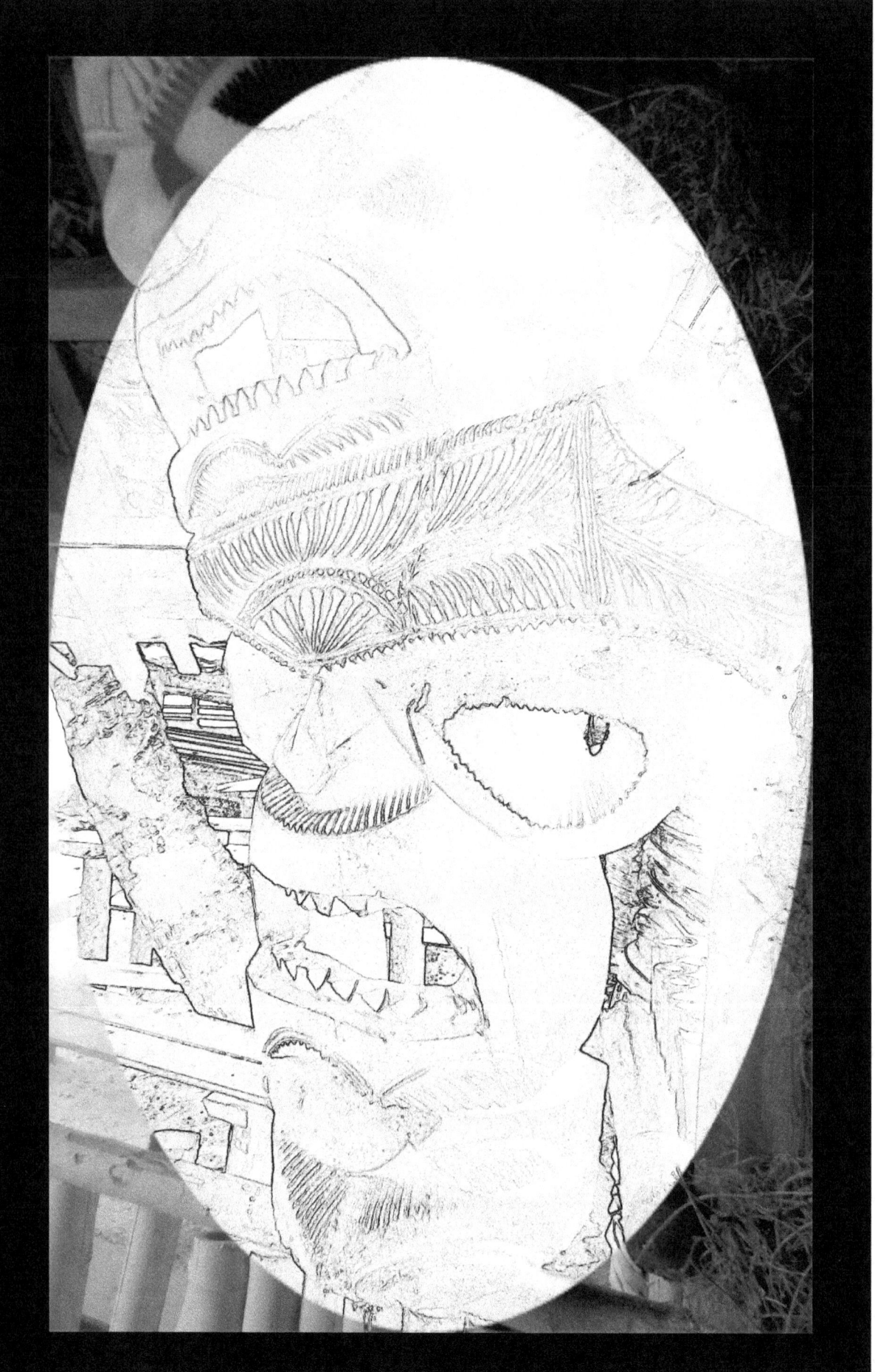

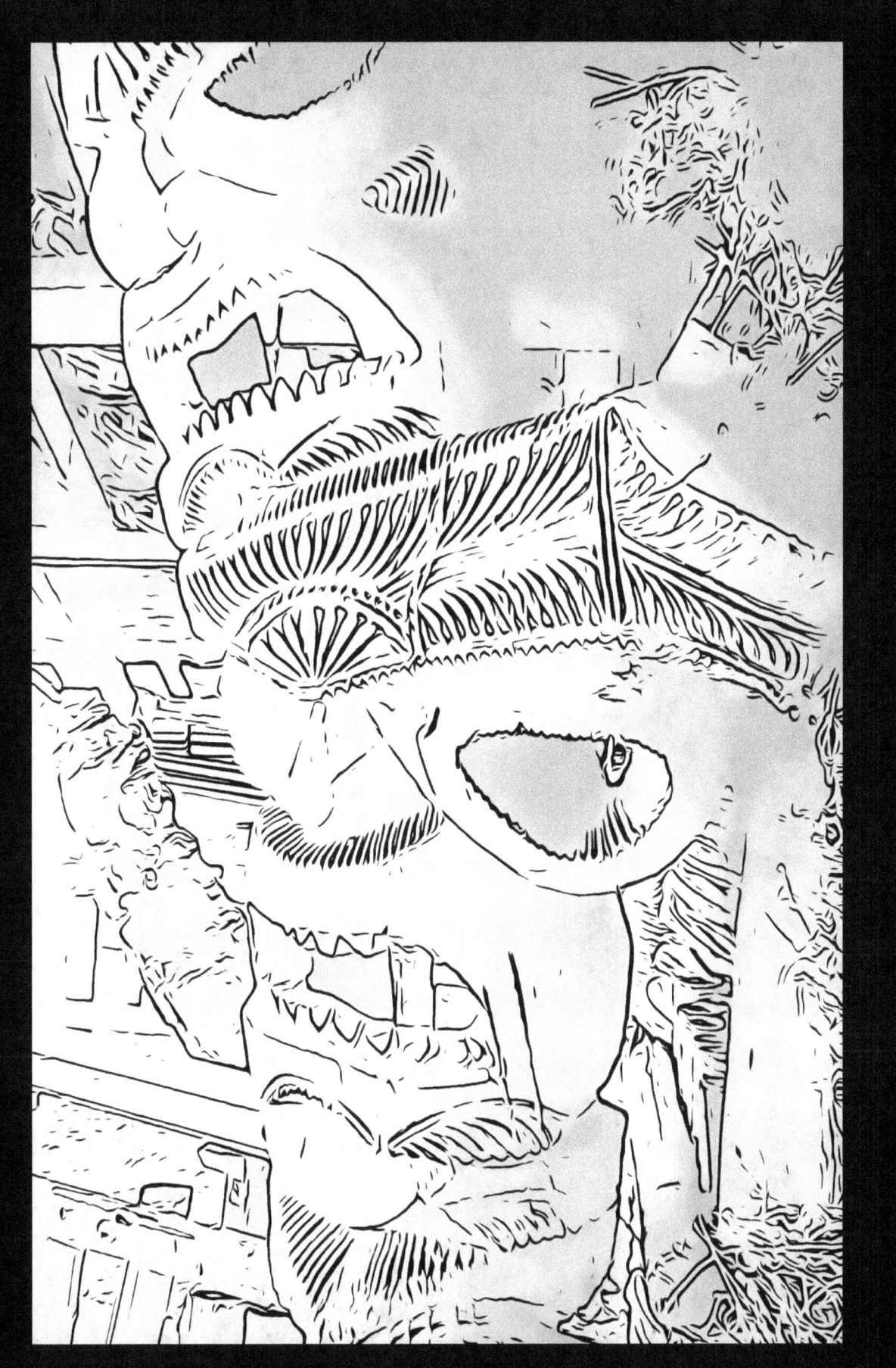

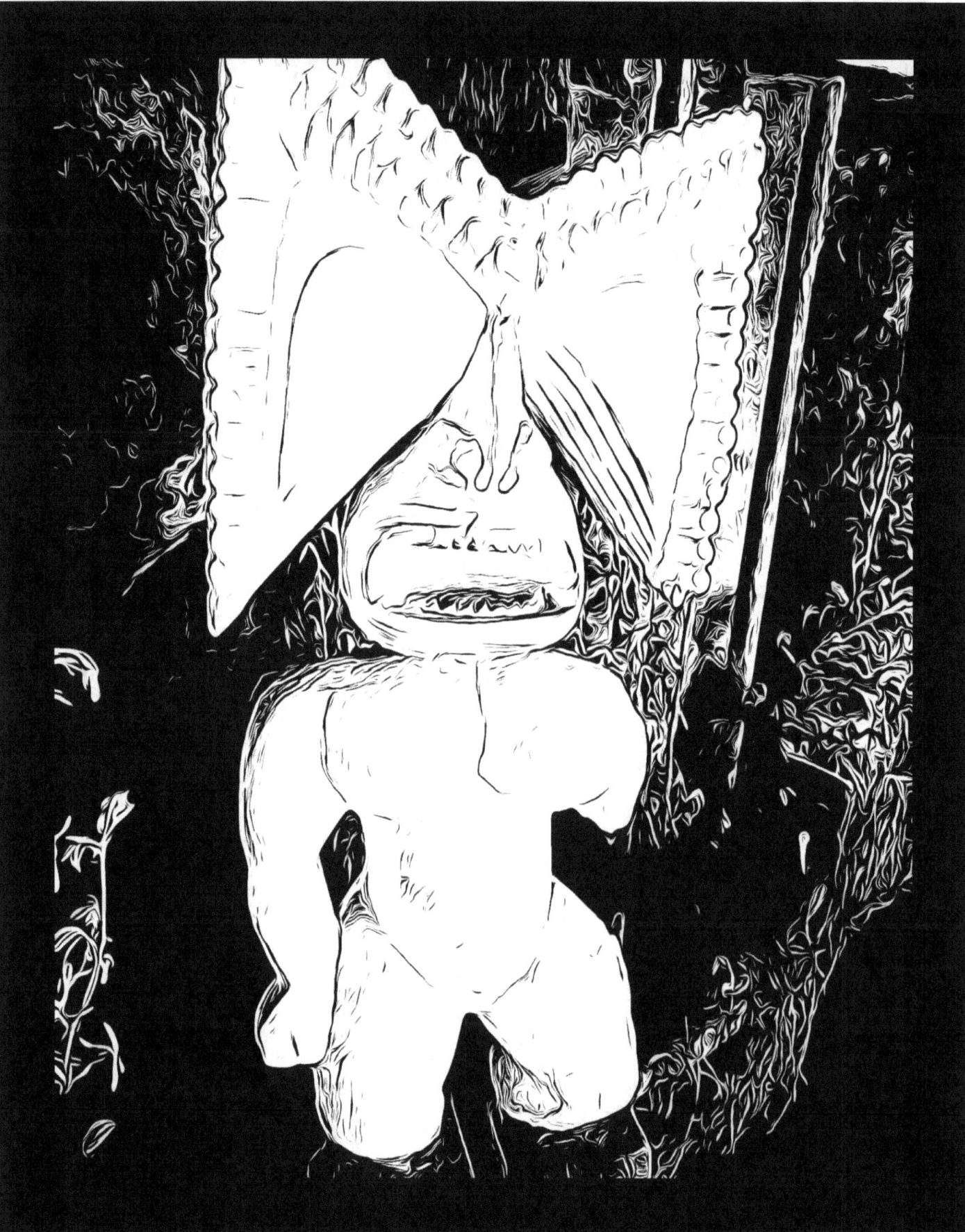

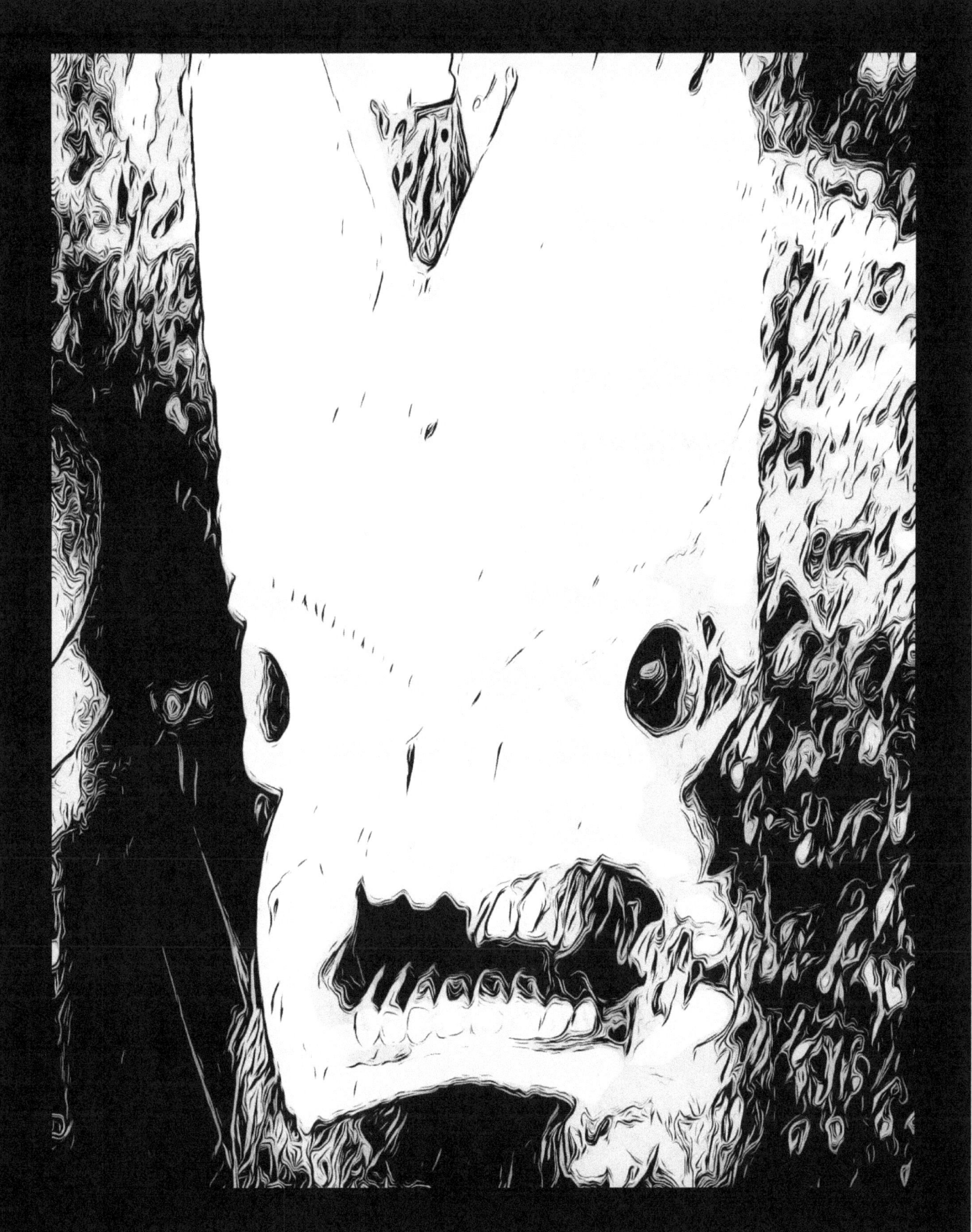

Why do the nations say,
"Where is their God?"
Our God is in heaven;
he does whatever pleases him.
But their idols are silver and gold,
made by human hands.
They have mouths, but cannot speak,
eyes, but cannot see.
They have ears, but cannot hear,
noses, but cannot smell.
They have hands, but cannot feel,
feet, but cannot walk,
nor can they utter a sound with their throats.
Those who make them will be like them,
and so will all who trust in them.
Psalm 115:2-8, NIV

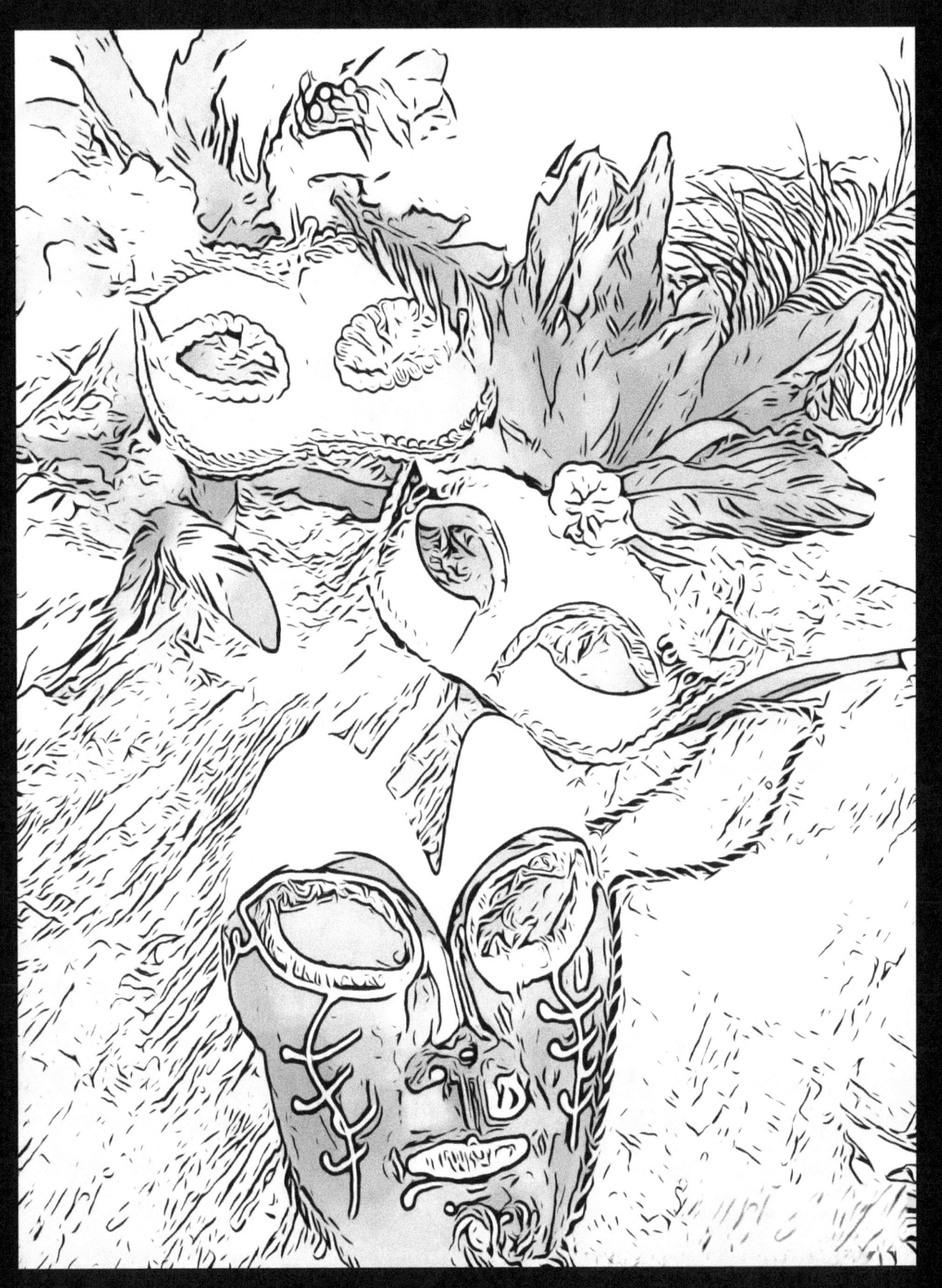

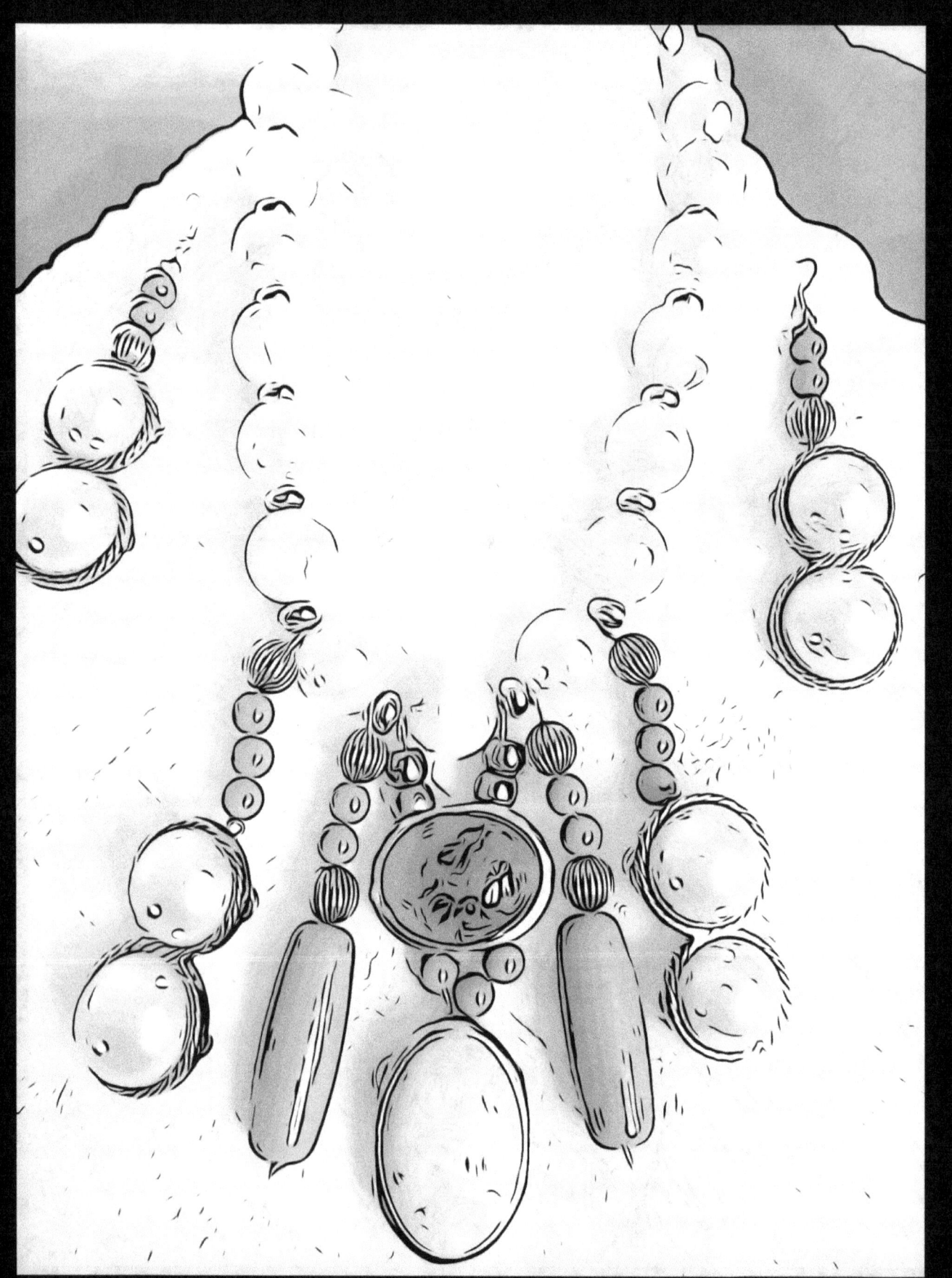

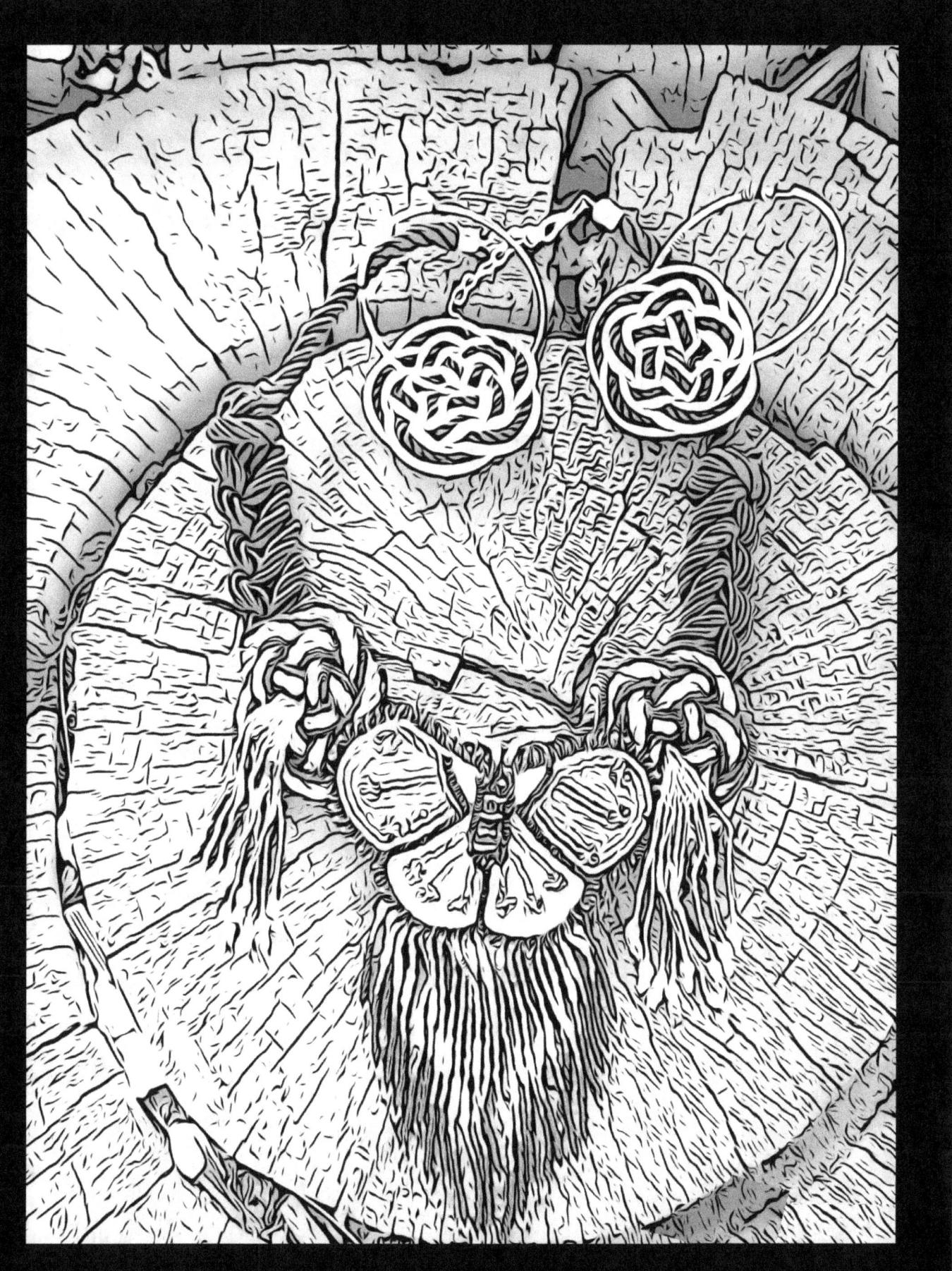

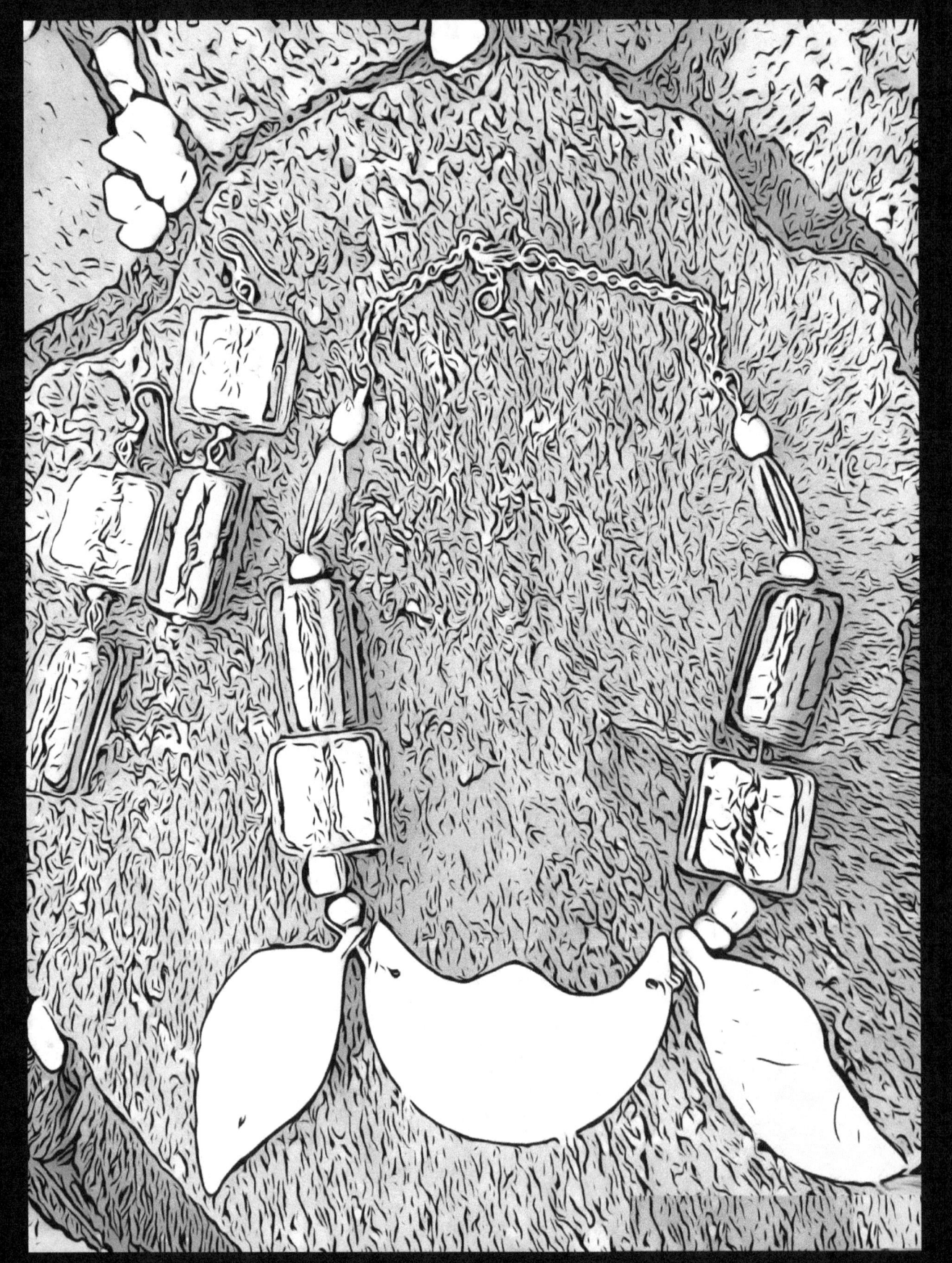

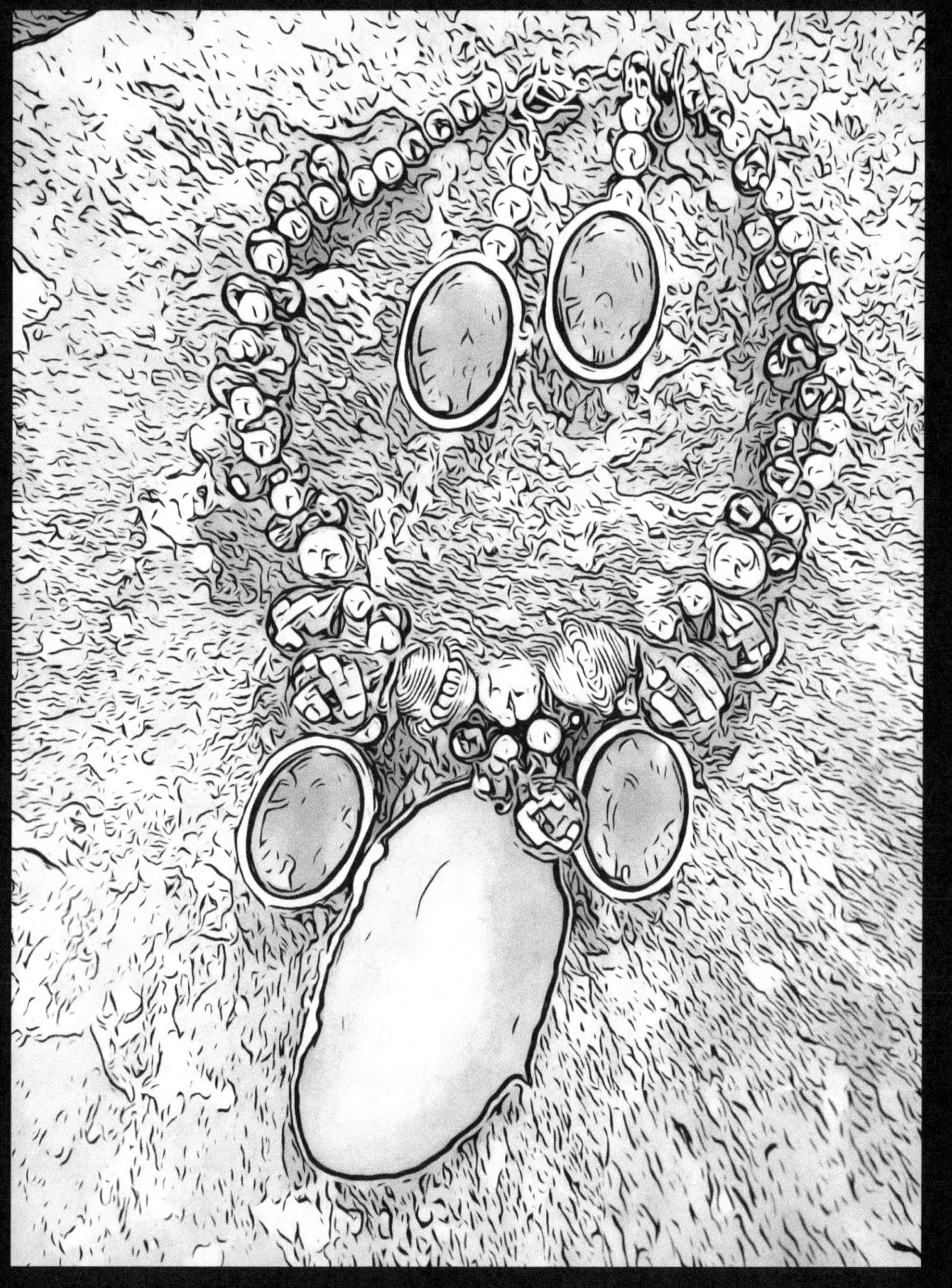

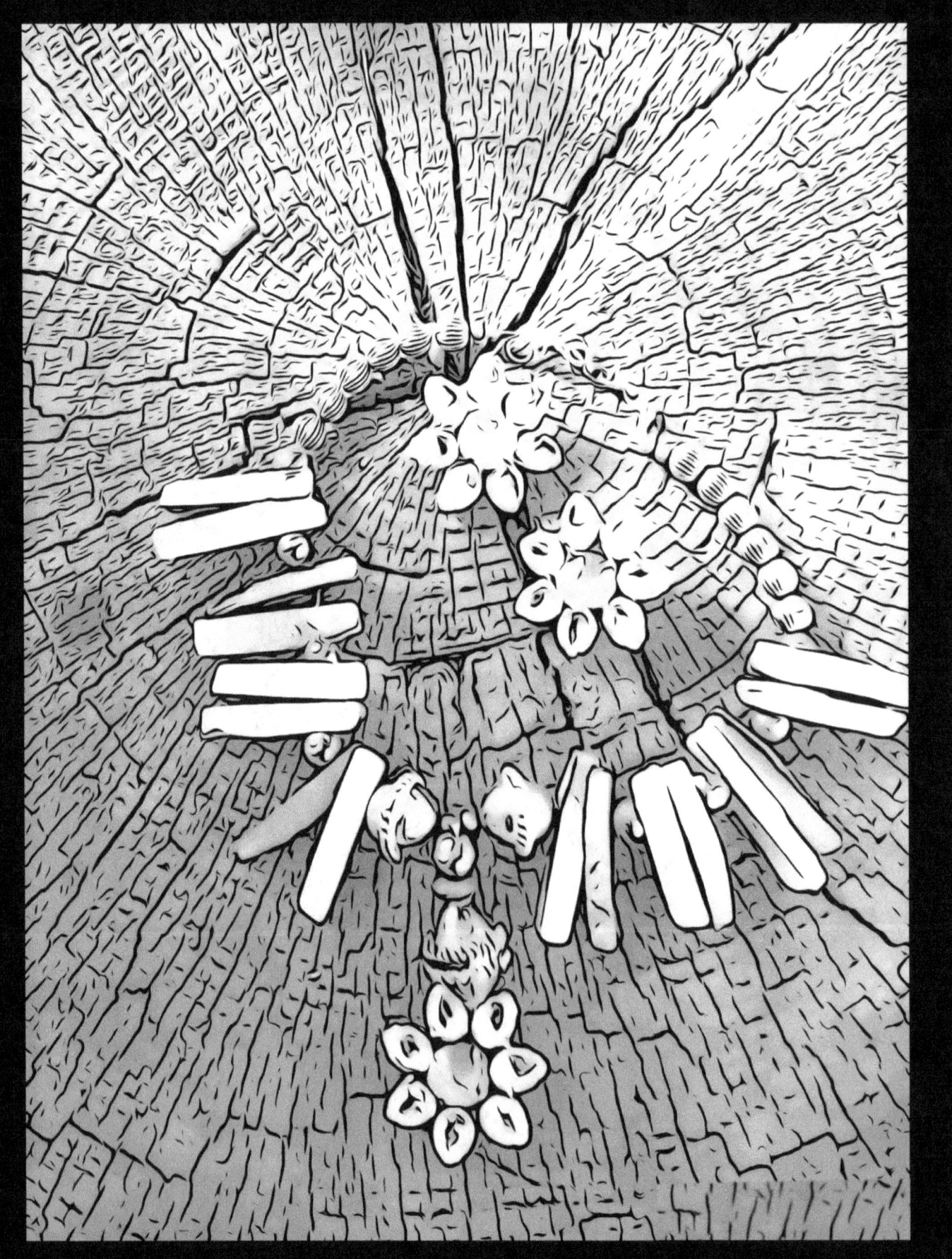

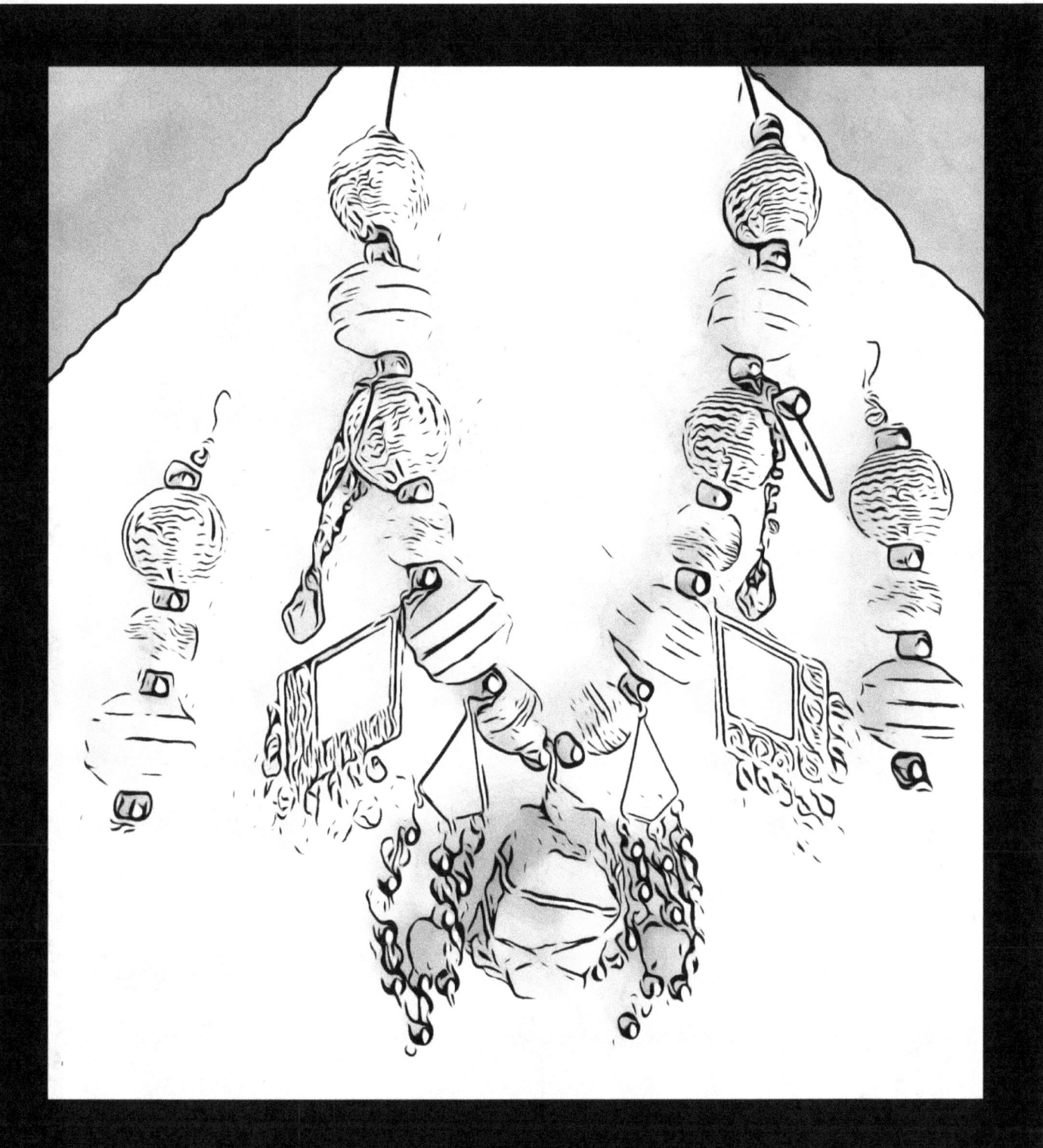

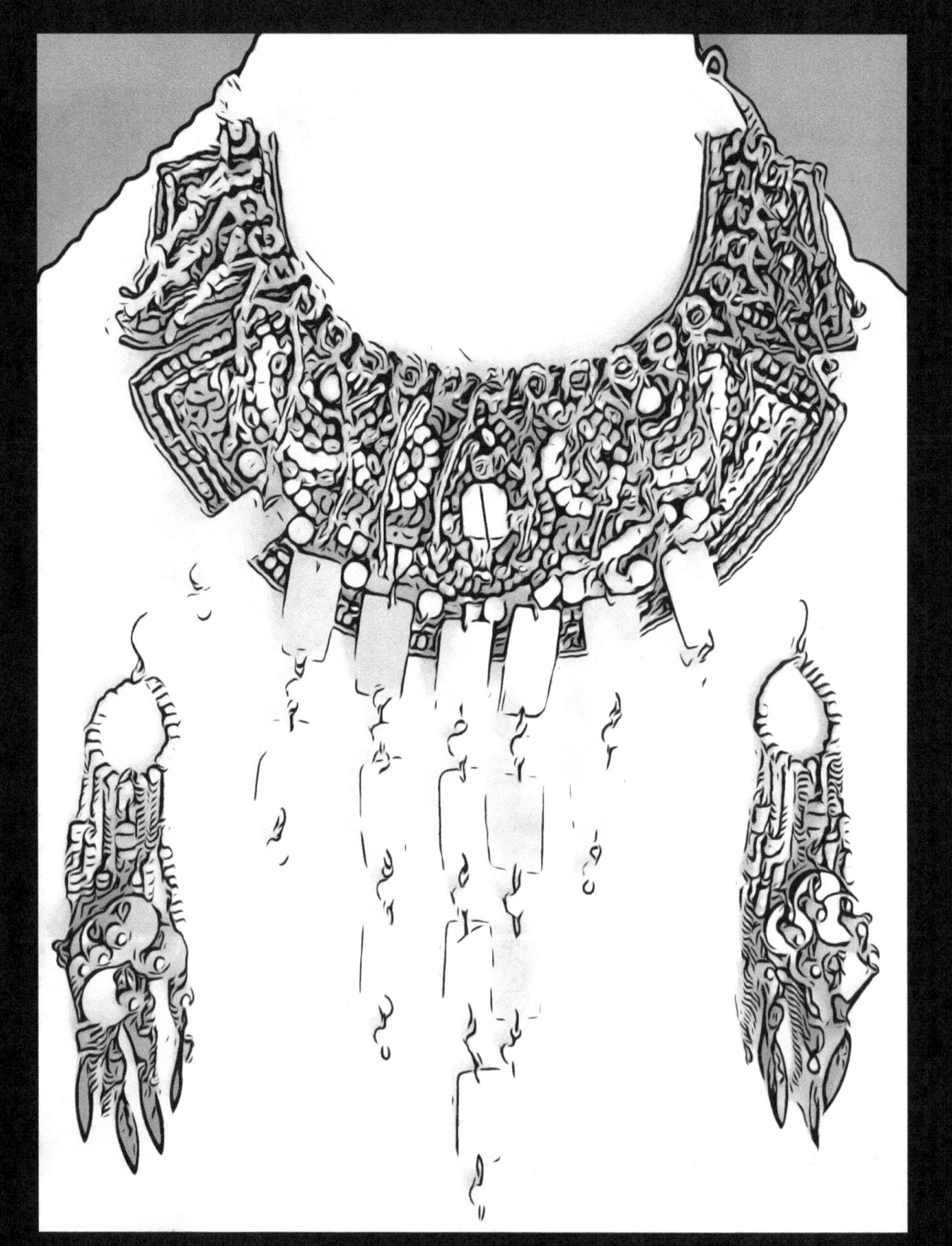

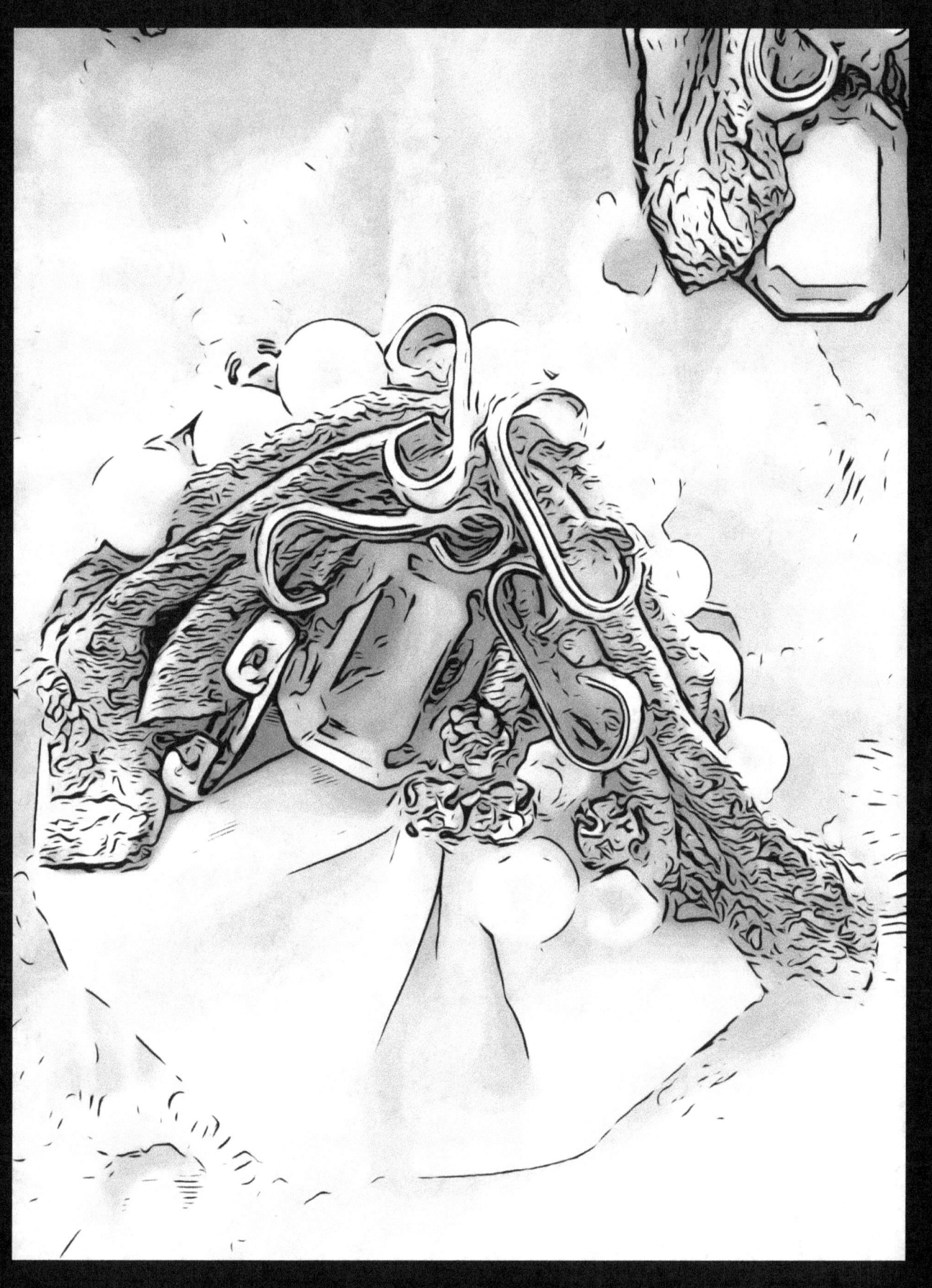

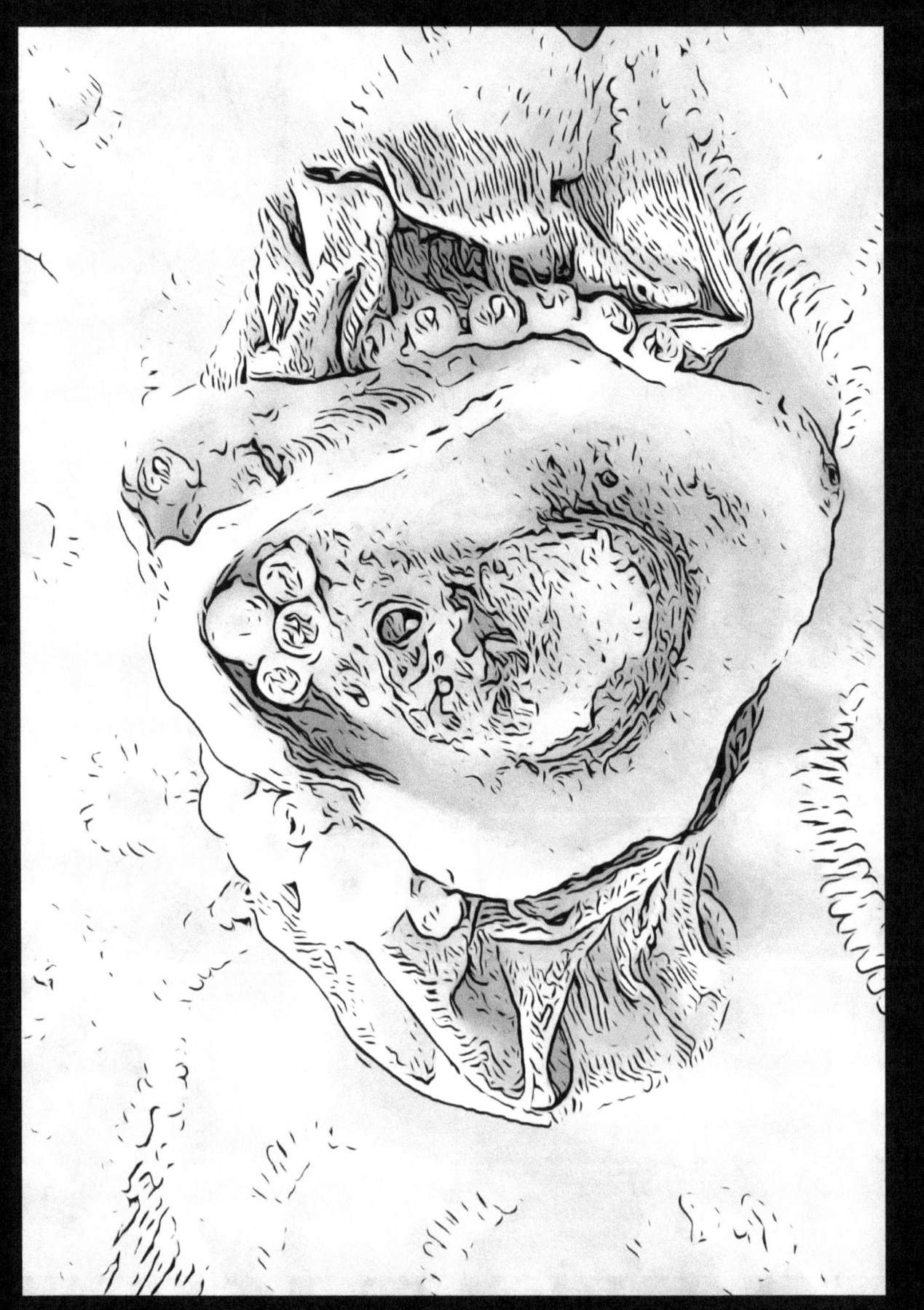

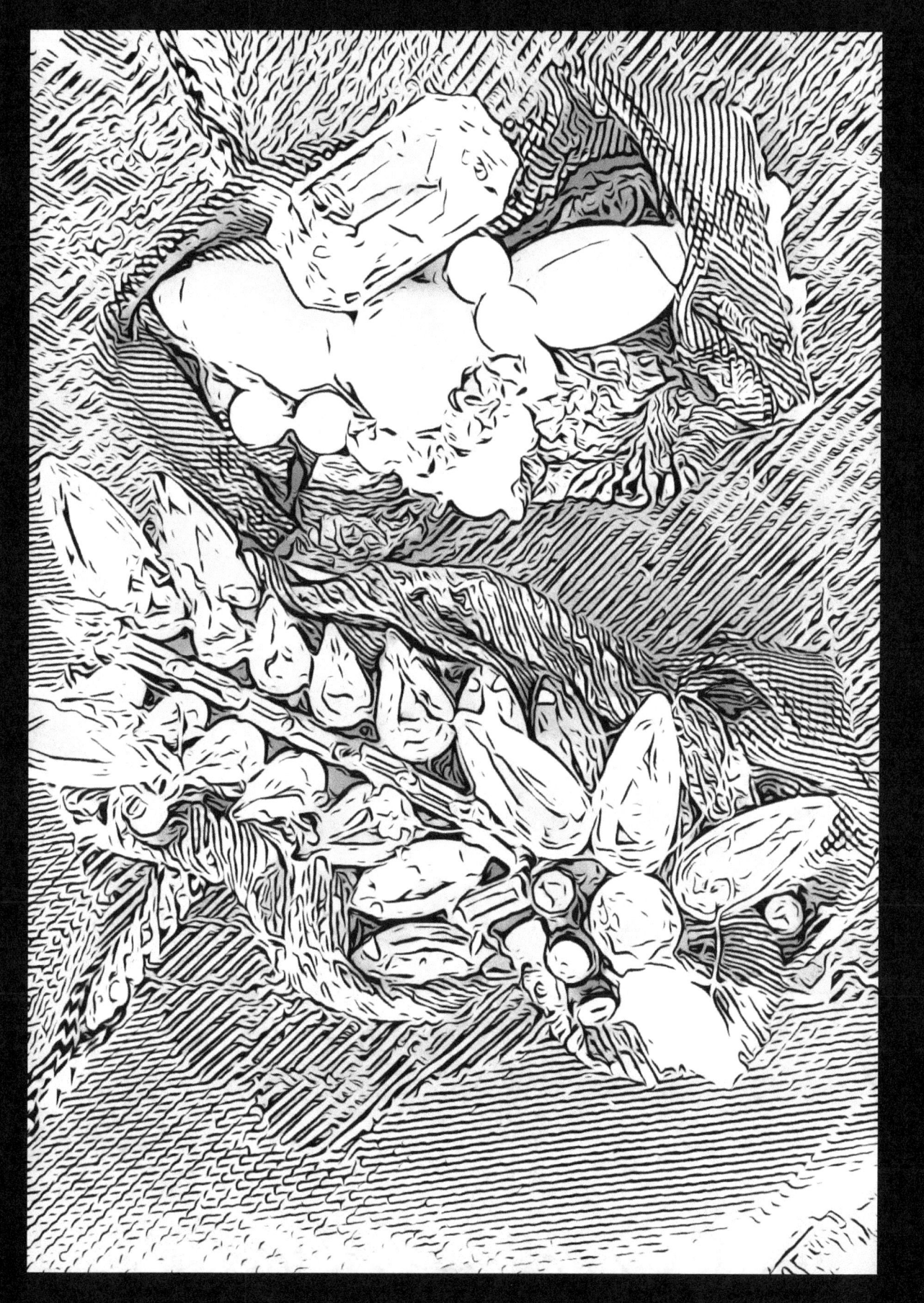

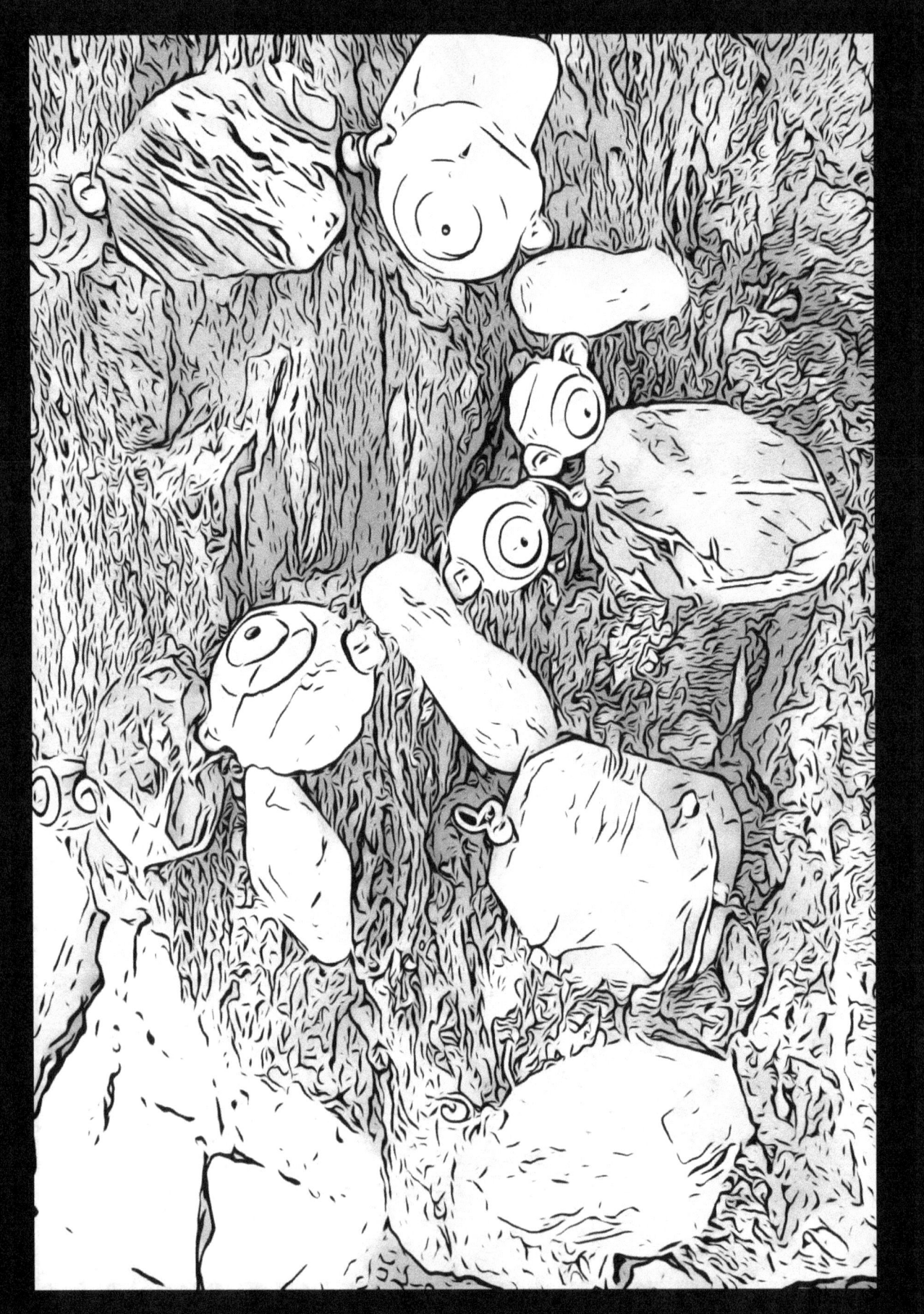

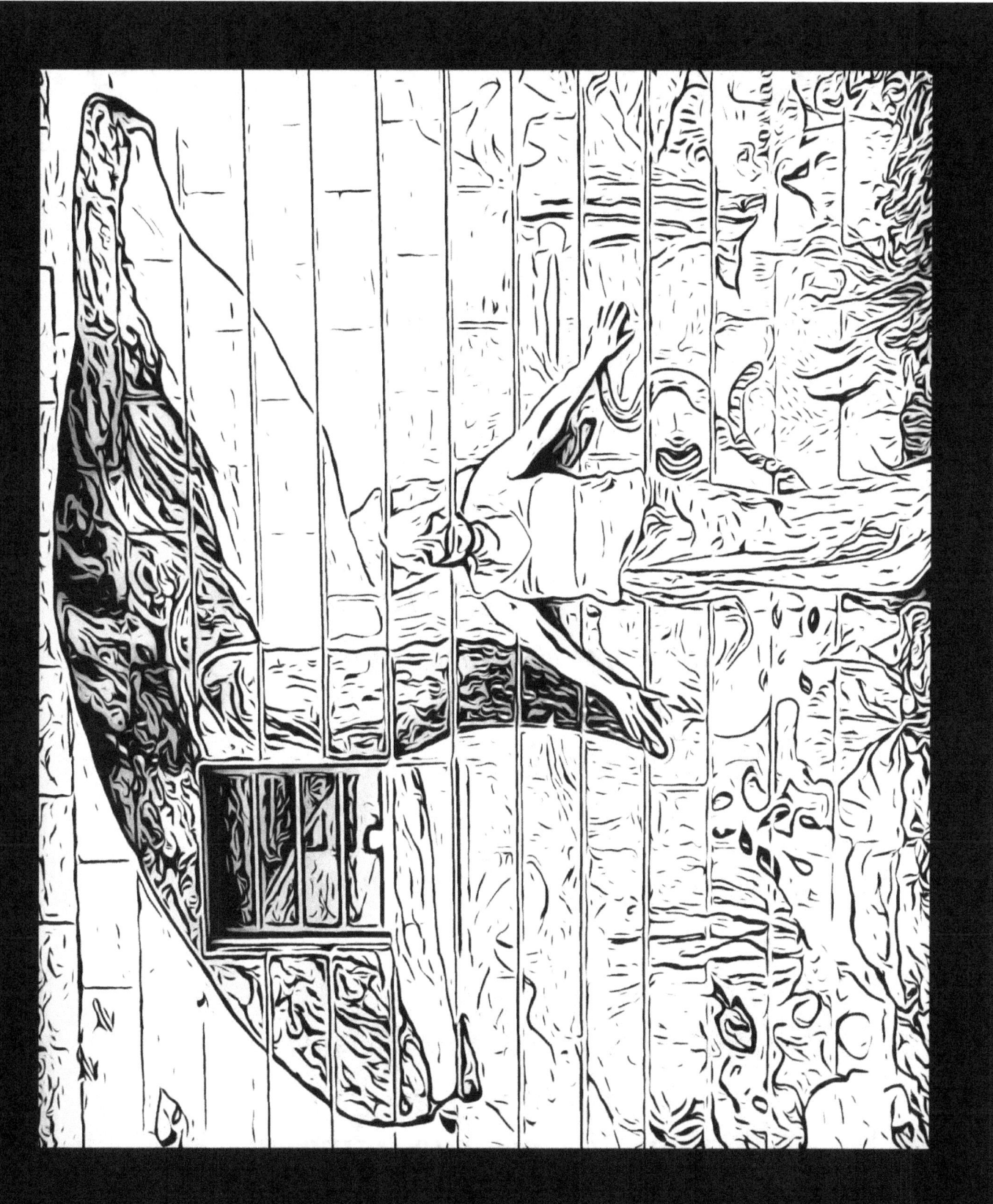

Great are the works of the Lord;

they are pondered by all who delight in them.
Glorious and majestic are his deeds,
and his righteousness endures forever.
He has caused his wonders to be remembered;
the Lord is gracious and compassionate.
He provides food for those who fear him;
he remembers his covenant forever.
He has shown his people the power of his works,
giving them the lands of other nations.
The works of his hands are faithful and just;
all his precepts are trustworthy.
They are established for ever and ever,
enacted in faithfulness and uprightness.
He provided redemption for his people;
he ordained his covenant forever—
holy and awesome is his name.
The fear of the Lord is the beginning of wisdom;
all who follow his precepts have good understanding.
To him belongs eternal praise.

Psalm 111:2-10, NIV

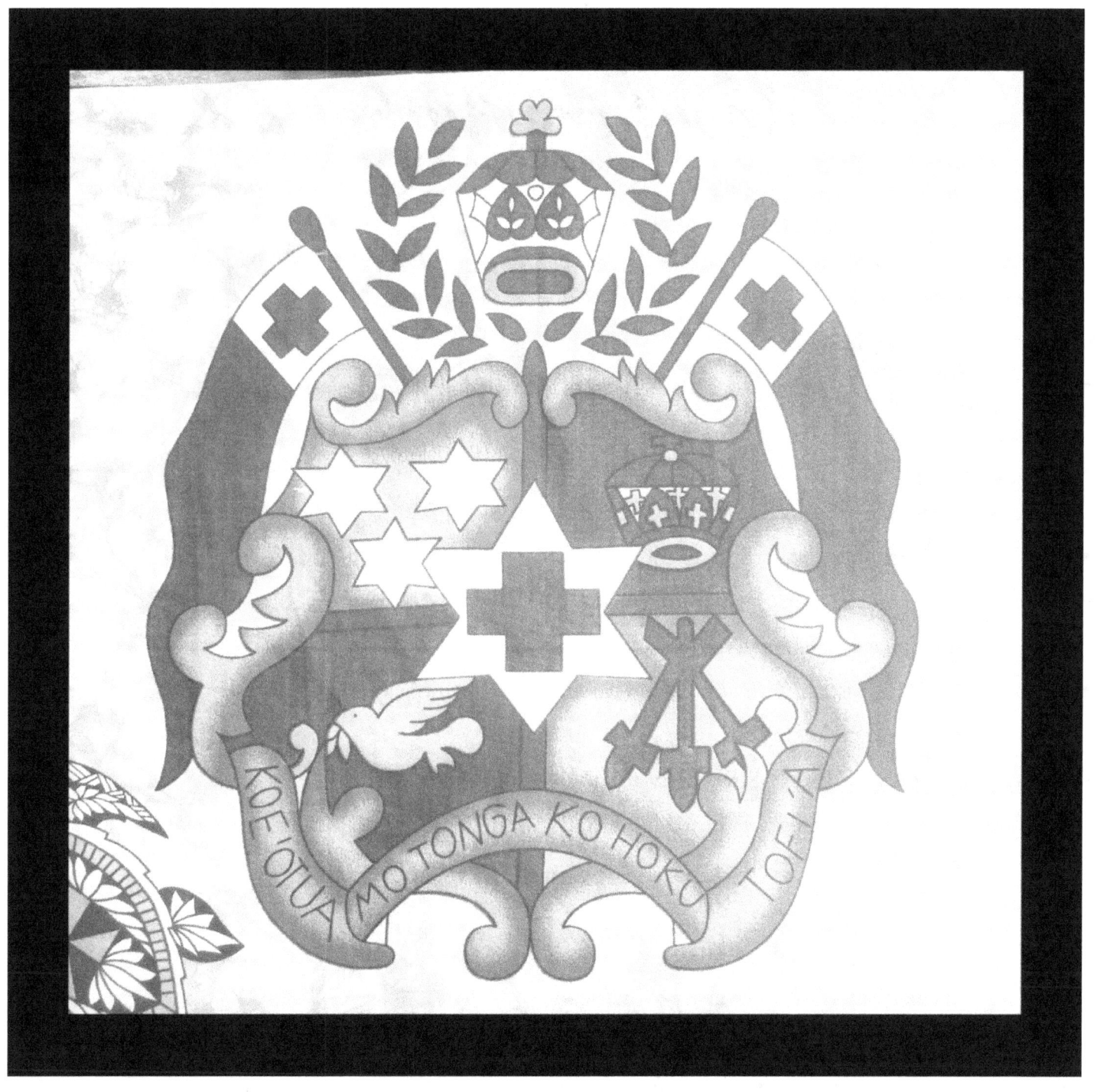

Most of the images are created and taken by Ghitta from her book Exhilarating Kingdom of Wonder: Hurricane Gita over Tonga – Mission, Faith, Prayer. All jewellery are designed by Ghitta. Art documentary taken from the beautiful tropical island The Kingdom of Tonga. Get the book through Ghitta's website www.ghittalejeune.com

About the Author

Past Career - Europe

- Fashion runway model Paris.
- Model agency and ladies school owner and hostess training and uniform design.

Canada

- Entrepreneur with her husband of interior design business and fashion jewelry designer.
- Shaw cable TV producer in of youth talent show.
- Developer of youth programs for self-esteem and life skills.
- Lecturer for women's fashion makeovers and workshops.
- Public speaker of Christian Women's Club retreats and conventions.
- Personal testimony speaker in Christian church outreaches.
- Guest speaker on 100 Huntley Street, national TV.
- Builder, owner, and operator with husband of God's Mountain Crest Chalet.

Private Present Life – Canada

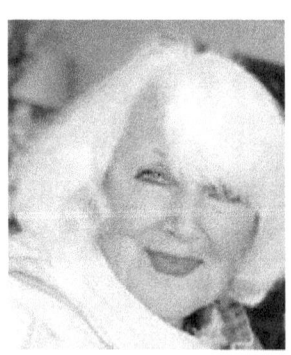

- Retired senior over seventy, dynamic and young at heart.
- Bold and visionary, married for over forty-five years.
- Parent of two daughters and five grandchildren.
- Committed foster parent for over thirty-five years.
- Caregiver for more than eighty teenagers during this time.
- Ghitta is passionate and motivating mentor, sharing their life experiences.
- She is a secret writer and believer, reaching out to everyone who wishes to learn new skills, to give hope, better their lives, relationships, and to trust in God.

www.ghittalejeune.com   www.almightysummitestate.com

www.ingramcontent.com/pod-product-compliance
Lightning Source LLC
Chambersburg PA
CBHW080912170526
45158CB00008B/2084